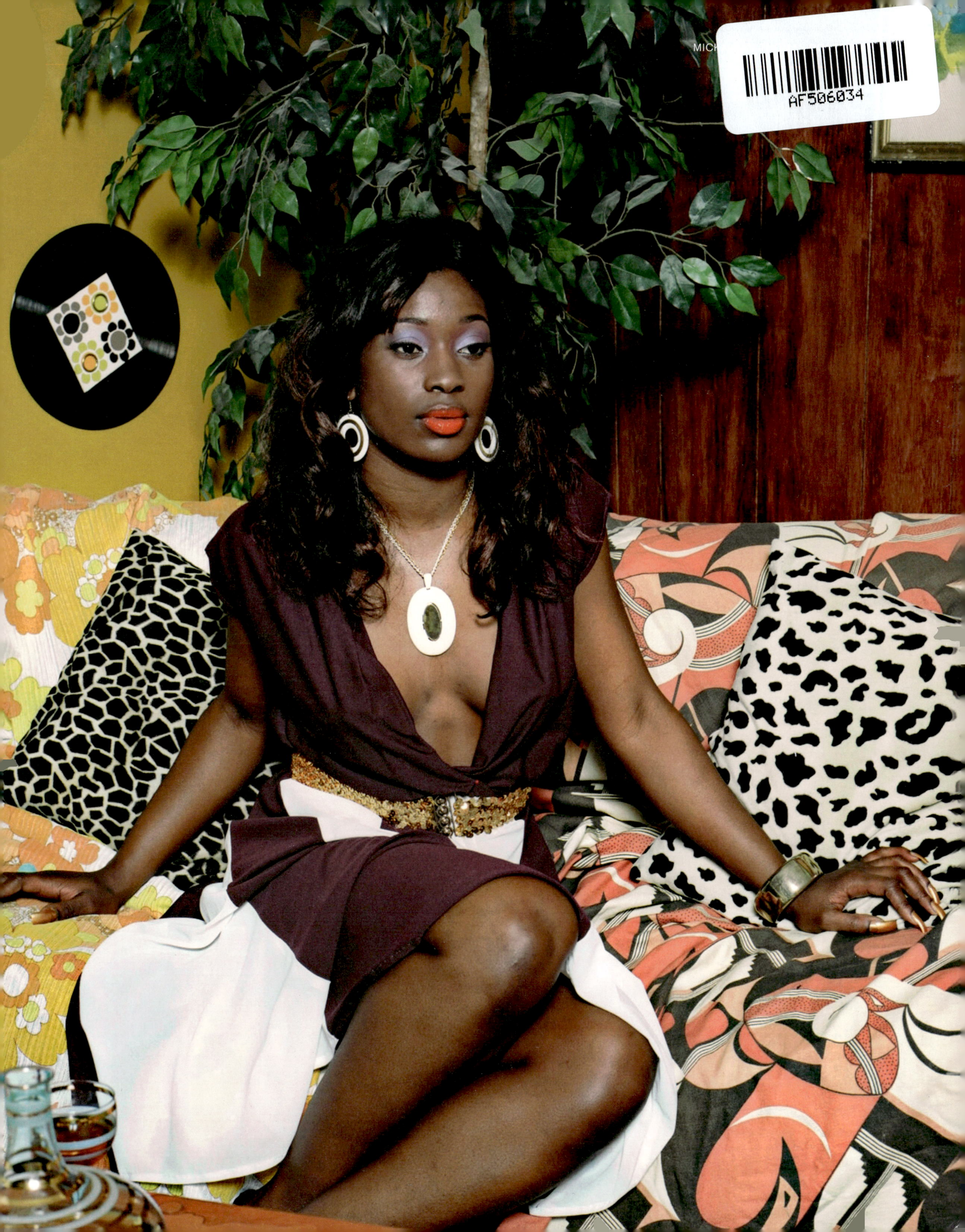

AF506034

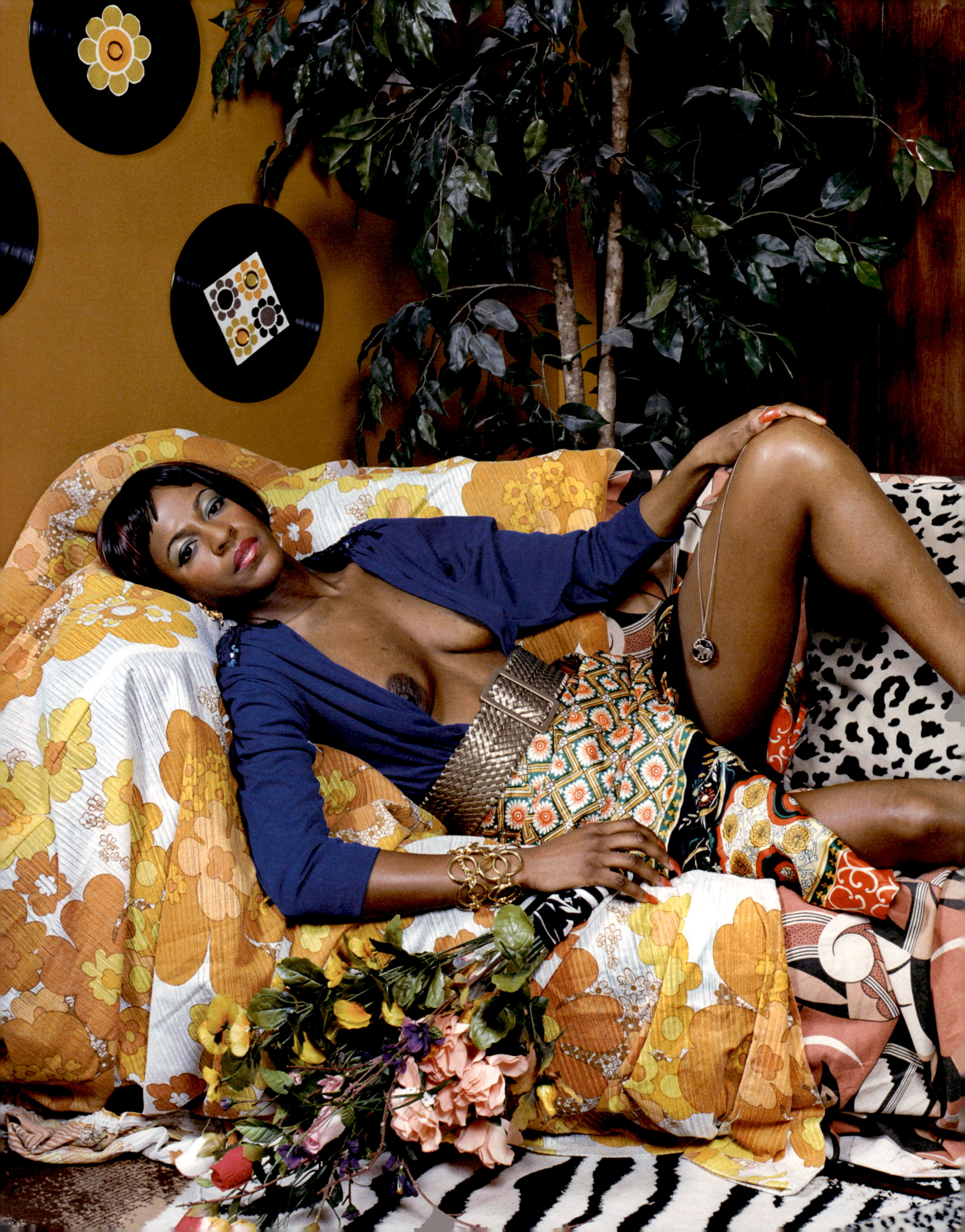

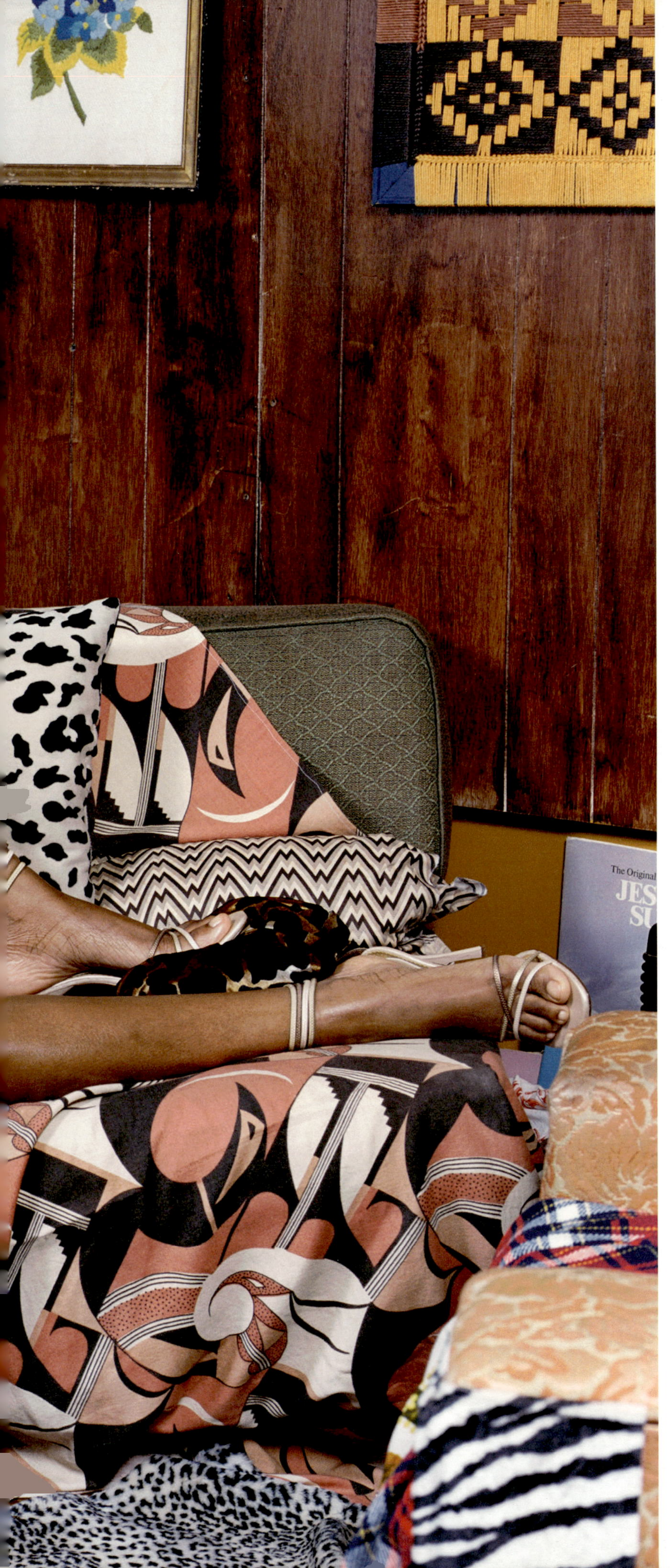

MICKALENE THOMAS Portraits "One of the things I look for in the women I work with is a unique, sometimes unexpected interpretation of what it means to be a woman. I love photographing powerful women who possess their own particular strength and charisma and I like to think that my photographs capture the way they see themselves, reflecting their personality. Most are friends and family members. For example, Sandra: She's A Beauty is a photograph of my mother, one of the main subjects of my work since 2001. I started working with her as my model for a photography class I was taking at Yale. Over the past few years, I have started to include women I have met through friends and involving women I have known for a long time. I met Qusuquzah through a friend and found Tamika from a Craigslist posting. Fran, from Just An Old Fashioned Girl, is actually the person who cuts my hair and has done the makeup for my photo shoots for the last five years. I met Keri, the model in Da Ya Think I'm Sexy and Hot! Wild! Unrestricted! through Fran. All of these photographs were shot in my studio where I build installations that suggest domestic interiors using a collection of objects and furniture that I have altered. I use brightly colored and patterned fabrics, furniture, and objects to create figurative tableaux that display a complexity of space usually found in paintings. All of the titles are song titles or lyrics from artists such as Eartha Kit, Donna Summer, and Millie Jackson, that add another complicated layer and context to the image." - Mickalene Thomas, born in Camden, New Jersey, in 1971, is a painter and photographer currently living and working in Brooklyn. She earned her Master of Fine Arts at Yale in 2002 and had exhibitions at Santa Barbara Contemporary Arts Forum; Detroit Museum of Contemporary Art; The Renaissance Society in Chicago; and New York's Dumbo Arts Center, Studio Museum Harlem and P.S.1/MoMA.

Opening page Portrait of Qusuquzah, 2008, 60 x 75 cm. *Previous spread* Tamika sur une chaise longue, 2008, 75 x 61 cm. *On the right* Da ya think I'm sexy, 2009, 61 x 76 cm. *Following spread* Hot! Wild! Unrestricted!, 2009, 76 x 61 cm. *Page 10* Just an old-fashioned girl, 2009, 50 x 76 cm. *Page 11* Sandra: She's a beauty, 2009, 76 x 114 cm. *All images mounted c-prints* © *the artist, courtesy Lehmann Maupin Gallery, New York*

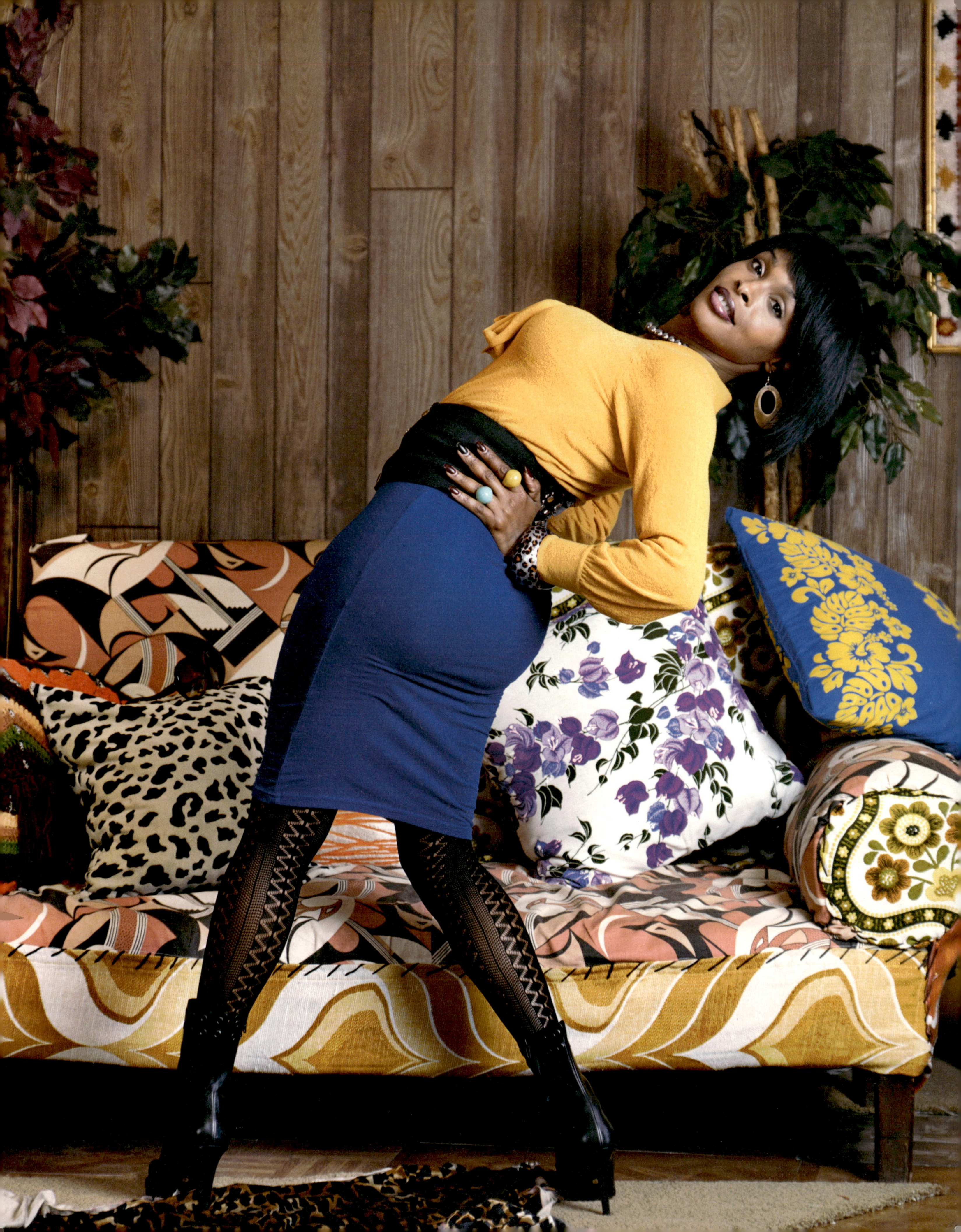

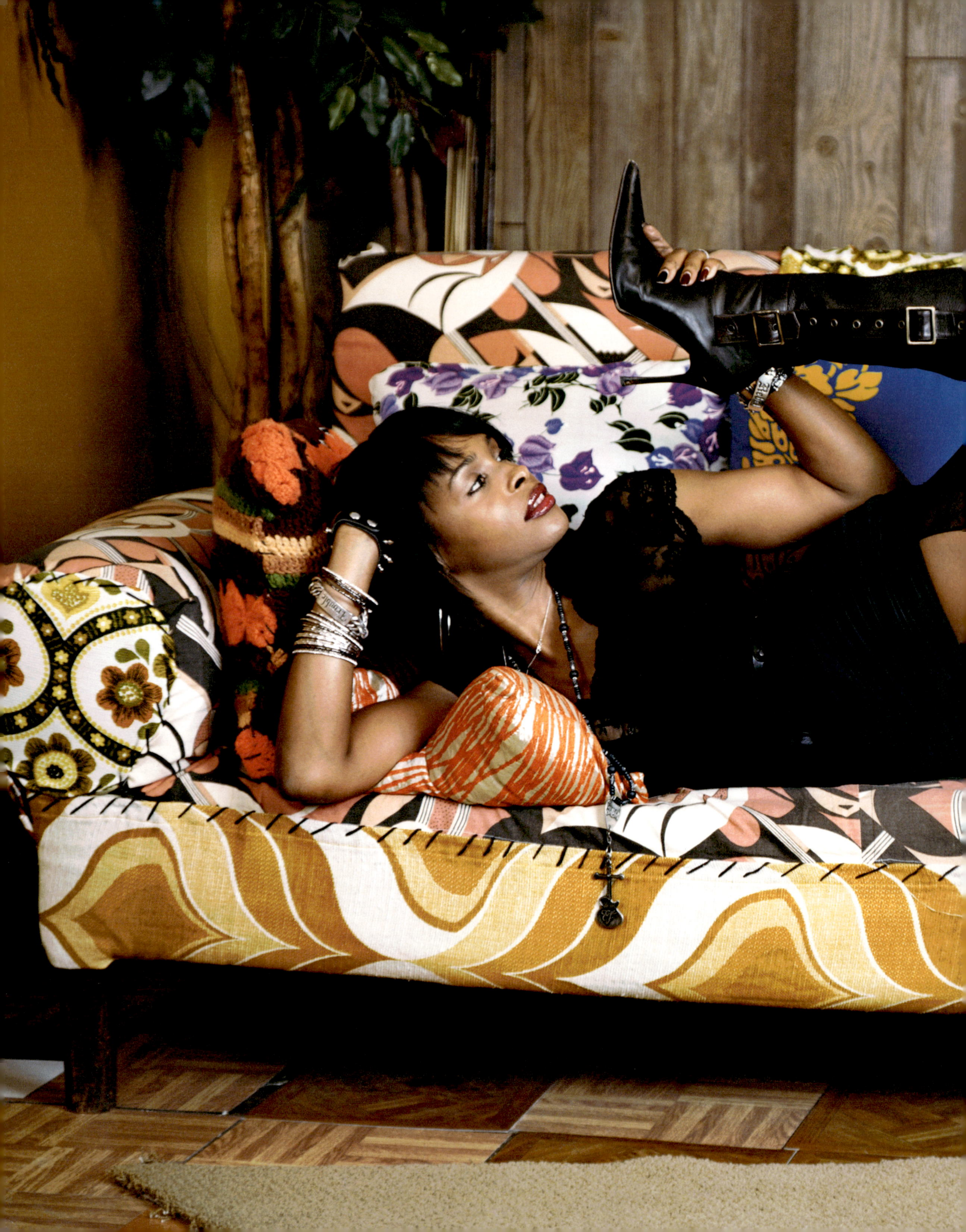

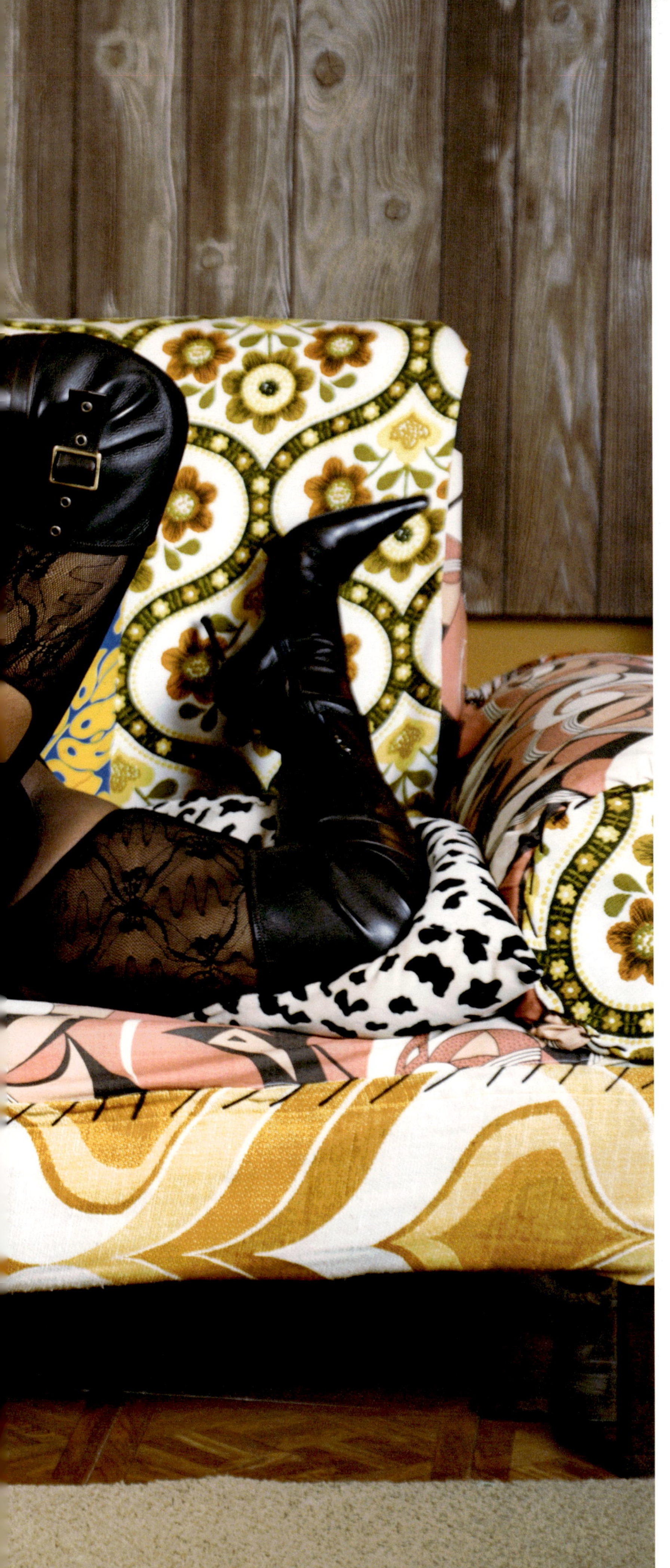

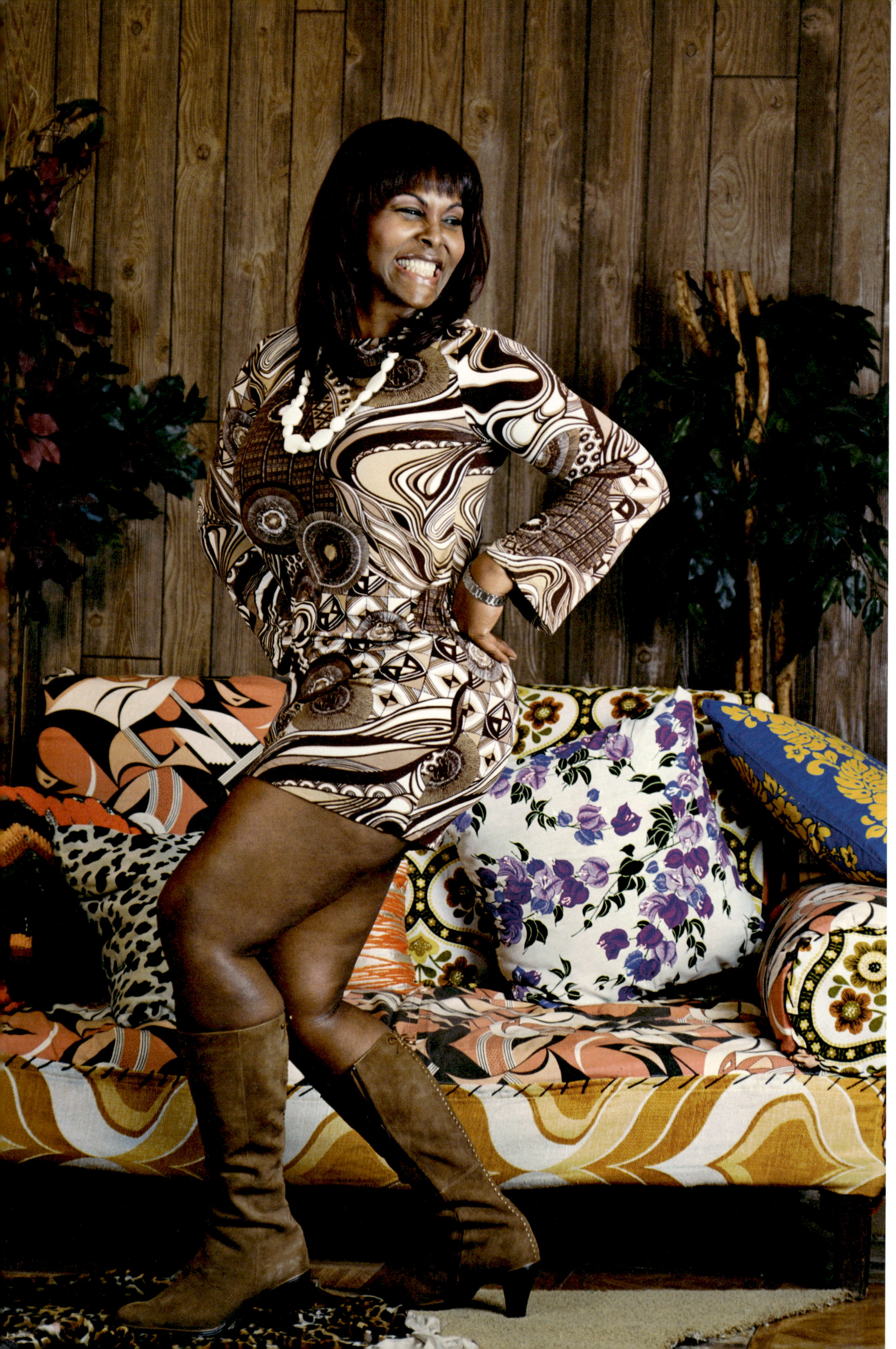

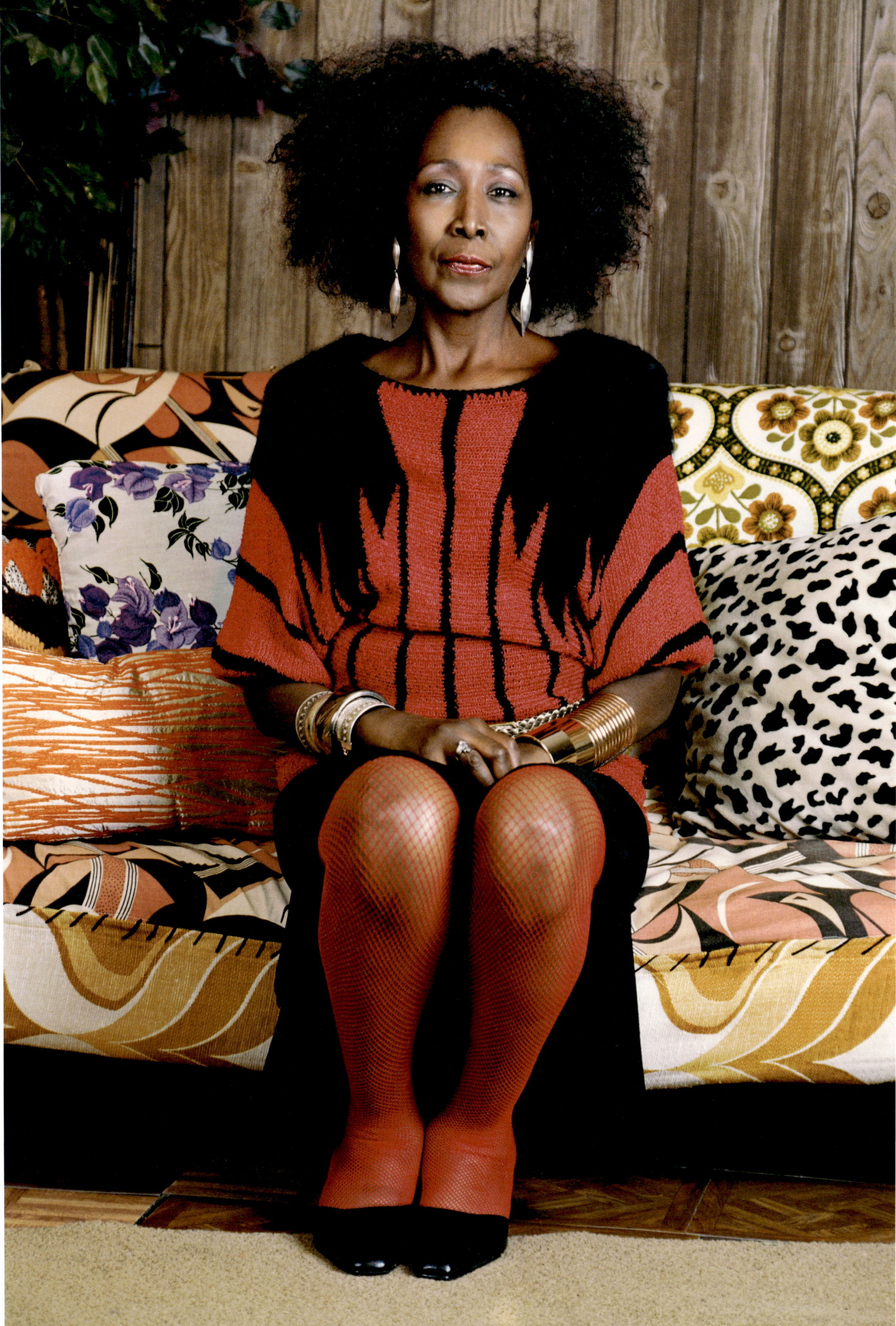

Simon Starling
THREE BIRDS, SEVEN STORIES
INTERPOLATIONS AND BIFURCATIONS
introduced by his gallerist
Franco Noero

The work presented here began in Turin while Simon Starling was finishing his previous project for our gallery. In that period, a few days after a conversation he had with Pierpaolo Falone on Manik Bagh and Eckart Muthesius, in an apartment in Turin he accidentally came across the double portrait of the Maharajah and Maharani of Indore in their wedding outfits. The sum of these coincidences was, in a certain sense, the start of a short circuit which the artist would address with a research that would take up, on and off, two years of his work. The series of twenty-one photographs - 11 of which are presented here - are both the result of a complex project and the cue to start discussing it.

Here we encounter the cosmopolitan culture of a young Indian prince, the modernist architecture of Muthesius and some of his conjuring tricks, the magnificent residence of Manik Bagh in Indore, the materials used for building the palace and their provenance, the cream of industrial design of that period, the art of Costantin Brancusi, Hinduism, the cinema of Fritz Lang, the technology we know best, that of the memory contained in a laptop, the possibilities provided by software in processing an ancient material like stone and, finally, a triangle formed of Berlin, India and Turin, broken up in a legendary auction and put back together in its current shape by Starling.

They are key images which narrate in fragments or, rather, illuminate the most complex angles of this journey. They are images which might also exist in isolation, especially those more obscure and indecipherable. They are images that are able to trigger a "chain of production", of ideas and complex associations, which transport us to the end of the story, but they are also images which are, in inverted commas, timeless, with their intense brightness and the absolute sophistication of their printing technique.
Indeed, Simon Starling has, for years, used the technique of platinum salts and palladium, a field of experimentation that explores and materialises the sculptural qualities of photography and beyond, skilfully analysed in the work *One Ton*. Using this medium, Starling is able to achieve dizzy heights in terms of image quality and is able to make another journey, back in time perhaps; putting man in charge of a technique and no longer at its service.
Over the years we have had the opportunity to personally meet the printer of these photographs. Paul Caffell and his son have travelled to see the result of the work they have done with Simon, from a small town in England to London and as far as Turin, almost as though they had become the protagonists of the circular route plotted by the artist.

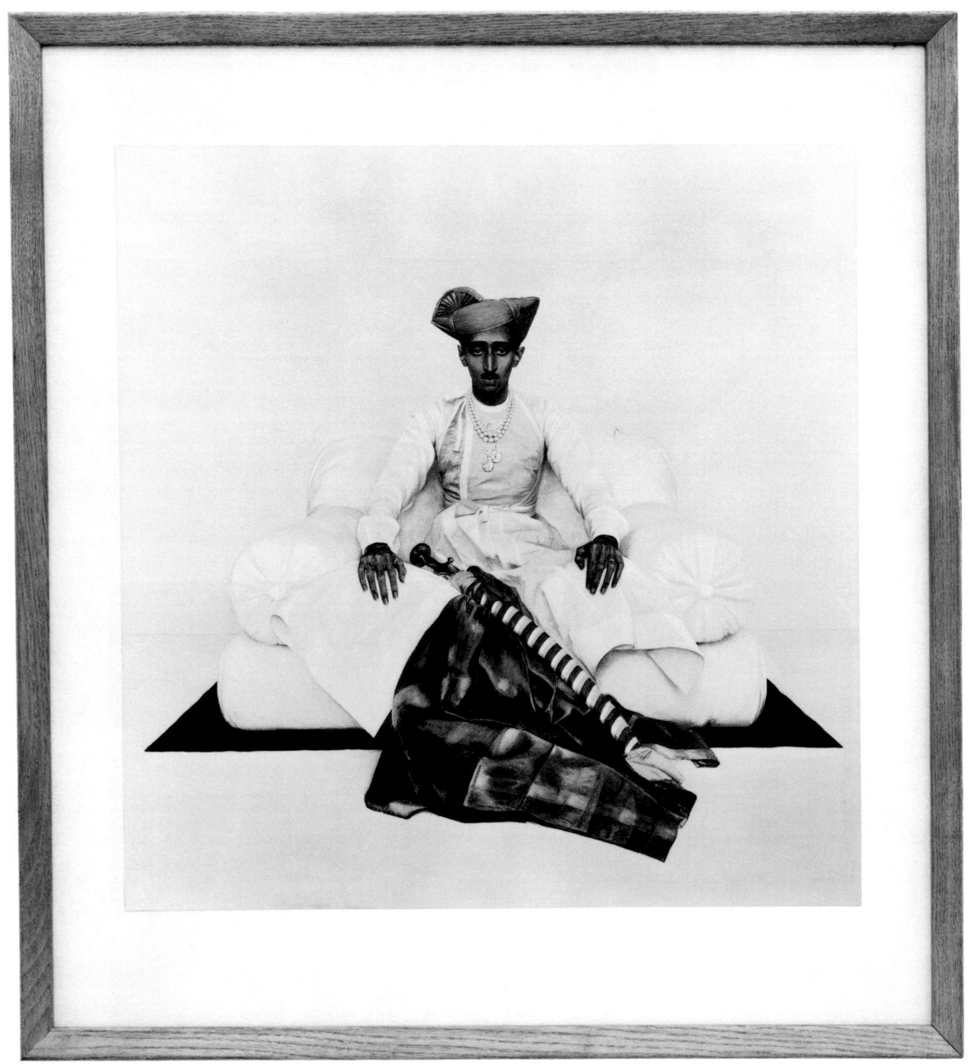

Maharaja Yeshwant Rao Holkar Bahadur, 1924. Photograph by Peter A. Juley & Sons, New York to commemorate the Maharaja's wedding. Found and re-photographed in Turin 2008, 40.5 x 50.8 cm. (framed 93.5 x 106.9)

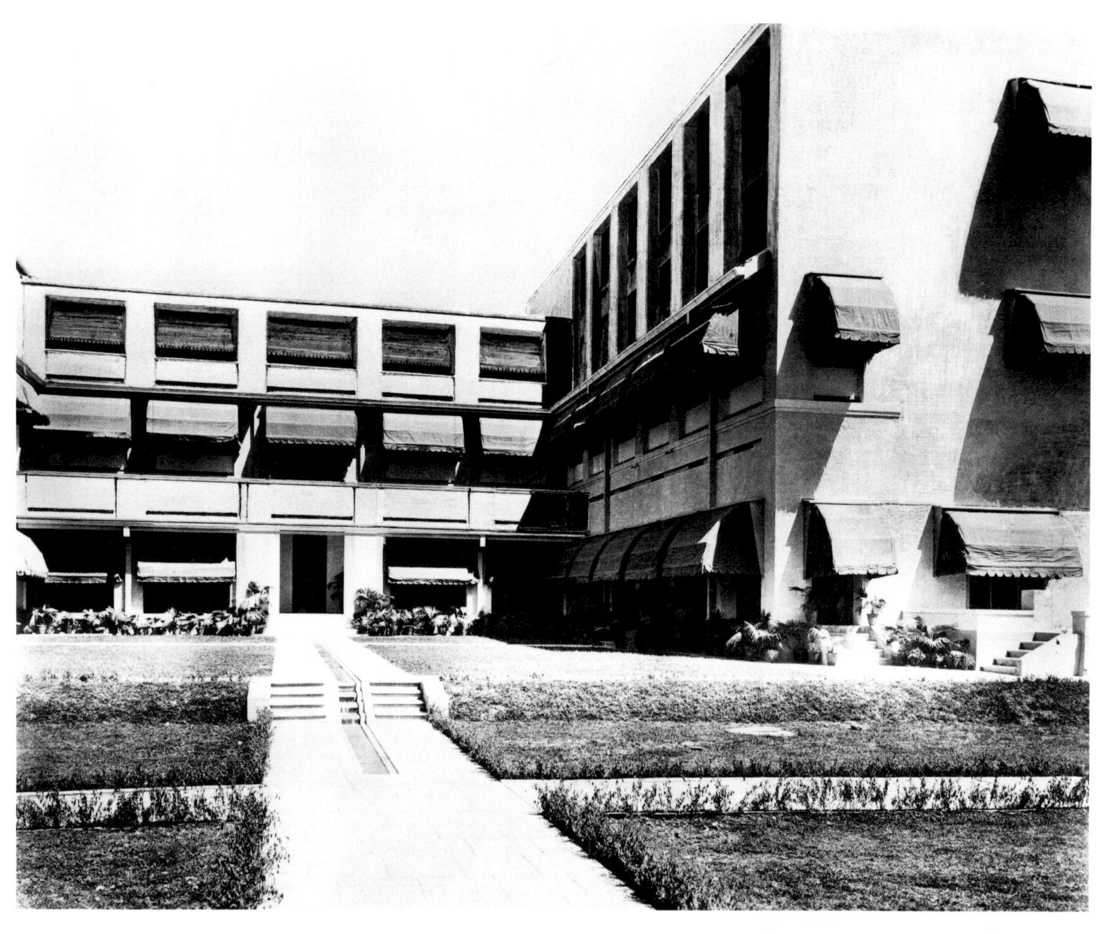

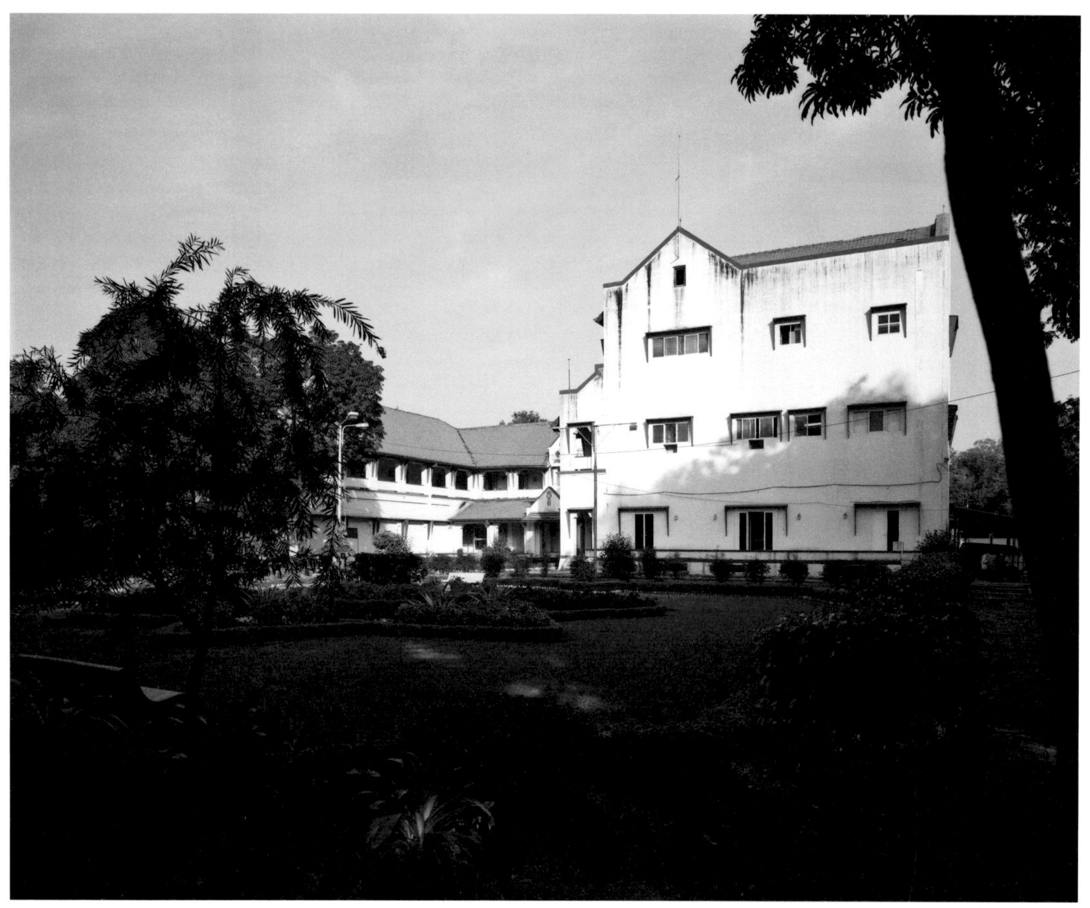

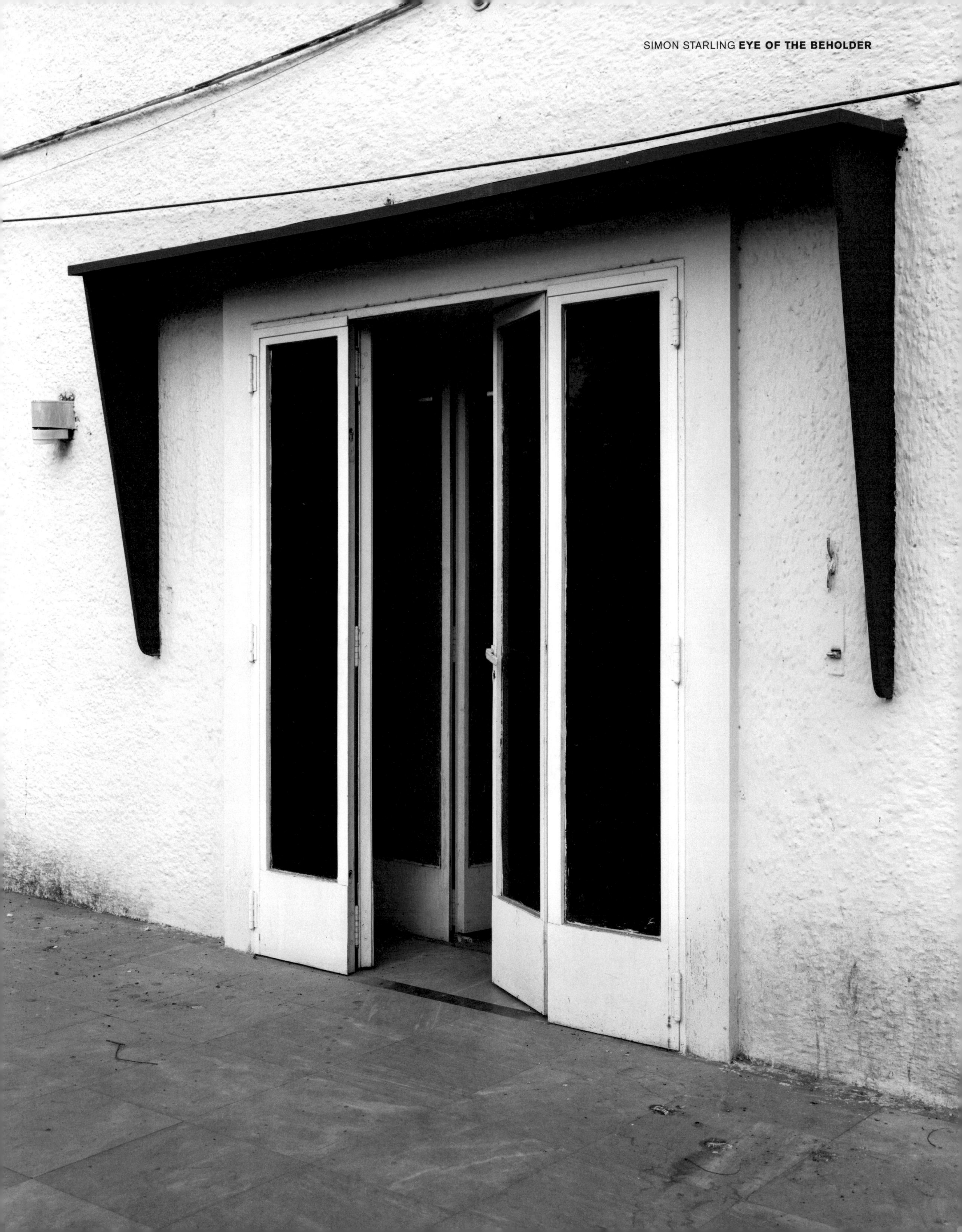

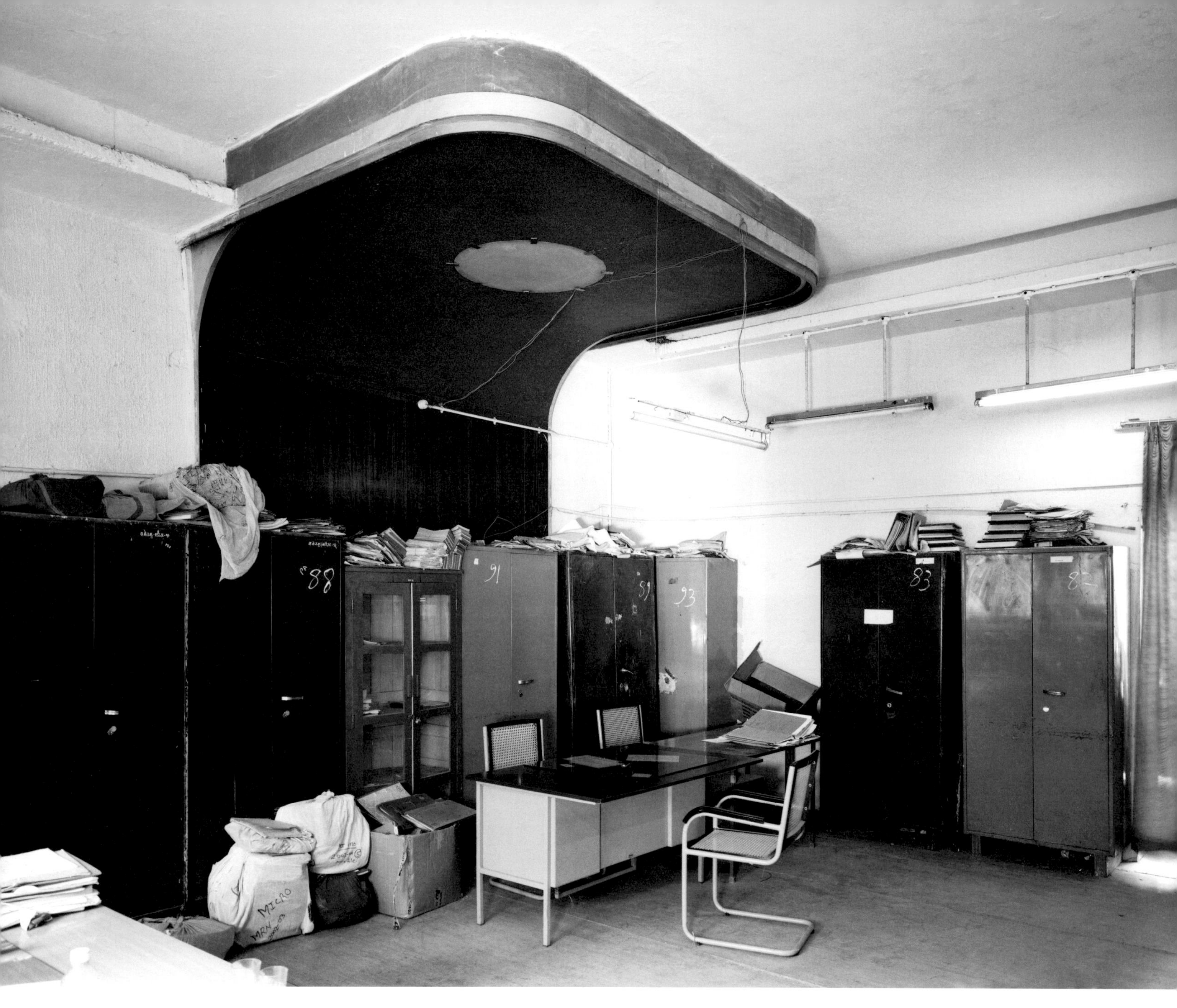

Page 14, top Off-Set Print of a Photomontage of the Exterior of Manik Bagh Palace,1933, 2008, 40.5 x 50.8 cm. (framed 93.5 x 106.9). *Page 14, bottom* Manik Bagh Palace, Indore. The Former Home of Maharaja Yeshwant Rao Holkar Bahadur, now the Office of the Commissioner, Customs & Central Excise, Indore 2007, 40.5 x 50.8 cm. (framed 93.5 x 106.9). *Page 15* Ballroom Doors, Manik Bagh Palace, Indore (open) 2007, 50,8 x 40.5 cm. (framed 106.9 x 93.5)

In this page Former Bedroom of Maharaja Yeshwant Rao Holkar Bahadur, Manik Bagh Palace, Indore 2007, 40.5 x 50.8 cm. (framed 93.5 x 106.9). *Right* Former Bedroom of Maharani Sanyogita Raje, Manik Bagh Palace, Indore 2007, 40.5 x 50.8 cm. (framed 93.5 x 106.9)

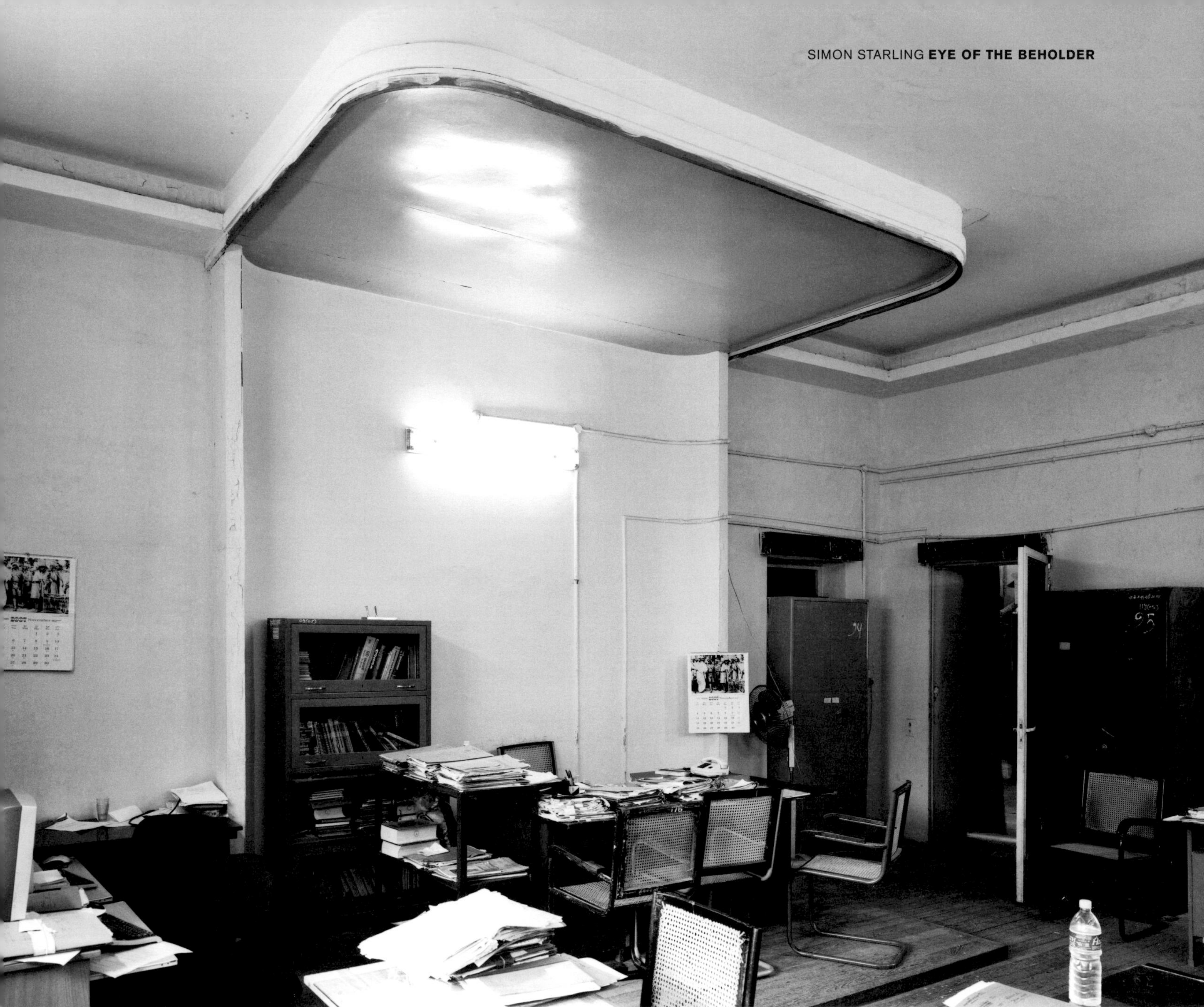

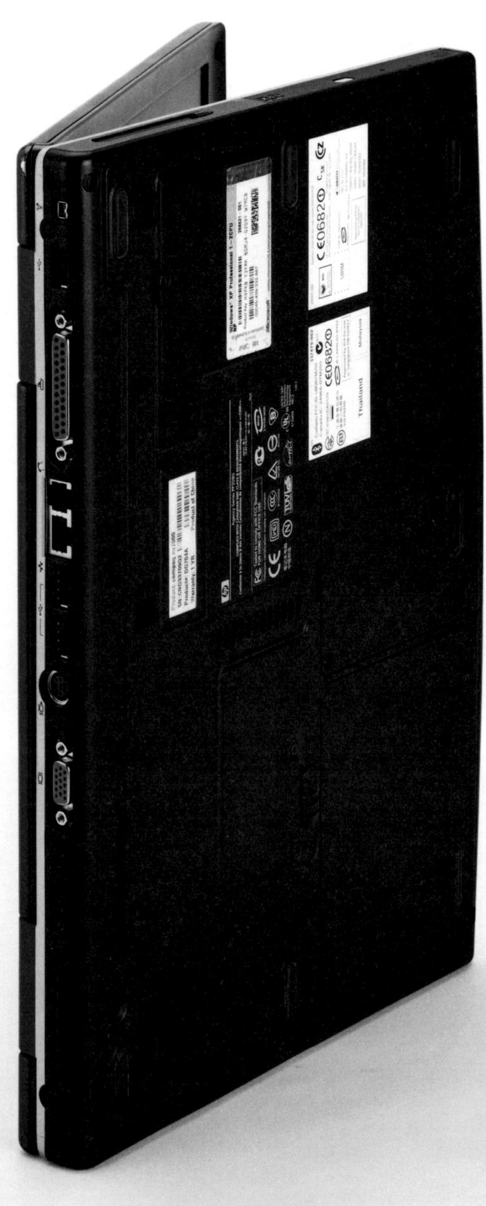

In this page Compaq nk 7000 computer. Laptop computer manufactured by Hewlett Packard in China, Thailand, Malaysia and Taiwain (2001) containing a 800 megabyte file of a 3D scan from a rough-cut block of Belgian black marble generated with a Scantech 3D scanner and stored in ASCII format, 2008, 40.5 x 50.8 cm. (framed 93.5 x 106.9). *Right* Copies of *The Tiger of Eschnapur* and *The Indian Tomb* by Joe May, Richard Eichberg and Fritz Lang, Film Museum, Frankfurt-am-Main, 2008, 40.5 x 50.8 cm. (framed 93.5 x 106.9)

Page 20 Main Staircase, Manik Bagh Palace, Indore 2007. 50,8 x 40,5 cm., (framed 106,9 x 93,5). *Page 21, top* Rough-Cut Block of Belgian Black Marble, Catella Marmi, Moncalieri, Italy (Negative) 2008, 40.5 x 50.8 cm. (framed 93.5 x 106.9). *Bottom* Rough-Cut Block of Belgian Black Marble, Catella Marmi, Moncalieri, Italy, 2008. *All images Platinum/Palladium print © Simon Starling, courtesy Galleria Franco Noero, Turin*

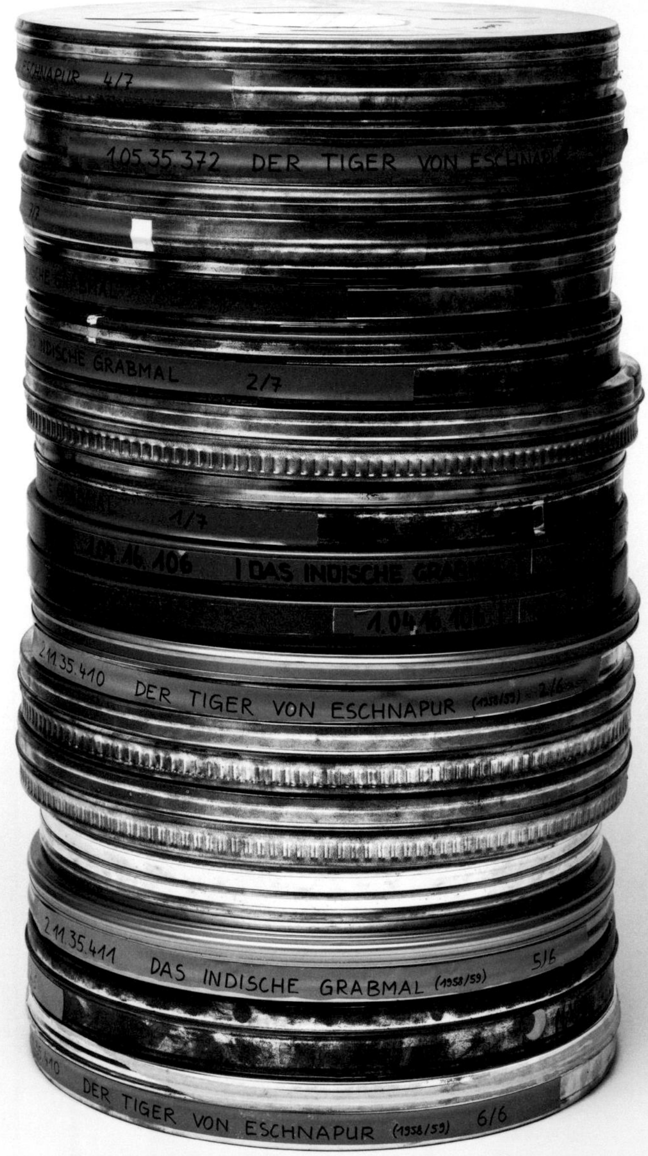ESCHNAPUR 4/7
105 35 372 DER TIGER VON ESCHNAPUR
INDISCHE GRABMAL 2/7
1/7
104 35 106 DAS INDISCHE GRAB
104 35 105
2 11 35 410 DER TIGER VON ESCHNAPUR (1958/59) 2/6
2 11 35 411 DAS INDISCHE GRABMAL (1958/59) 5/6
DER TIGER VON ESCHNAPUR (1958/59) 6/6

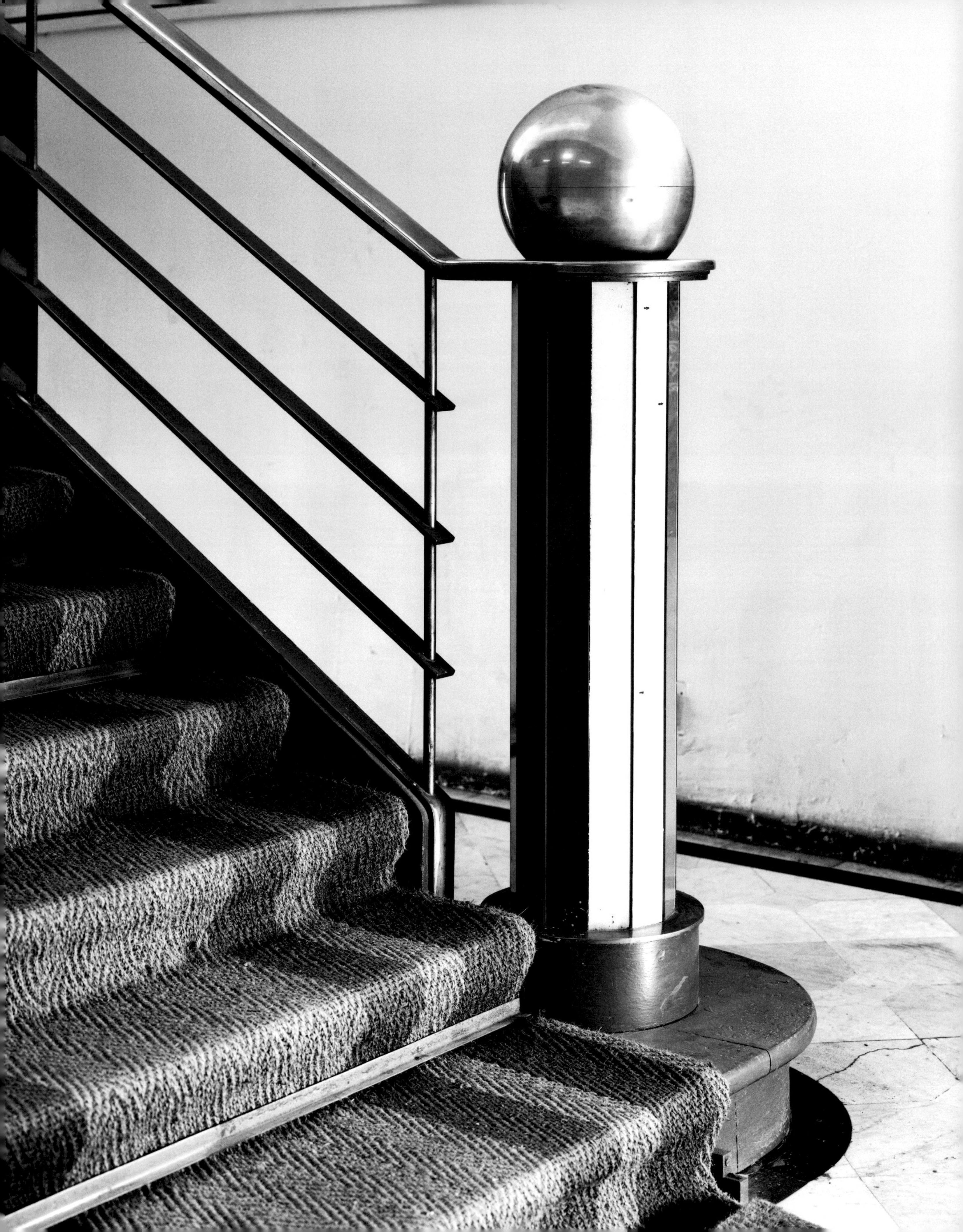

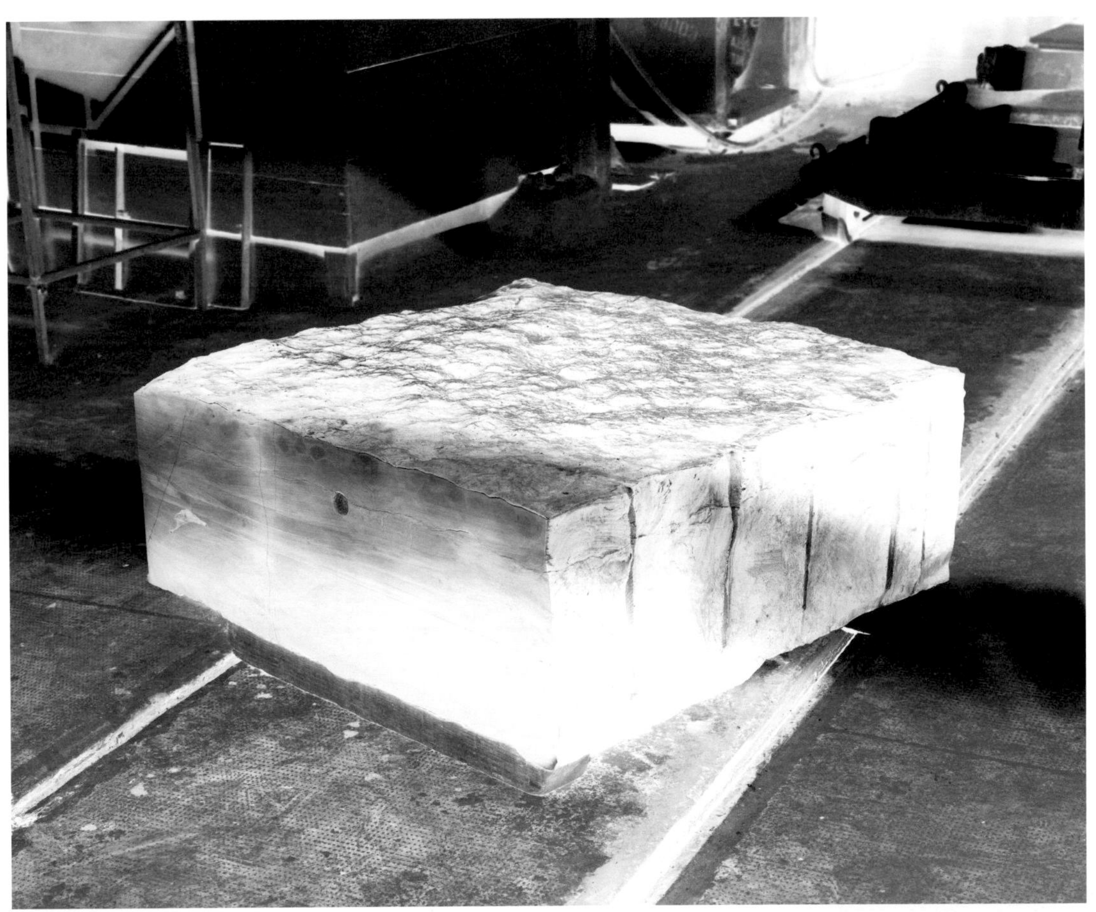

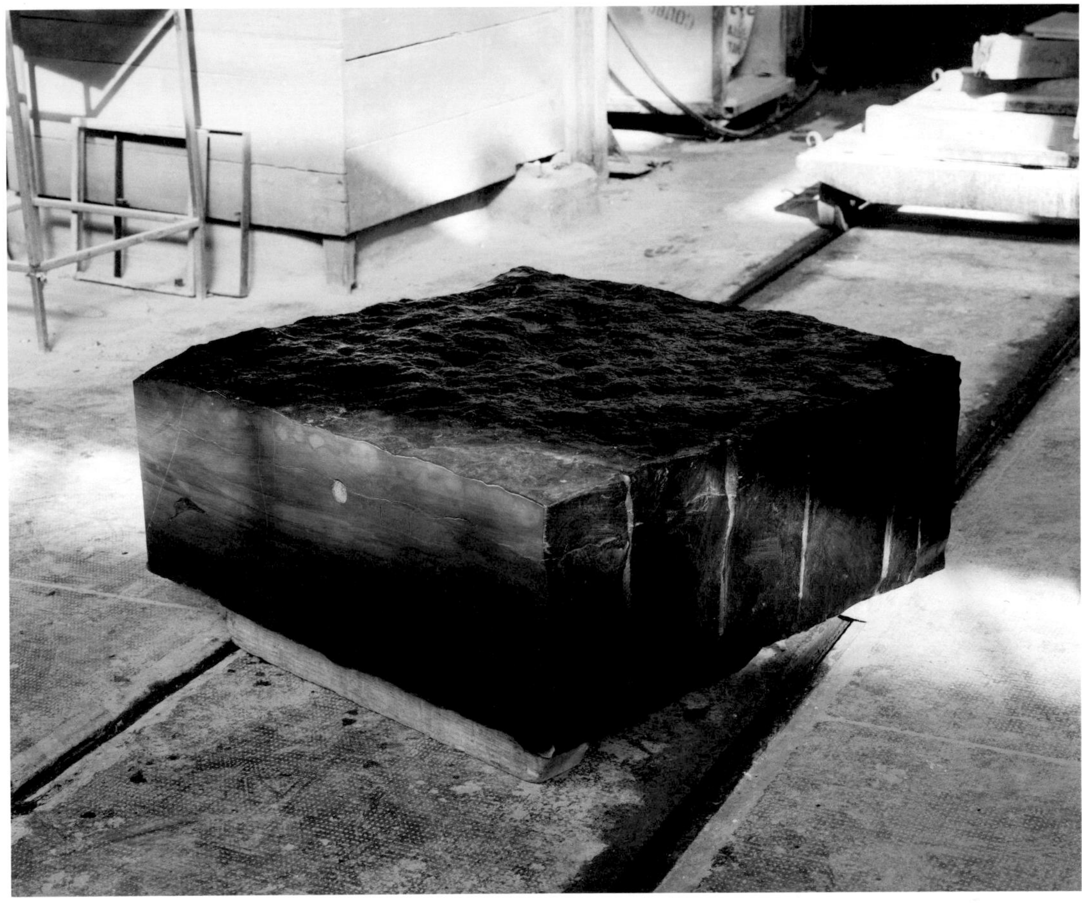

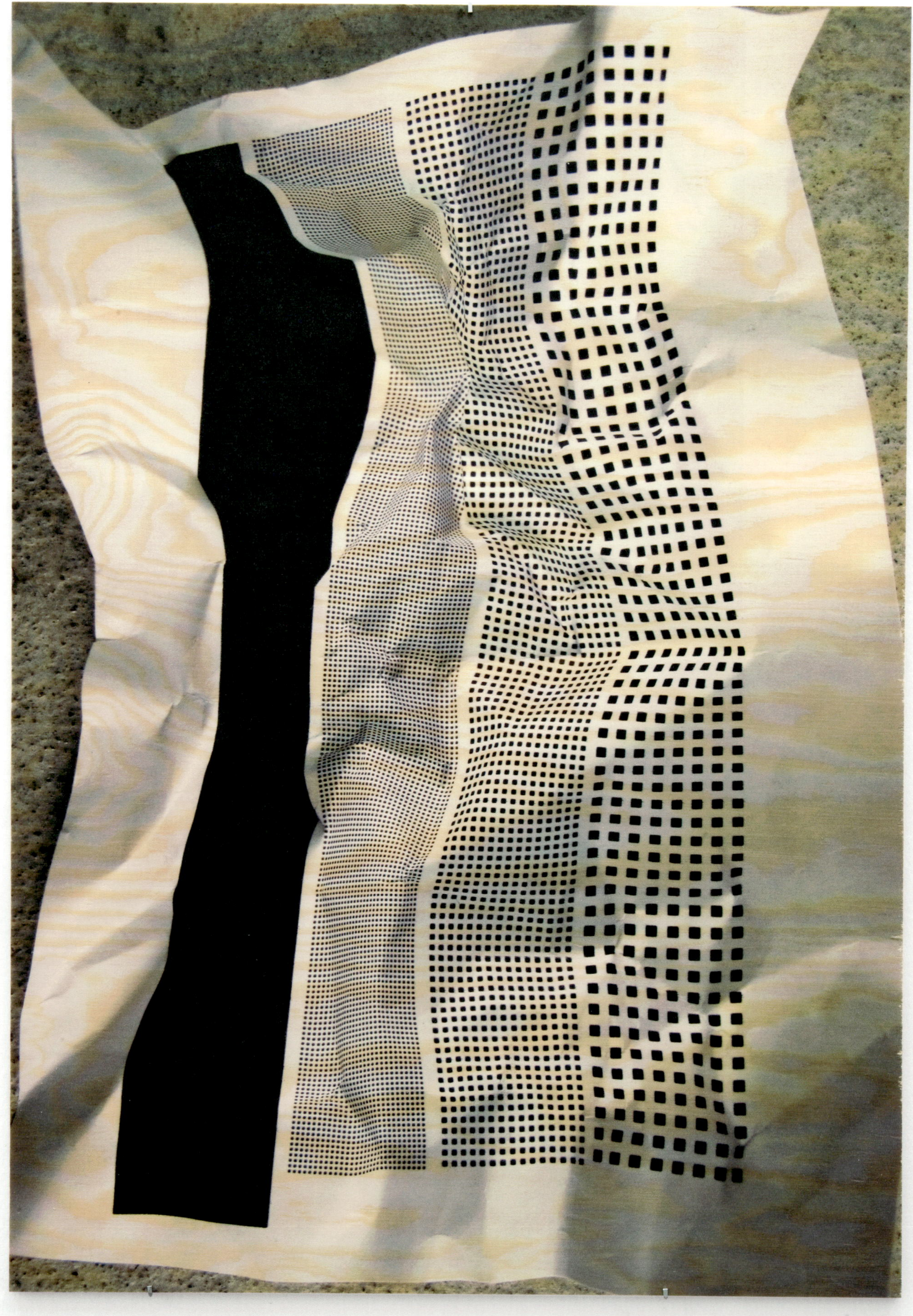

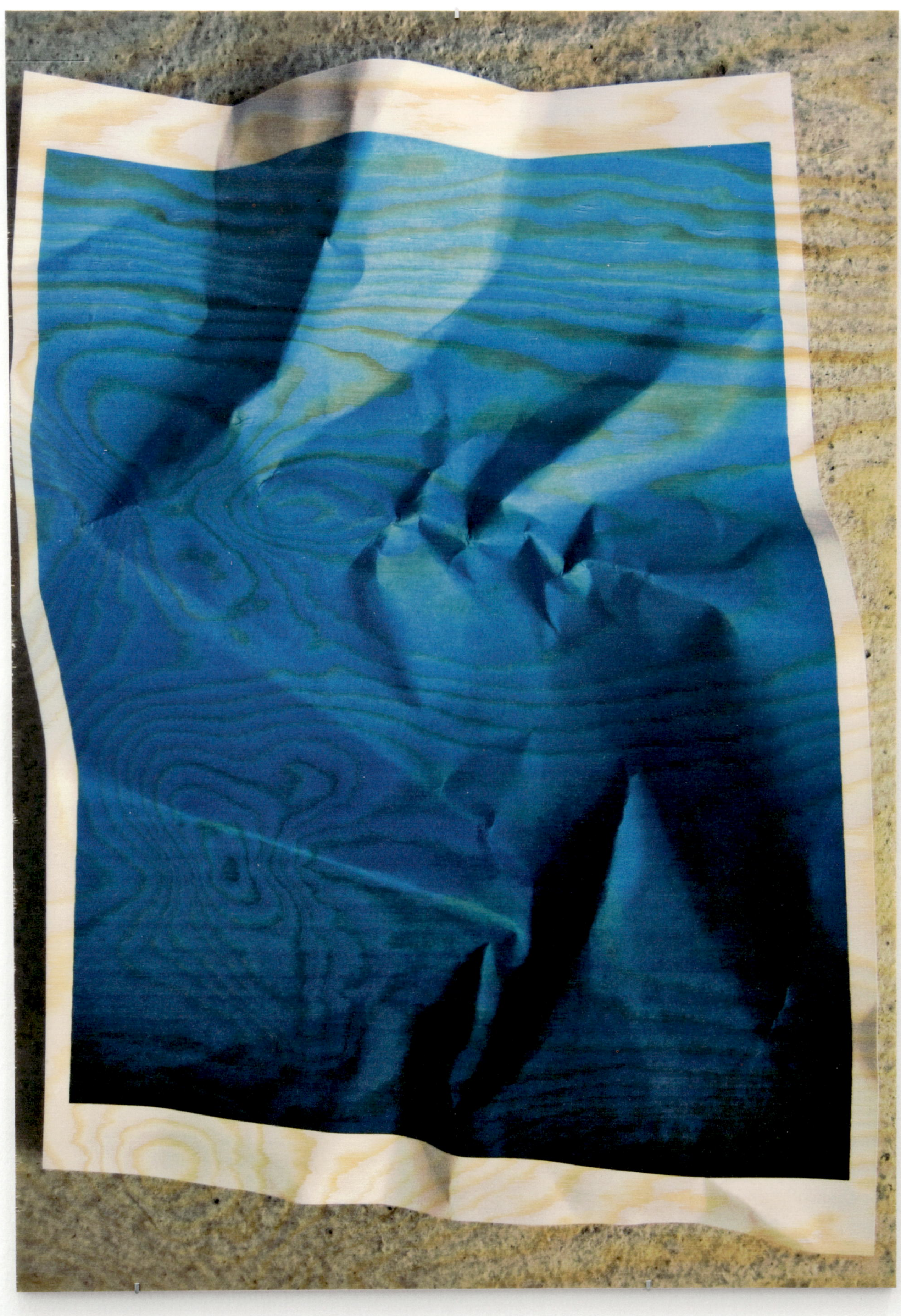

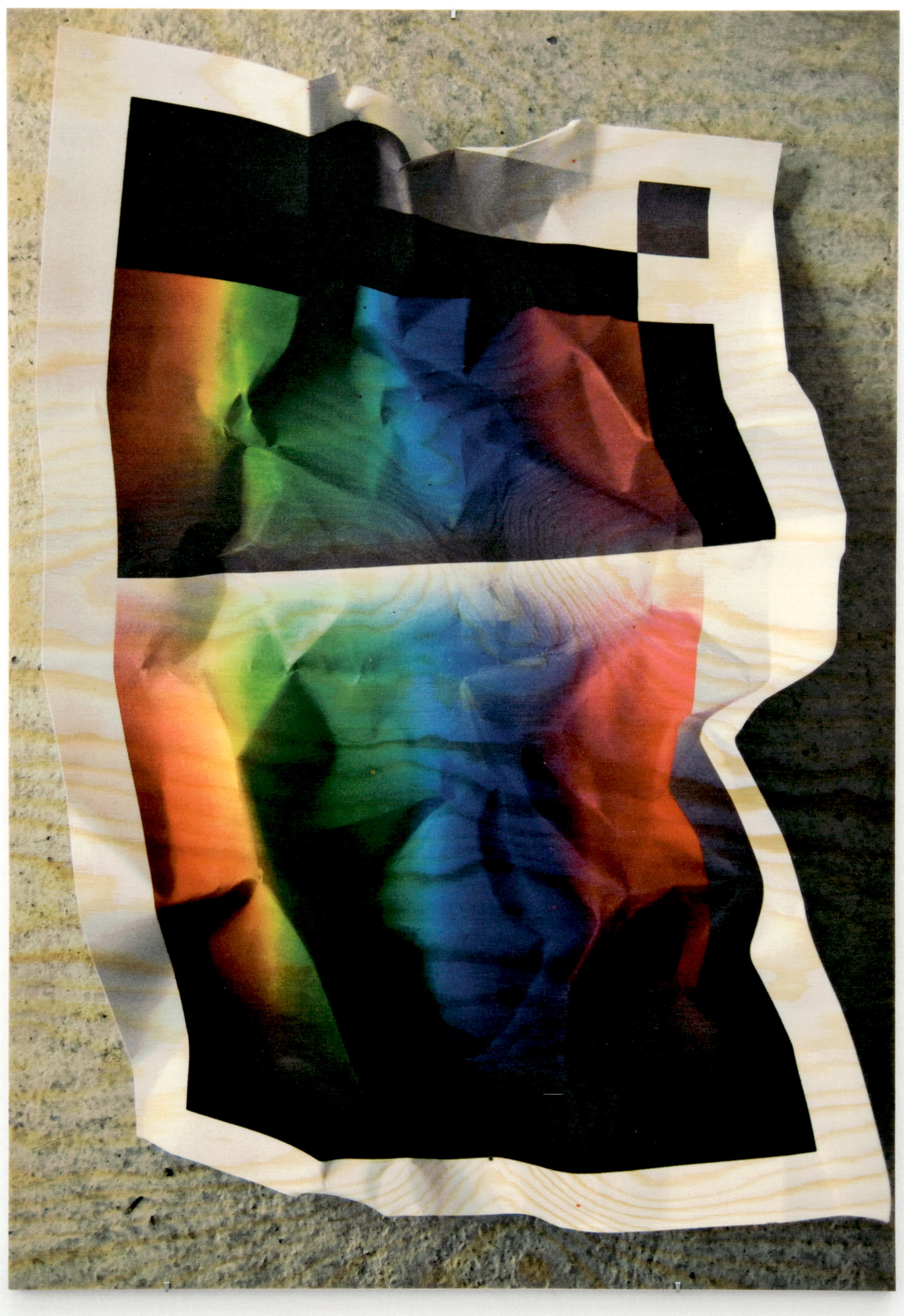

The Materialization of Absence
CHRISTODOULOS PANAYIOTOU by Denis Pernet

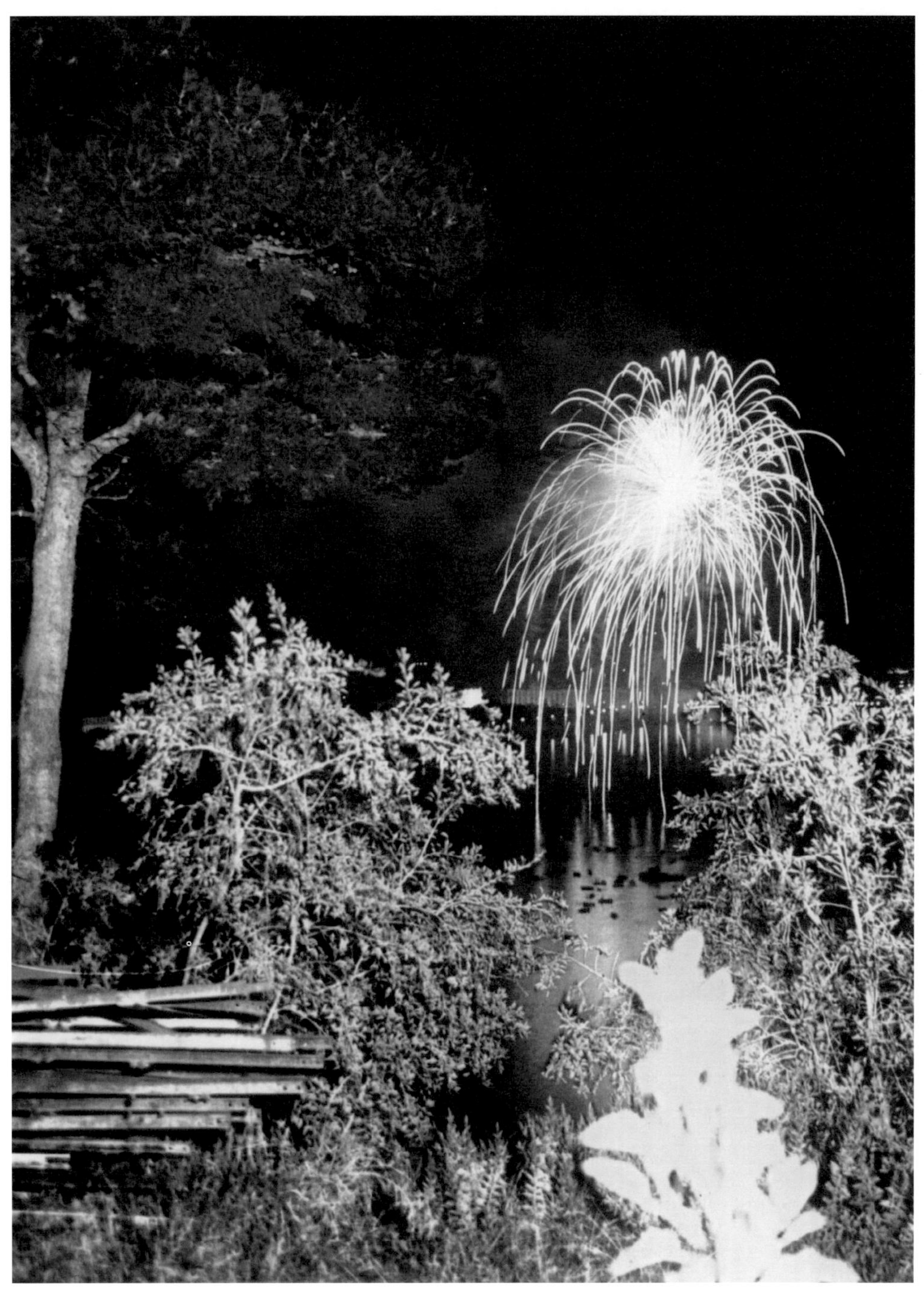

Among the various themes that crisscross the work of Christodoulos Panayiotou (1978, Cyprus), one in particular seems to relate to the medium of photography: the representation of an absent object, and the emotions arising from that absence. In a number of works, the materialization of absence is manifested in redundant documentary gestures relying on the use of photographs, installations and videos, as well as slide projections, performances, posters advertising the performances and publications relating to the projects at hand. Absence, in Panayiotou's work, is a plural topic: from the absence of the beloved in *Slow Dance Marathon* to the body's absence in *Untitled* (2007) and *Le fauteuil de Sarah Bernhardt* (2008), and the absence of the represented object in *Untitled (Act I: The Departure, Act II: The Island, Act III: The Glorious Return)* (2007), *The End* (2009) and *Wonder Land* (2008). These works revolve around the emotions associated with the act of recalling and the memory work. The artist's practice interrogates our relationship to the past, and by extension to society, history (with or without a capital H), and the construction of identity.

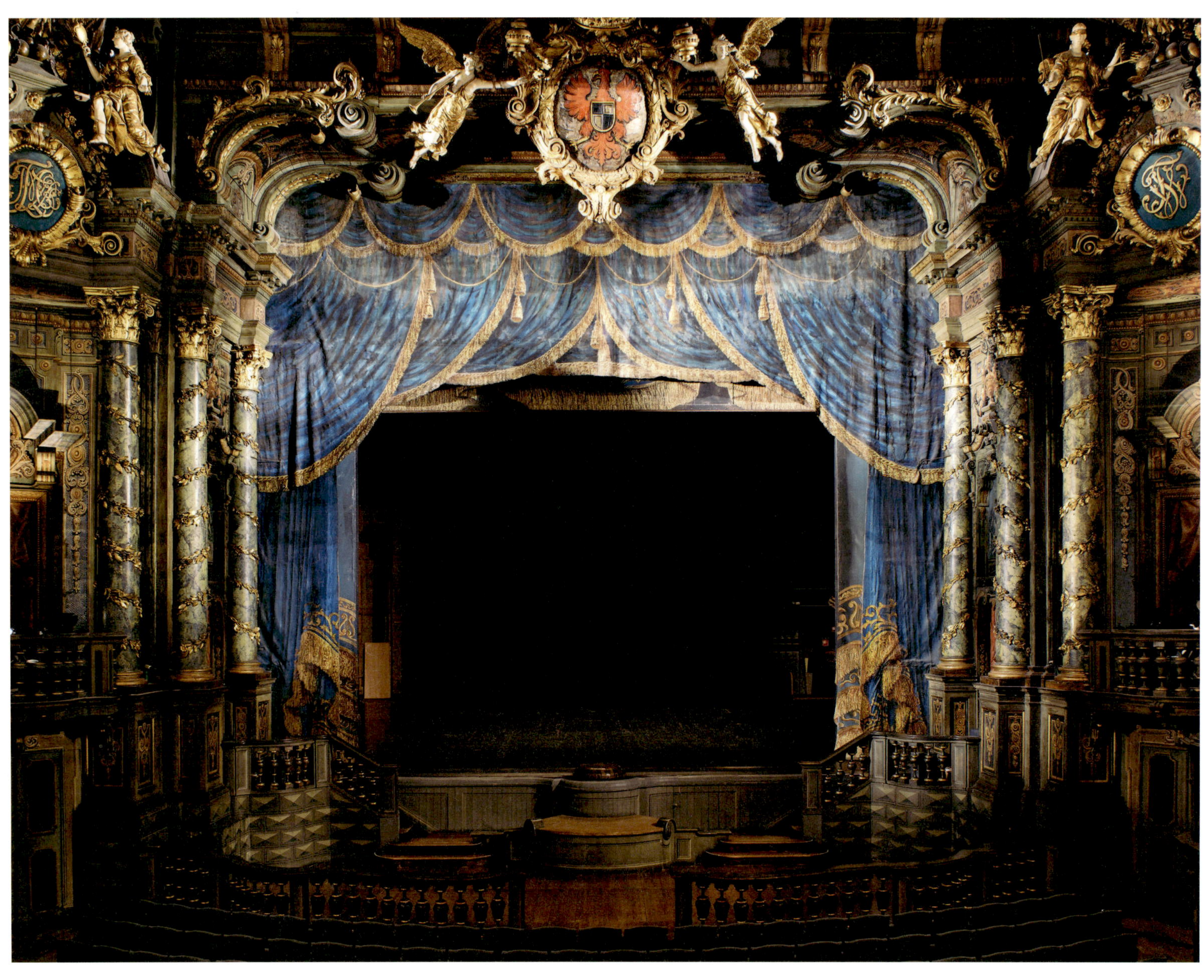

Previous page If Tomorrow Never Comes, 2007. From a series of 27 black and white slides, realized with the collaboration of Archivio Fotografico Parisio and Archivio Mario Carbone, Naples

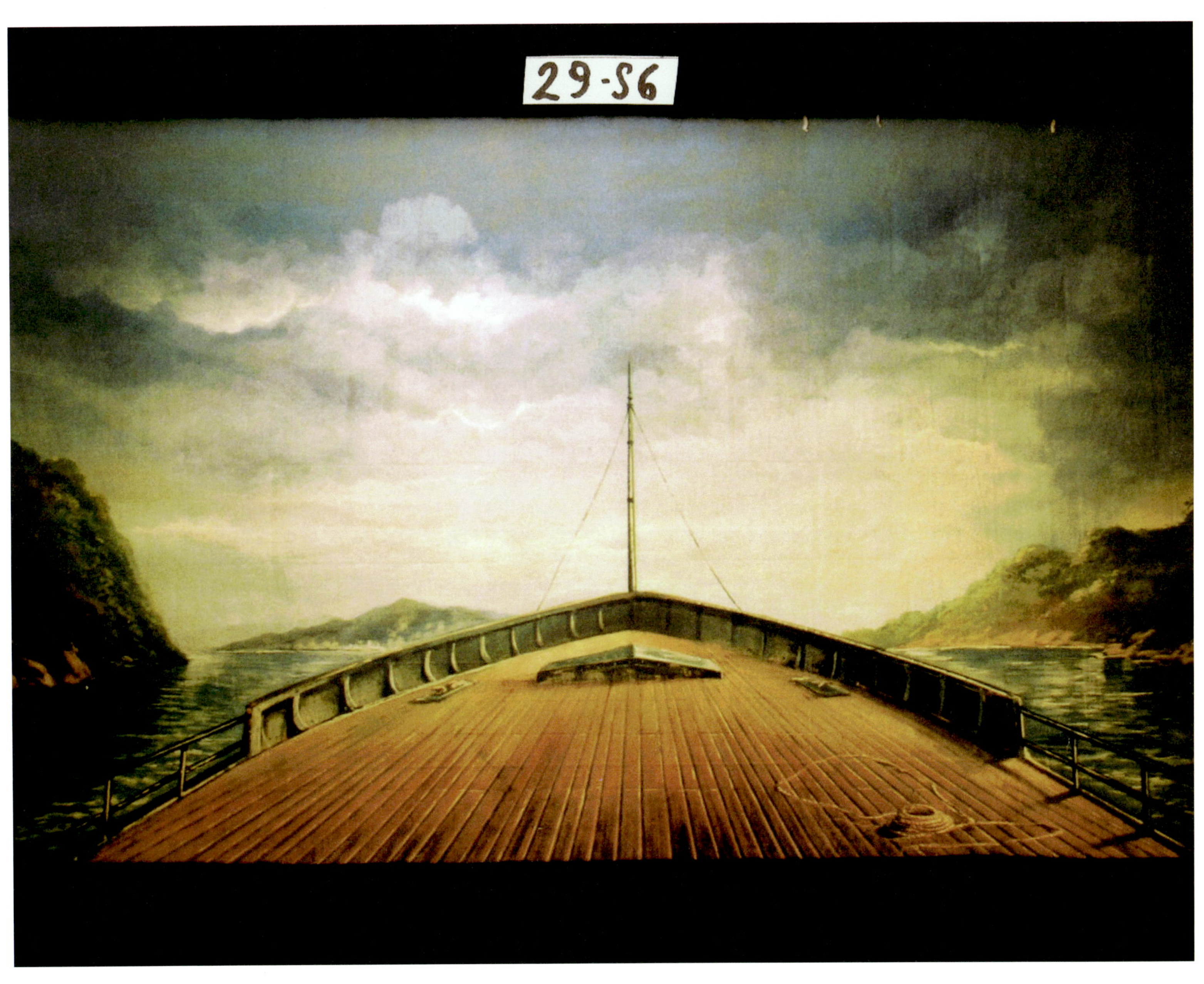

Left The End, 2009. Documentation of performance. *In this page* Untitled (Act I): The Departure, 2007. Folded theater backdrop (9 x 5 m.) and framed photo. *Courtesy the collection of Nikos Pattichis*

Using re-appropriation strategies, Panayiotou mines documentary lodes in order to extract materials that will act as supports for collective memory.

The slide projection *Wonder Land* (2008) consists of images culled from the archives of the city of Limassol documenting this Cypriot city's carnival parade. Panayiotou selected a series of photographs from 1974 to today focusing exclusively on costumes inspired by Walt Disney characters. The remaining traces of the festivities acquire a strange ambivalence, hovering between nostalgia and critique, between personal memory and the political structuring of a collective identity. The mode of presentation reinforces this impression of eeriness: the mechanical nature of the slide projection is both familiar and obsolete. The question of Cyprus' situation at the crossroads between East and West is evoked here, as it is again in the later slide work, *Never Land* (2008), which grew out of Panayiotou's research into the archives of the island's main daily paper.

Remaining in the realm of popular culture, Panayiotou created a faceless portrait of Marilyn Monroe. *Untitled* (2007) is a color photograph documenting the presentation of a dress that once belonged to the Hollywood star and was bought at auction by a pioneer of Danish pornography. In order to display the garment, the collector had an armature produced to the star's exact measurements. This ghostlike portrait acts as the trace of a tangible element: the dress, retaining the body's imprint. The collector carefully displays these materials in front of a red curtain. Panayiotou photographs the dress frontally. The image is so familiar that viewers can automatically summon up the absent figure, recalling characters like Lorelei Lee in *Gentlemen Prefer Blondes*.

Panayiotou questions the dialectic of love in the performances gathered under the title *Slow Dance Marathon* (2005-2006). The artist organized 24-hour slow dance marathons in different cities, adding an extra day for each new edition of the piece. With the soundtrack, a mix of commercial music, Panayiotou explores our relationship to love and romanticism and reminds us how tender feelings may surge irrepressibly at the sound of a vapid love song, when heard while in an enamored state. "Love is overrated", claimed the artist in a publication of the same title (2006) that accompanied the marathon project, and he went on to consider the extent to which our experience of love is formatted by commercial and cultural parameters.

The dialectic of love appears in several other works by Panayiotou and may illuminate the question of the materialization of absence. In *A Lover's Discourse: Fragments* (1977), Roland Barthes analyzed various stages of the lover's experience and defined "disreality" (déréalité) as "the sentiment of absence and withdrawal of reality experienced by the amorous subject" in the absence of the loved one. Everything seems vain. The surrounding world is neither unreal nor surreal: it simply no longer exists. In some way, Panayiotou confronts us with the discomfort caused by this state of *disreality*, when the absence of the beloved (or of the represented object) gives rise to an eerie feeling, like an echo of melancholia.

With *Le fauteuil de Sarah Bernhardt* (2008), Panayiotou evoked the physical trace left by the world's most famous stage actress. In a bout of inspiration worthy of a Land Art artist, Sarah Bernhardt had a seat carved out of the cliffs at Belle-Ile-en-Mer so she could contemplate the ocean. The photographic diptych presents two views: in one, the hollowed rock in the shape of a chair seat; in the other, the view of the open sea past the Pointe des Poulains. The two images are displayed in a corner so as to blur their shot/countershot dialectic. The simplicity of the black and white shots also calls tomind the actress' connection with the history of photography. Among the most famous portraits by Nadar around 1860 are several shots of a very young Sarah Bernhardt, her shoulders all but bare. As she later became aware of the power of images, Bernhardt had herself photographed asleep in a coffin, promoting in the American press the myth of her eccentric and melodramatic persona. Thus choosing to represent her death she, too, played with the emotions stemming from her future disappearance.

A student of dance and anthropology, Panayiotou approaches the realm of the spectacle from a critical perspective, using stage strategies to activate his propositions.

Theatricality is at the core of the series of installations that comprise *Untitled (Act I: The Departure; Act II: The Island; Act III: The Glorious Return)* (2007). The work consists of three theater backdrops made of painted canvas found in a theater in Naples, Italy. They show the departure, the journey and the arrival of a ship. The work exists in three discrete parts that cannot be exhibited simultaneously. The backdrops are shown folded on the floor, with the painted colors barely discernible through the canvas. A small photograph on the wall documents the actual subject of each backdrop when unfolded. The physical presence of the folded object stands in contrast with its concealed content, which can only be seen on the modestly scaled photographic reproduction. The spectacle of colonialism is put in question, and with it our relationship to history. But isn't the *disreality* of the deactivated object also being materialized?

The link between performance, object and photographic representation takes on an additional dimension in the work titled *The End* (2009), which conflates a performance and its own documentation. The performance, announced on a poster and presented at the baroque Markgräfliches Opernhaus in Bayreuth, consisted in displaying an entirely black backdrop on stage. The resulting installation recalled *Untitled (Act I, II, III)*. The black backdrop was then folded on the ground and shown along with the poster and the photograph documenting the performance. The image revealed the sumptuous and excessive ornamentation of the opera house, designed in the 18th century by Giuseppe Galli-Bibiena, a member of a prestigious family of architects specializing in opera house interiors. Driven by her desire to turn Bayreuth into an ideal city, Princess Wilhelmine of Prussia undertook the construction of many new buildings and surrounded herself with a court of renowned intellectuals and artists. The opera house is one of the rare remaining examples of the splendor of baroque theaters, many of which were destroyed by fire. In the 18th century the whole theater would stay lit for the entire duration of the show (as shown on the photograph), because the ornamentation surrounding the stage was considered as much part of the spectacle as what was happening on it.

With these works, Panayiotou imagines the ongoing elaboration of a possible play, in which *The End* and *Untitled (Act I, II, III)* act as elements. But *The End* extends the hypothetical narrative fourfold: to the actual space in which the performance unfolds, to the audience's participation, to the displacement of the object and to its exhibition. The object is unveiled in a performative presentation and deactivated in the exhibition space. A black theater backdrop conjures emptiness, the void, the absence of ornament and action, but it is also the sum of all possible backdrops (as for instance in stand-up comedy). In the context of Bayreuth, the black backdrop acts as an oxymoron: a void at the core of abundance. The folded backdrop is visible but mysterious; the photograph documents it, but above all reveals the space of the performance. Again, the materialization of absence gives rise to eeriness. The veiled object activates our imagination and connects it with the photographic document. This device evokes the process of recollection: a dissociated, syncopated and perhaps *disreal* form of recollection.

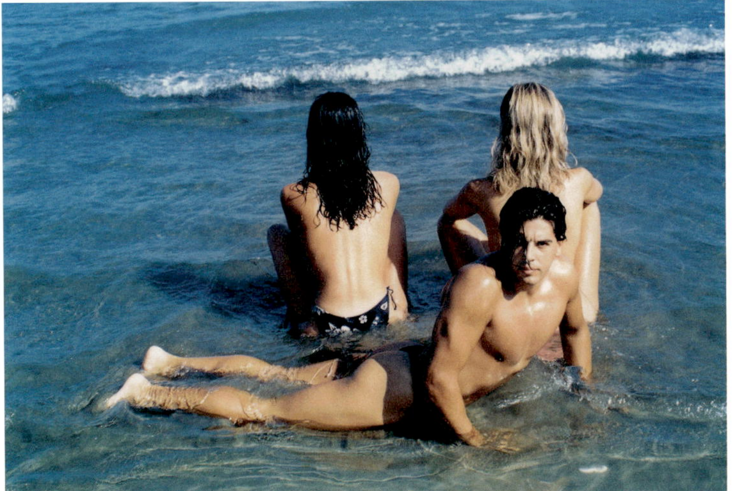

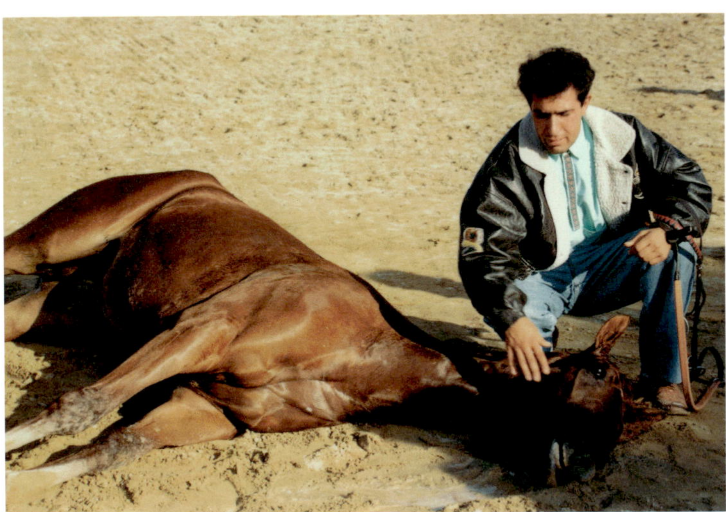

Never Land, 2008. From a series of 153 color slides with 3 synchronized slide projectors. Realized with the collaboration of the archive of the newspaper *Phileleftheros*, Nicosia, Cyprus.

All images courtesy of the artist and Rodeo Gallery, Istanbul

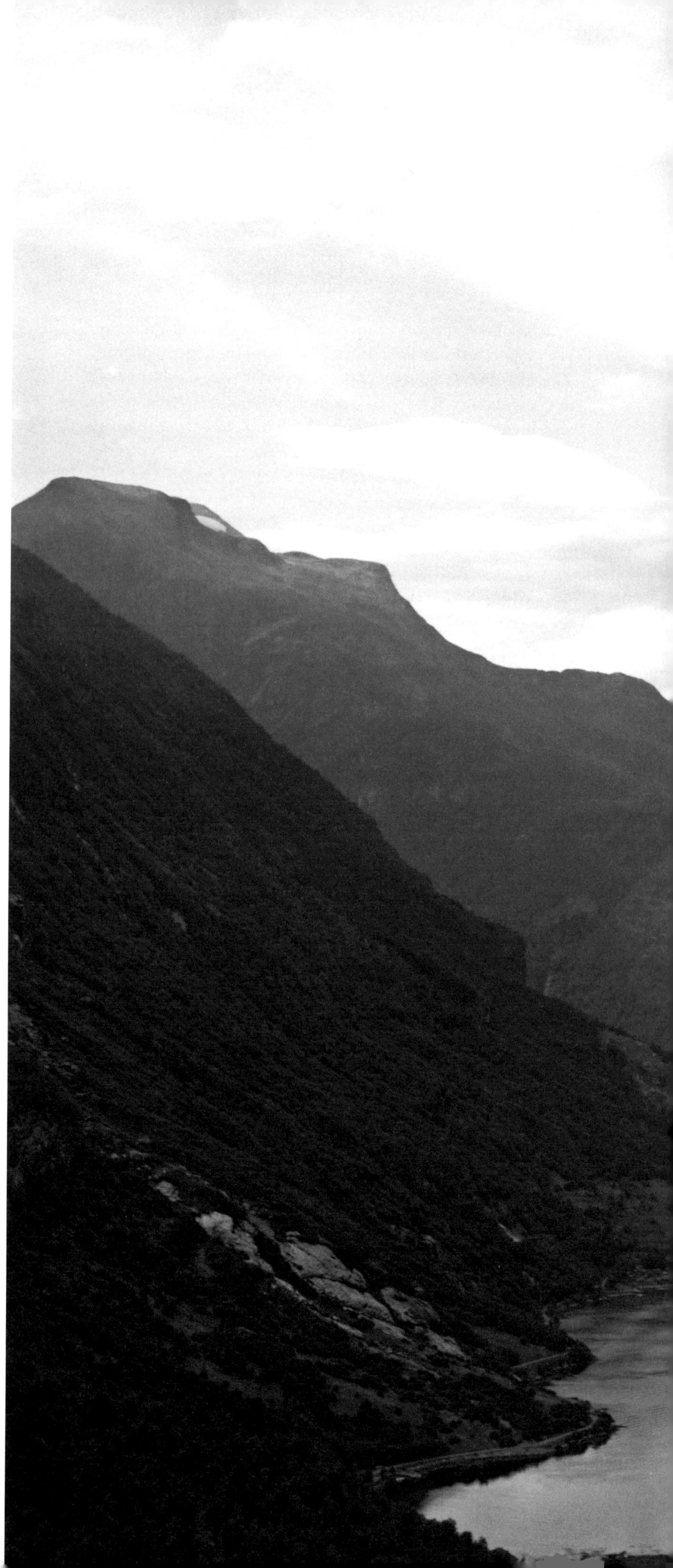

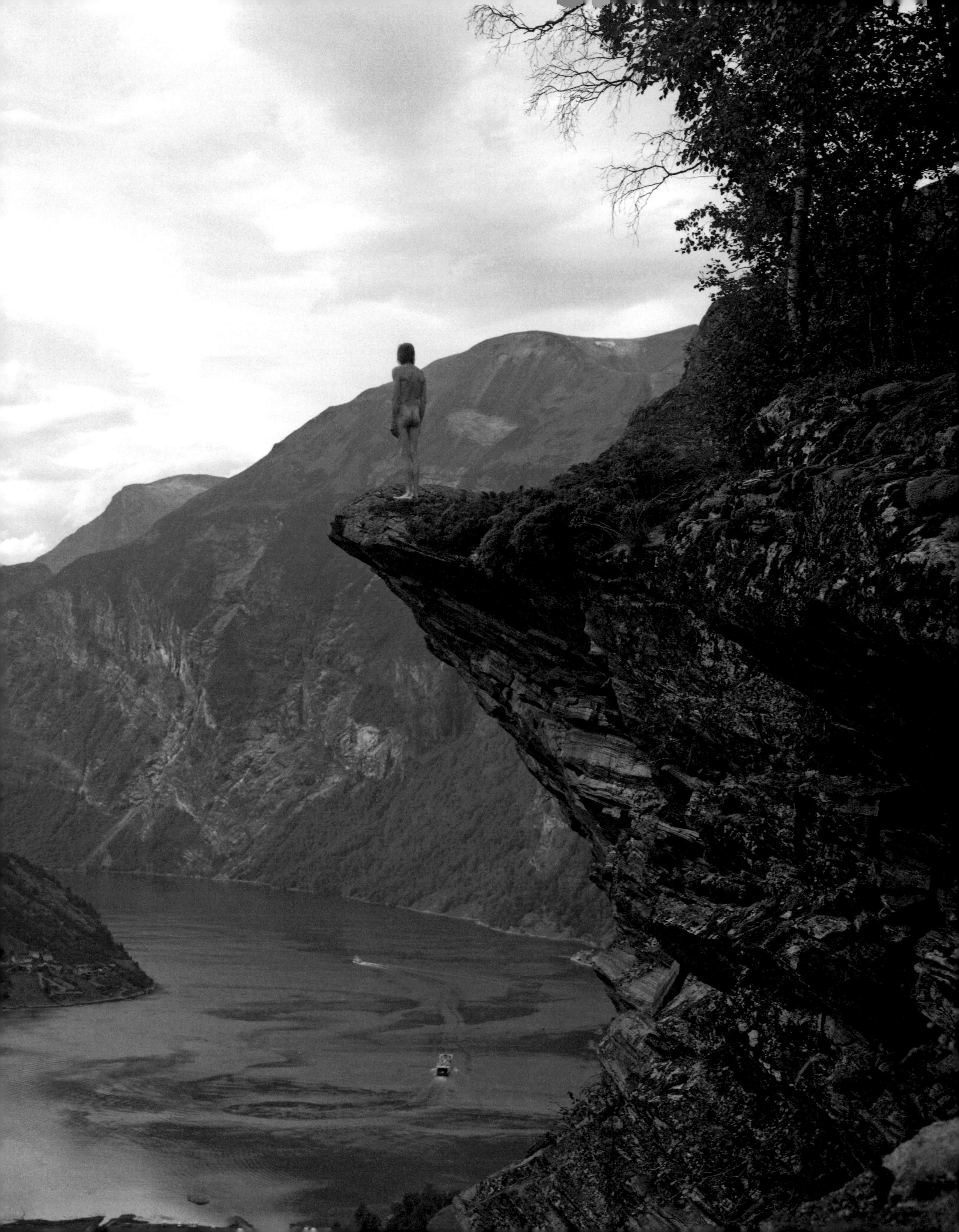

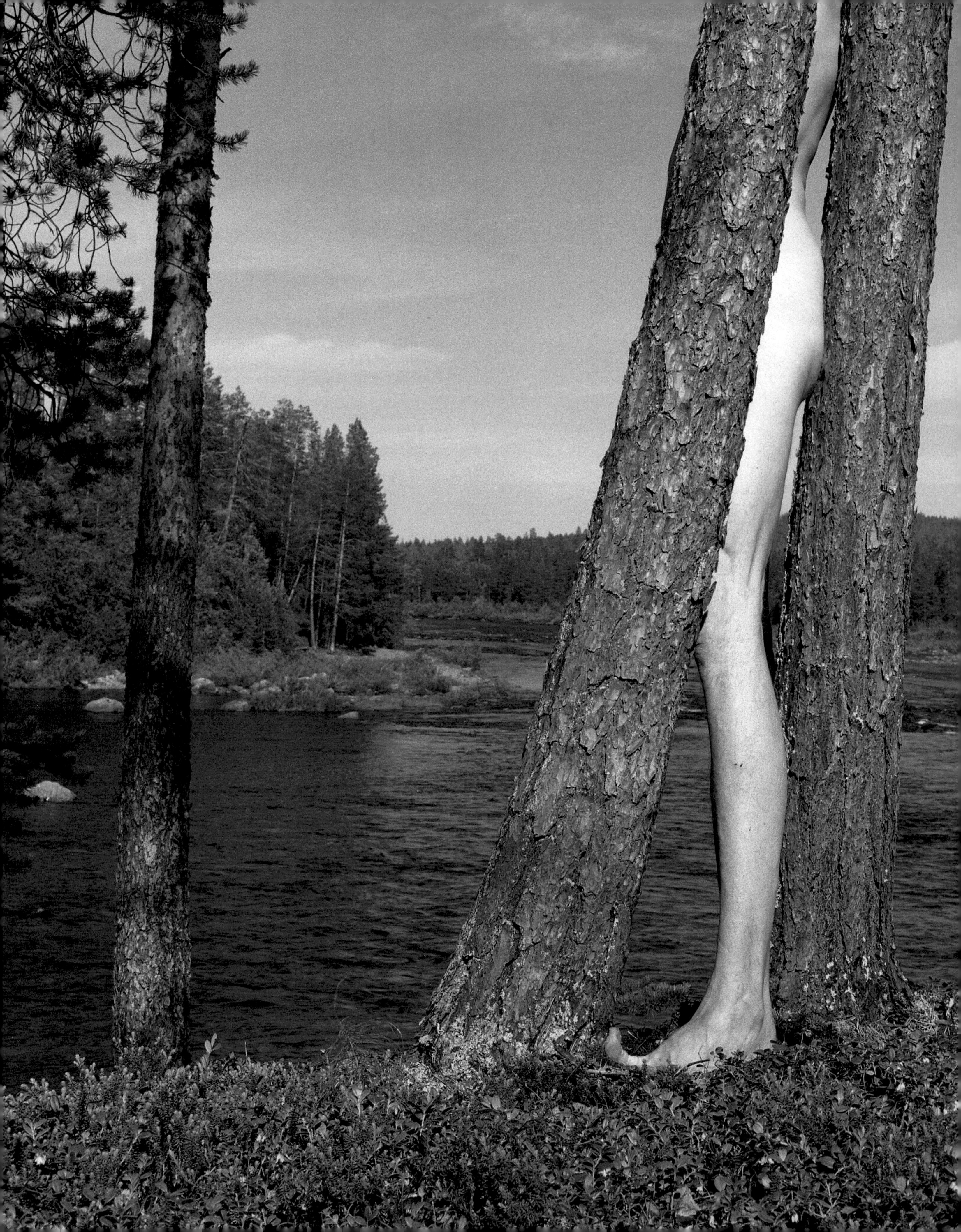

Parallels
Photographers in conversation
Jorma Puranen meets
ARNO RAFAEL MINKKINEN

"I consider myself to be a documentary photographer. If you see my arms coming up from under the snow, I am under the snow. What happens in front of my camera happens in reality. There are no double exposures, no digital manipulations". Arno Rafael Minkkinen has been taking self-portraits in relation with nature for 40 years. Questioning with wit, sensitivity, inventiveness, and risk our connection with our environment(s), and thus ourselves. He was born in Helsinki, Finland in 1945, moved to the US with his family in 1951, and now lives with his wife Sandra on Fosters Pond in Andover, Massachusetts. We invited Minkkinen's fellow Finnish photographer and friend, Jorma Puranen (1951), to engage him in a conversation about his work.

"If you would find yourself, look to the land you came from and to which you go" (Henry David Thoreau)

JORMA PURANEN *Dear Arno, I wanted to open our dialogue with this quote from Thoreau to address my interest in the landscape, northern landscape in particular, the one in which we both have worked, a stage for craving and visual dreaming. Whatever cosmologies, belief systems or lived experiences may have shaped our relation to landscape or the ways we see it, one thing seems to remain the same to us both; belonging, being a part. I remember from years back the title of your show, One Foot in Finland, which in itself says so much to me. Now looking at your work years later it seems to me as if your foot has become deeply rooted in this northern land. Limpid horizontal lake scenes and vertical upright birch trees aim to represent latitudes and longitudes within the map of your personal life.*

ARNO RAFAEL MINKKINEN You are right. Finland epitomizes the idea of the landscape as a place for belonging in both of our works. Within a few years of becoming a photographer, Finland became my primary background source and continues to this day to be my single most sacred hunting ground for new photographs as always. Just a few weeks ago, in fact, I was in Kajaani, some two hours south of the Arctic Circle, photographing on the shallow shores of Oulunjärvi

(the lake of Oulu). Half of my body was under the water, the other half above water. Hopefully my back, rounded like a stone with no head, arms, or feet to connect the shape to a human figure, might suggest the possibility of flesh becoming stone. A stone the size of my back (another version of which you can see in the images I made on Hainan Island in China a few years ago) doesn't travel far so you could say most stones belong to the landscapes in which they are found. Thus I was trying to suggest - at least in the moment the shutter fired - that I too belonged to the landscape. And should the photograph turn out to be a good one, I will always belong to - and be part of - the lake and reflecting clouds of Oulunjärvi. All this is not to say, of course, that I have not ventured to other parts of the world as well, especially in recent years. In an effort to create a broader connection between the natural world and the human body, I have tried to adopt new terrains of inspiration and to expand the work in new directions through geography. Thus I have journeyed to Isle of Wight in Southern England, to the fjords of Norway, to the cliffs of Gozo in Malta, to Hainan Island and the Lianzhou mountain ranges of Lower Central China, or the back roads outside Oaxaca in Mexico. Italy has been especially rewarding as a source of imagery since 1995. The Tuscan landscape with its ever-present mysteries and natural light, not to mention some of the most alluring women in the world, could form a complete body of work in itself. But all in all, perhaps my use of diverse locations could ultimately be viewed as an unconscious desire to belong to something larger: the wholeness of the one world we live in. Is this the case for you as well in the *Icy Prospects* project? Aren't those landscapes really landscapes that exist the world over?

I do hope they are and will remain as such. When staying in Greenland I used to watch icebergs, bearing in mind the time span, the number of years it takes for those enormous sculptural pieces to sail with dignity along the coastline wherever they were traveling to. Get yourself adapted to the rhythm of icebergs and you will understand a bit of the scale of the globe. I guess for me land is an idea. My work, Icy Prospects *for example, is very much about fantasy and geographical imagination. I keep thinking of possible fates and histories, places and encounters of indigenous people and travelers in icy vistas of Arctic landscape. I try to point to the twilight zone of what might have happened and what are the consequences of these encounters. For me thinking of landscape is very much about imagination of "what it might be to be someone else or to be somewhere else". When I look at your images I very much think of what Paul Virilio wrote some while ago saying that he is nostalgic about the magnitude of the world, about its scale. Even that modern communication technology is polluting the idea of the magnitude, distance and scale, it is still there. This is perhaps why some of us keep looking for new places, being attracted time after time to a spatial experience, a secret kind of thing, which is very hard to explain or translate. Your images constitute a kind of a visual travelogue of all these locations in which you use your own body in various fascinating ways seducing us to consider the scale of the world and that of a human. Identifying with your images, perhaps saying "it could be me" your photographs help us to find one´s feet in the world. But then what about the mood of being quite on your own in those fantastic places? What possibilities do you find in remoteness, stillness and silence?*

The remoteness, while cosmically radiant, can be frightening too, in a spiritual sort of way, knowing that if you get totally lost in the wilderness or fall or go unconscious and die, your body will not easily be found. If it happened, in my case, it would be a nude body that the helicopter line would draw up out of some slot canyon in Utah, or a nude body they would lift on to the snowmobile in Lapland. The nude part I would like. Not having any life left in me? That part would suck. But because I have never really been lost or fallen beyond a bloody shin or rock-scrapped butt, I became more and more intrepid I suppose. Seeing me coming out of the shower once I was home, my wife would ask, "what happened to you?". Well, the stillness and the silence part? That was a whole other thing, gifts to the soul. We are lucky, aren't we, to get to work in such remote places where we can experience these metaphysical celebrations of aloneness. It's where we finally do find ourselves. Then on to another idea: something that occurred to me shuffling through old images that never quite saw the light of day. In a review of Szarkowski's *Looking at Photographs*, from a *New York Times Book Review* article from the early 1970s, the essayist Edward Hoagland wrote that one could always tell who was a photographer at the end of their life by looking in the closet. There one could theoretically find all the shoes the photographer ever walked to get his or her pictures. Unlike poets, writers, painters, and thinkers of all sorts, who in their final years could easily reflect back on their life in the comfort of a studio, photographers were doomed, or blessed, with the knowledge that if they wanted to have a photograph from the top of a mountain at age eighty, they would have to climb that mountain. Eighty or eighteen, it makes no difference. A picture of the real thing doesn't come any other way.

That got me thinking. Was there something we, as old-timers (meaning me, not you), could do to save shoe leather in the later years of life? Then the answer appeared out of the blue. Create triptychs from images that never made it. Bring them to light and to life again in the later years, at the comfort of our laptops when we can no longer roam in the wildernesses of our heart's desire. Triptychs, diptychs, it doesn't matter. But like the poet reflecting on times past, we could invent new works without ever leaving home.

Old age? Is it true that in your twenties you make your discoveries? In your thirties, you make your best work and become famous. In your forties, you answer your critics and fall out of favor. In your fifties, you regain your worth by going for quantity. In your sixties, quality is supreme as you reap in the harvest. Award ceremonies become part of the creative calendar. In your seventies, you tack on new horizons and re-invent yourself. In your eighties, you make your masterpieces. In your nineties, you drink good wine.

Reading your experiences somewhere in the wilderness of Rocky Mountains perhaps, quite on your own and what might have happened it´s like a script to a movie. And I´ve been into the same kind of situations so many times. Perhaps not risking my health in the way you do. Working in faraway remote places you lose yourself in breathtaking happiness. For us Finns, I think it is about discovering poetic pos-

Opening spread Dalsnibba, Geiranger Fjord, Norway, 2006. *Page 32* Pajakoski, Ivalo, Finland, 1995. *On the right* Kilberg, Vardø, Norway, 1990.

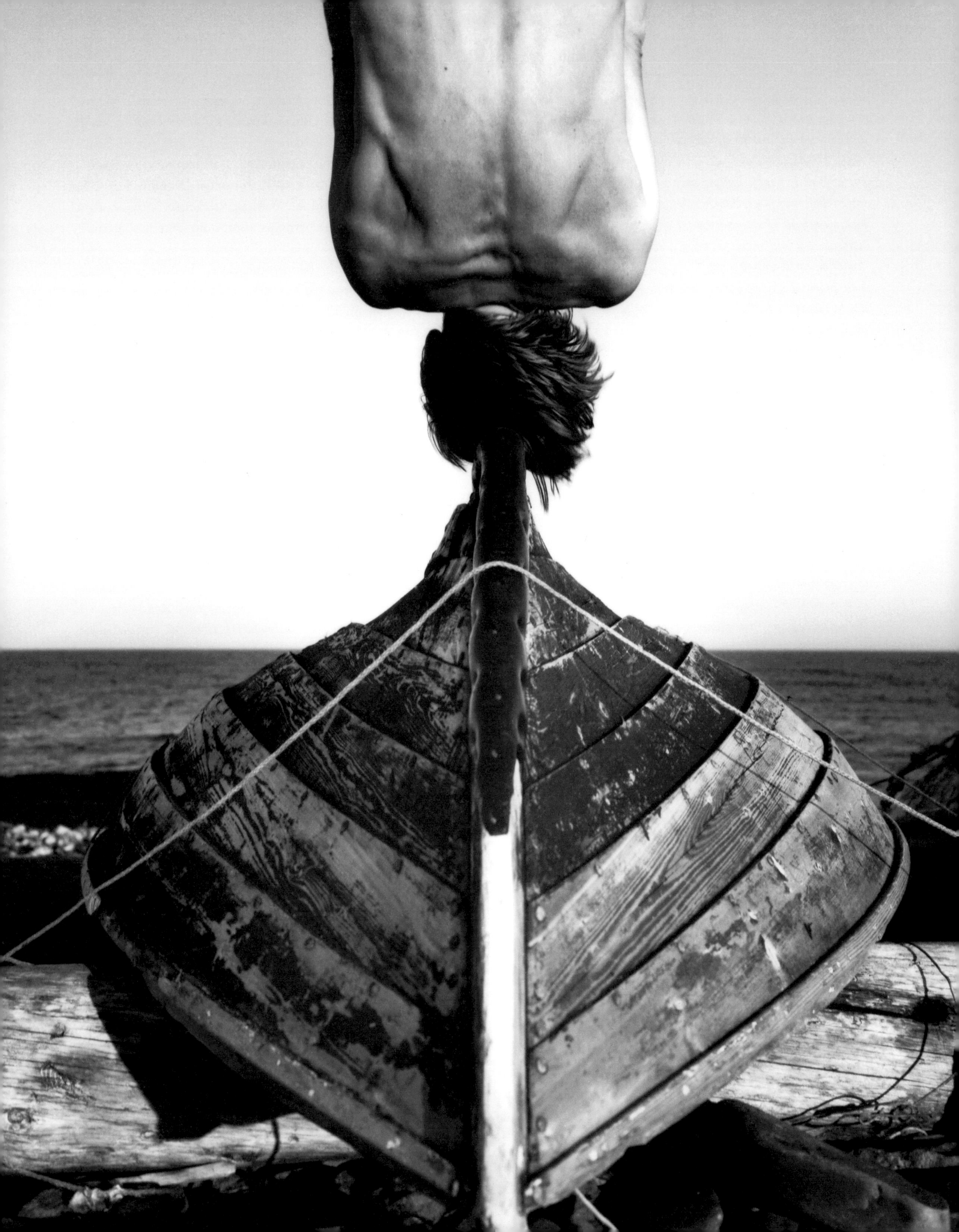

sibilities in silence. Why talk that much anyway. You may work for a day or two or more in isolation somewhere up in the mountains and see nobody, installing black/white transparencies in snowy fell slopes for example, as I did with "Imaginary Homecoming". You feel absolutely happy, hearing only sounds of migrating birds or see some reindeer or foxes, thinking that making art is a privilege, taking pictures a kind of an embodiment of hope, inspired by faith. Then suddenly you will see an occasional tourist coming closer and asking "what on earth are you doing?".

Your proposal of organizing images in triptychs or diptychs, in order to provide a paradigm of your career to produce new meanings made me look at your older works once more. I am in the process of working myself with a coming museum exhibition and looking for bridges between my pictures from different decades. I remember the first ever images of yours that I saw back in the early 1970´s, called "White Underpants" which really shook our understanding of photography in Finland, indeed. Then you organized your pictures as leading towards building a narrative, a series at the very least. And I think you still do, for me anyway.

I am sometimes a bit appalled nowadays about the tyranny of a single image, a work of art if you like, in our contemporary photography culture. It seems as if photography´s identity is distorted so as to obey the basic organizing principles of art history, for example emphasis to exceptional pictures or who did what first. As a consequence art history celebrates singular achievements.

For me photography was always about narrative and series instead of one single image. The issues I work with, past and present concerns intertwine like in a movie where the protagonist, perhaps me in this case, appears as a northern mountain taxi driver who narrates stories to his passengers about adventures and histories of people long gone and disappeared into this particular landscape. It is like talking to ghosts and you cannot say it all in one single image. How do you feel about it?

As much as I enjoy seeing single images in a collective whole, the singularity of the single image is what I recall and retain the most out of a body of photographs. A single image makes sense to me because it evolves from the moment something happened inside the viewfinder. Maybe because I am this half-blind photographer - who never sees the completed image in the view-finder - that single images take on such importance for me. I can't wait to open the developing tank and see what I got and, if it worked, share that view of the world with my audience. Naturally, without the accumulation of many single images, photography would be a poor storyteller. Single images, for that reason, only go so far. Without the whole body of work, we would have a house with just rooms, no structure, no foundation, and no roof.

The wholeness of the concept ultimately has the greater role and greater purpose. So, yes, I guess for me single images are what I am mostly after. The downside is that my hunger for them can never be satisfied. As soon as I am done with the latest success, I am searching for the next one. I leave rolls of film unprocessed in the darkroom for this reason. When the appetite for a new image becomes unbearable, I simply grab a roll like an alcoholic might grab a beer.

How about for you? Is the completion of anything ever fully satisfied? Is the creative life - if that is what it should be called - just one journey after another, as they say, no other destination than that?

I mostly work from one project to the following one. Once I have completed a project, which may take, say 3-5 years, I then know exactly how the work should have been done. From this discontent but not unhappiness will be found the seeds for the next work. And so the whole picture will never be finished or completed. Even that my work sometimes is informed and entangled with disciplines and interests beyond visual arts, such as social sciences or cultural studies, photography and art in general is a necessary dreaming process for me. Dreaming is a daily practice. Looking at your images I can see the same thing going on; small size universes measured by creativity, dreams and desires, all within one picture frame. Pointing to surreal and conceptual, your work is like an invitation, a subtle gesture towards balance with your body, consciousness and invisible possibilities of nature.

Right Wied il-Ghasri, Gozo, Malta, 2002. *Following spread* Dead Wood, Foster Pond, 2009. *Page 40* Afternoon, Oulunjärvi, Kajaani, Finland, 2009. *Page 41* Evening, Oulunjärvi, Kajaani, Finland, 2009. *All images © the artist, courtesy Robert Klein Gallery, Boston and Galerie Anhava, Helsinki*

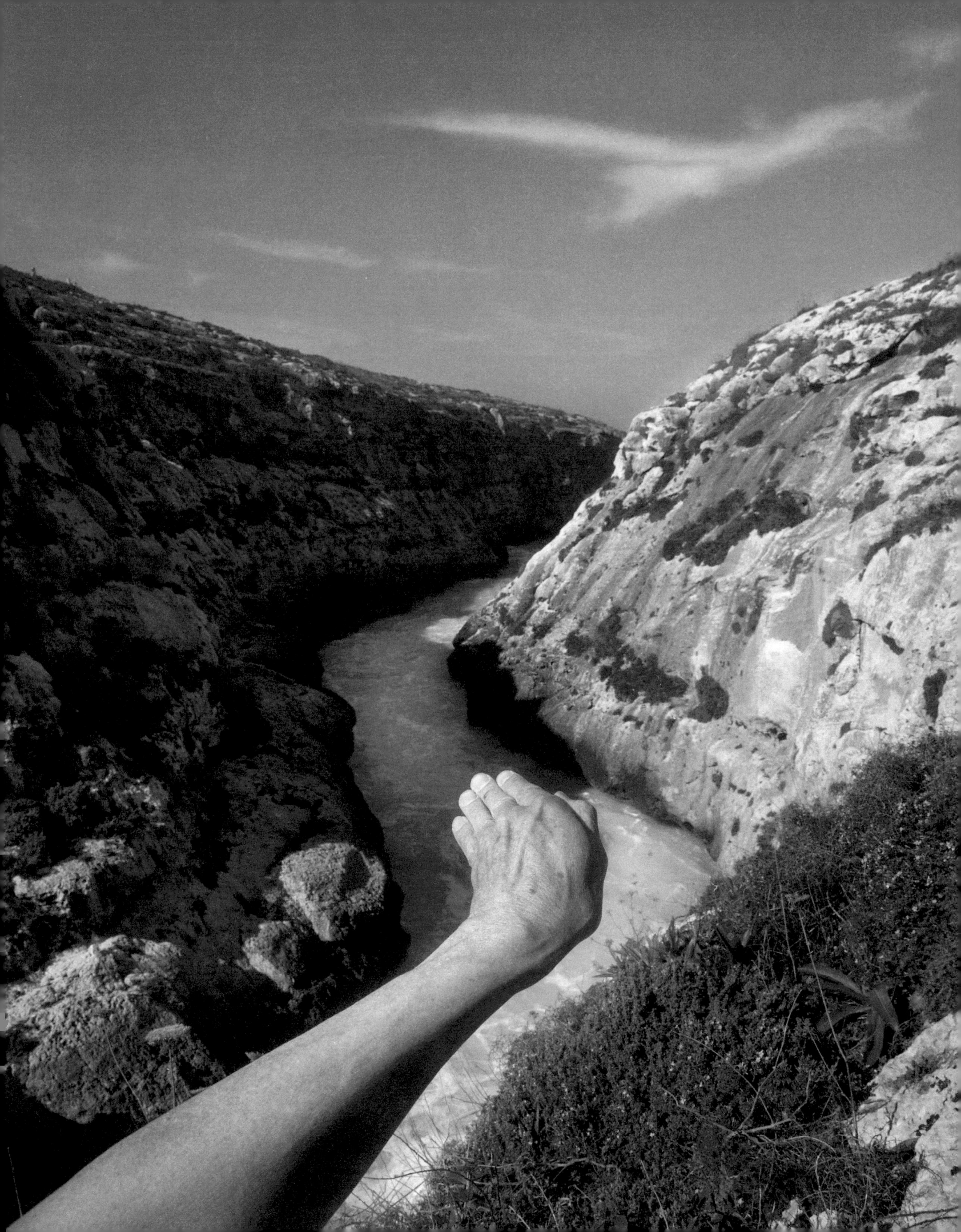

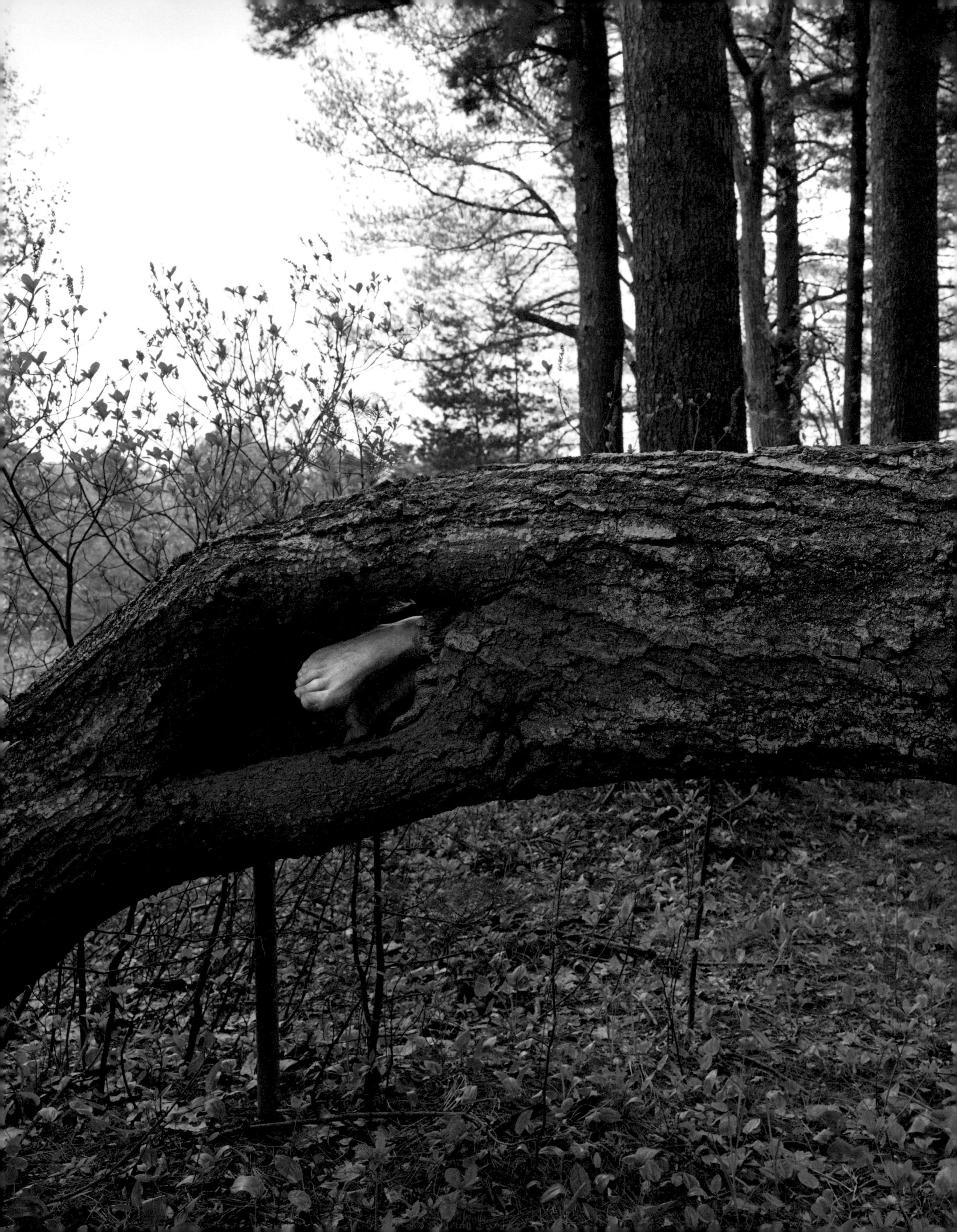

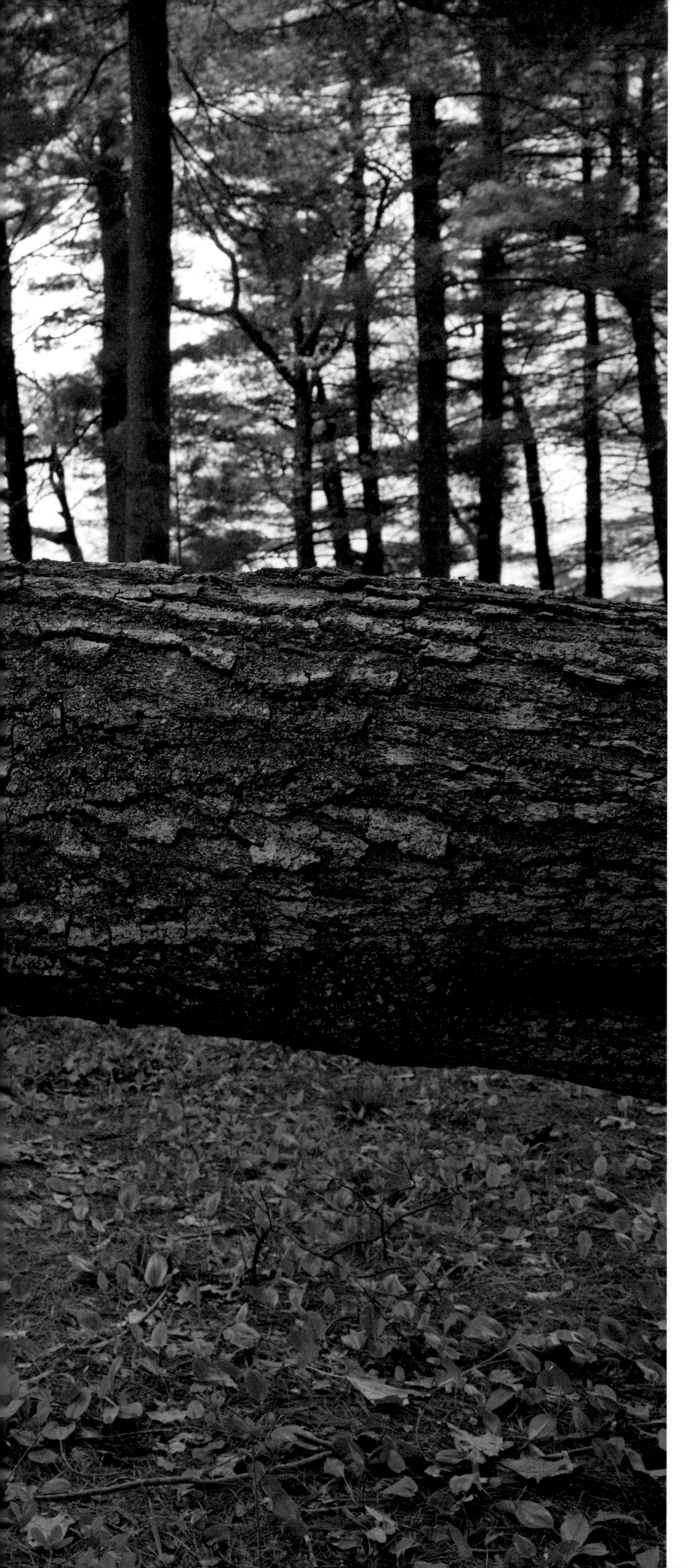

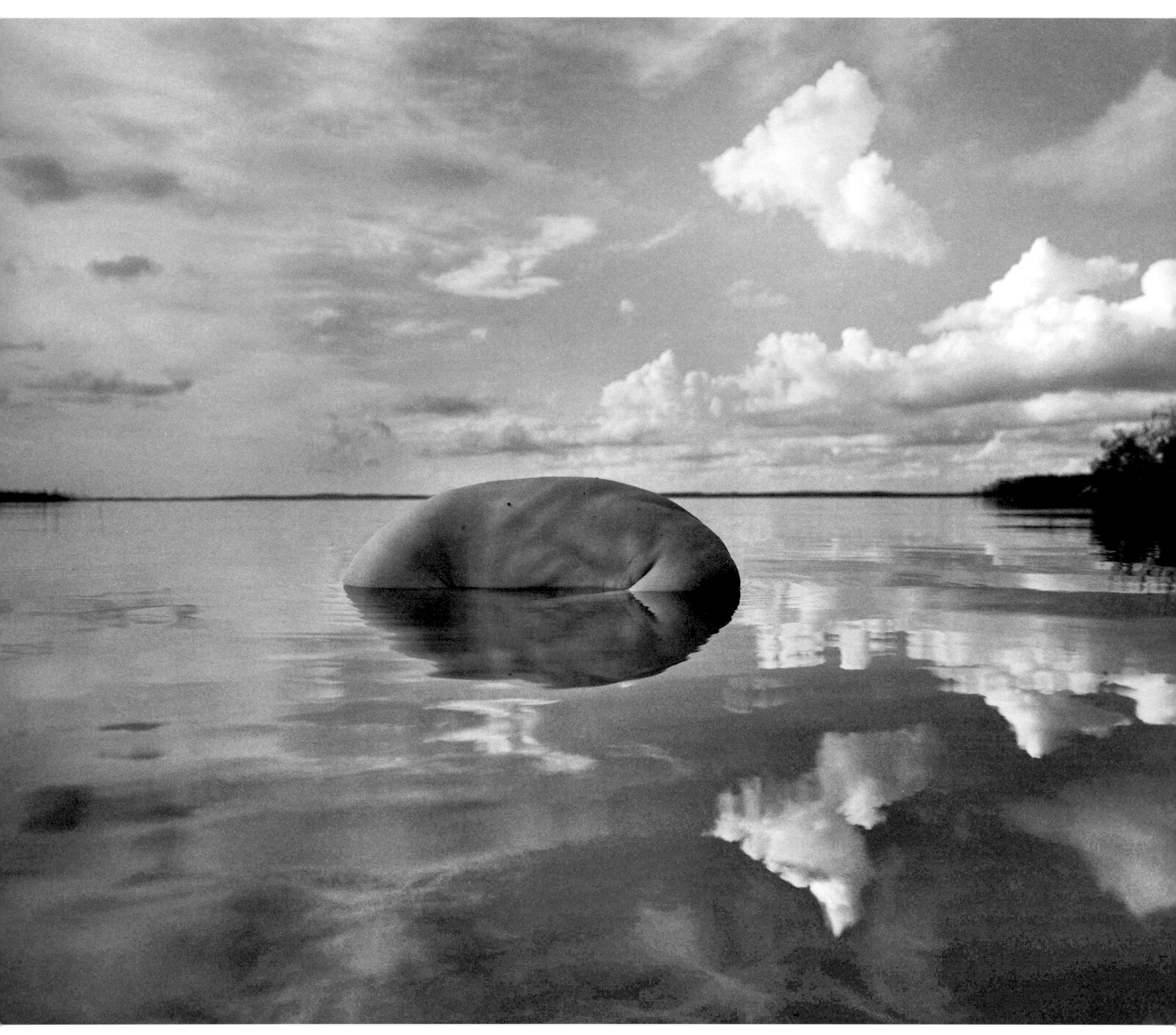

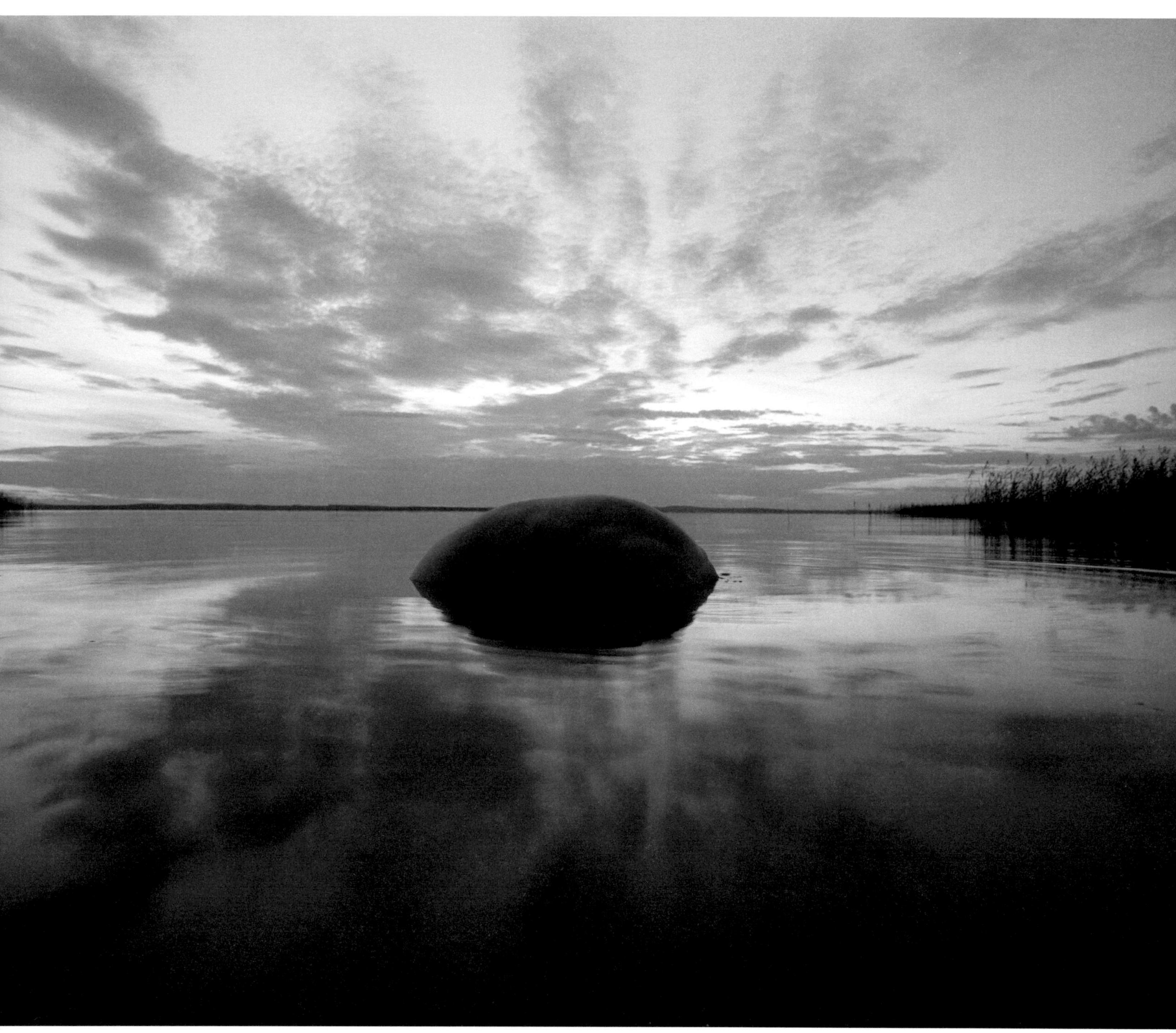

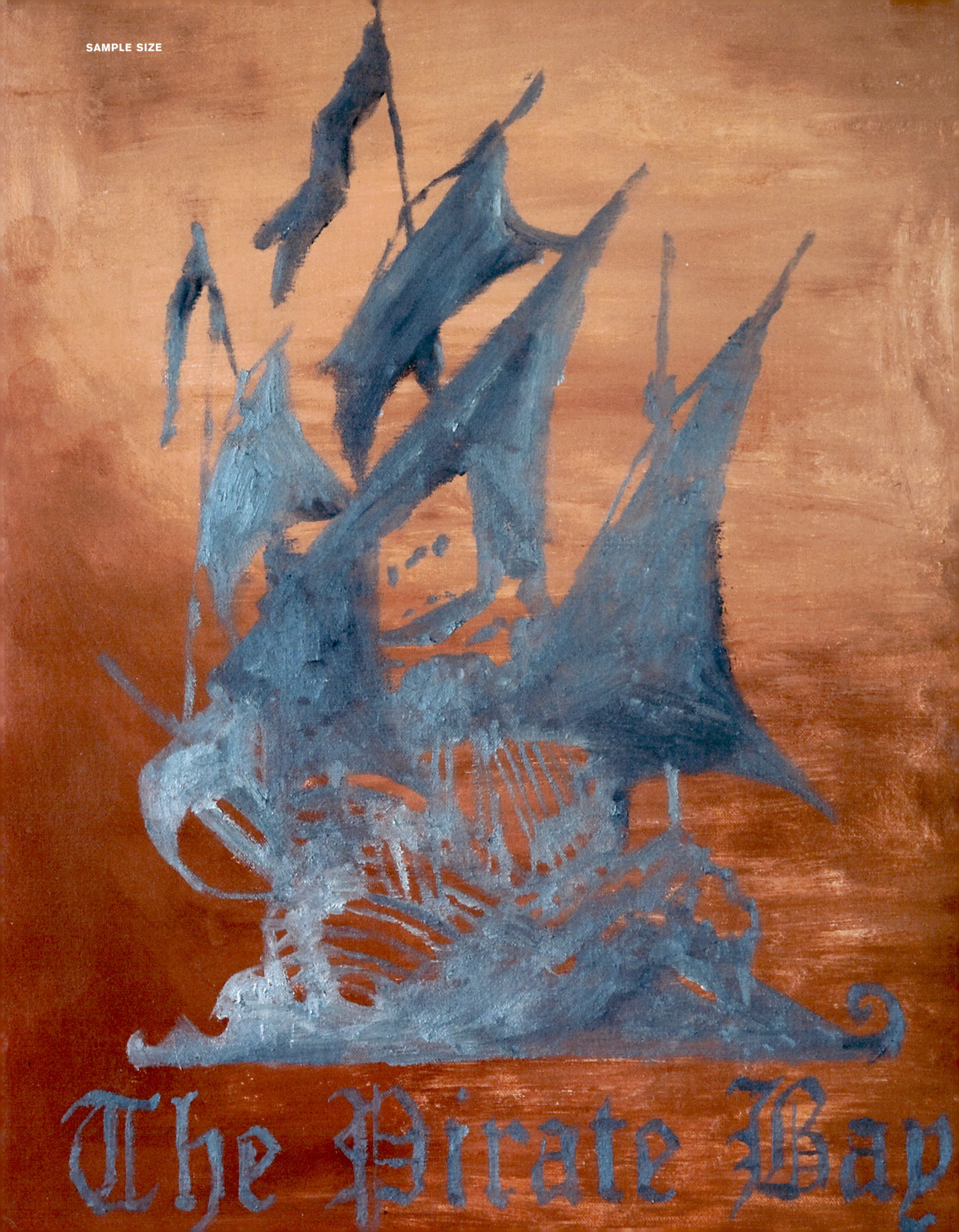
SAMPLE SIZE
The Pirate Bay

Pirates
of
the
Internet
Unite!
NEWS
FROM
A
FUTURE
NEWSPAPER
by
Miltos
Manetas

"A MAN WAS STOPPED YESTERDAY AT THE BOARDER OF ITALY AND FRANCE, HIS COMPUTER WAS SCANNED AND PIRATED MATERIAL WAS FOUND, MOSTLY ADOBE SOFTWARE AND SONGS BY BEATLES. THE MAN WAS ARRESTED AT THE SPOT".

FROM A POEM TO A DRUG, FROM A PIECE OF SOFTWARE TO A MUSIC RECORD AND FROM A FILM TO A BOOK, EVERYTHING THAT'S FAMOUS AND PROFITABLE, OWNS MUCH OF ITS ECONOMIC VALUE TO THE MANIPULATION OF THE MULTITUDES.

PEOPLE HAVEN'T ASKED TO KNOW WHAT THE COCA COLA LOGO LOOKS LIKE, NEITHER HAVE THEY ASKED FOR THE MELODY OF "LIKE A VIRGIN". EDUCATION, MEDIA AND PROPAGANDA TEACH ALL THAT THE HARD WAY; BY EITHER HAMMERING IT IN OUR BRAINS OR BY SPECULATING OVER OUR THIRST, OUR HUNGER, OUR NEED FOR COMMUNICATION AND FUN AND, MOST OF ALL, OVER OUR LONELINESS AND DESPAIR.

IN THE DAYS OF INTERNET, WHAT CAN BE COPIED CAN ALSO BE SHARED. WHEN IT COMES TO CONTENT, WE CAN GIVE EVERYTHING TO EVERYONE AT ONCE. AROUND THIS REALIZATION A NEW SOCIAL CLASS IS AWAKENING. NOT A WORKING CLASS BUT A CLASS OF PRODUCERS. PRODUCERS ARE PIRATES AND HACKERS BY DEFAULT: THEY RECYCLE IMAGES, SOUNDS AND CONCEPTS. SOME OF IT THEY INVENT BUT MOST THEY BORROW FROM OTHERS.

BECAUSE INFORMATION OCCUPIES A PHYSICAL PART OF OUR BODIES, BECAUSE IT IS LITERALLY "INSTALLED" IN OUR BRAIN AND CAN'T BE ERASED AT WISH, PEOPLE HAVE THE RIGHT TO OWN WHAT IS PROJECTED ON THEM. THEY HAVE THE RIGHT TO OWN IT THEMSELVES. BECAUSE THIS IS A GLOBAL WORLD BASED ON INEQUALITY AND PROFIT, BECAUSE THE CONTENTS OF A SONG, A MOVIE OR A BOOK ARE POINTS OF ADVANTAGE IN A VICIOUS FIGHT FOR SURVIVAL. ANY GLOBAL CITIZEN HAS THE MORAL RIGHT TO APPROPRIATE A DIGITAL COPY OF A SONG, A MOVIE OR A BOOK. BECAUSE SOFTWARE IS AN INTERNATIONAL LANGUAGE, THE SECRETS OF THE WORLD ARE WRITTEN IN ADOBE AND MICROSOFT: WE SHOULD TRY TO HACK THEM. FINALLY, BECAUSE POVERTY IS THE FIELD OF EXPERIMENTATION FOR ALL GLOBAL MEDICINE, NO PATENTS SHOULD APPLY. TODAY EVERY MAN WITH A COMPUTER IS A PRODUCER AND A PIRATE.

WE ALL LIVE IN THE INTERNET; THIS IS OUR NEW COUNTRY, THE ONLY TERRITORY THAT MAKES SENSE TO DEFEND AND PROTECT. THE LAND OF THE INTERNET IS ONE OF INFORMATION. MEN SHOULD BE ABLE TO USE THIS LAND FREELY, CORPORATIONS SHOULD PAY FOR USE - A COMPANY IS DEFINITELY NOT A PERSON. THE INTERNET IS NOW PRODUCING "INTERNETS", SITUATIONS THAT EXIST ALSO IN REAL SPACE, GOVERNED BY WHAT IS HAPPENING ONLINE.

THIS IS THE TIME FOR THE FOUNDATION OF A GLOBAL MOVEMENT OF PIRACY. THE FREEDOM OF INFRINGING COPYRIGHT, OF SHARING INFORMATION AND DRUGS, ARE OUR NEW COMMONS, THEY ARE GLOBAL RIGHTS AND AS SUCH, AUTHORITIES WILL NOT ALLOW THEM WITHOUT A BATTLE. BUT THIS WILL BE A STRANGE BATTLE AS IT IS THE FIRST TIME THAT THE MULTITUDES DISRESPECT THE LAW INSTINCTIVELY AND ON A GLOBAL SCALE.

TODAY, AN ARMY OF TEENAGERS IS COPYING, ADULTS AND SENIOR CITIZENS ARE COPYING, PEOPLE FROM THE LEFT AND THE RIGHT ARE COPYING. EVERYONE WITH A COMPUTER IS COPYING; LIKE A NOVEL GODDESS ATHENA, INFORMATION WANTS TO BREAK FREE FROM THE HEAD OF TECHNOLOGY AND ASSIST US IN OUR ENTERPRISE.

PIRATES OF THE INTERNET UNITE!

PIRACYMANIFESTO.COM

The Pirate Bay

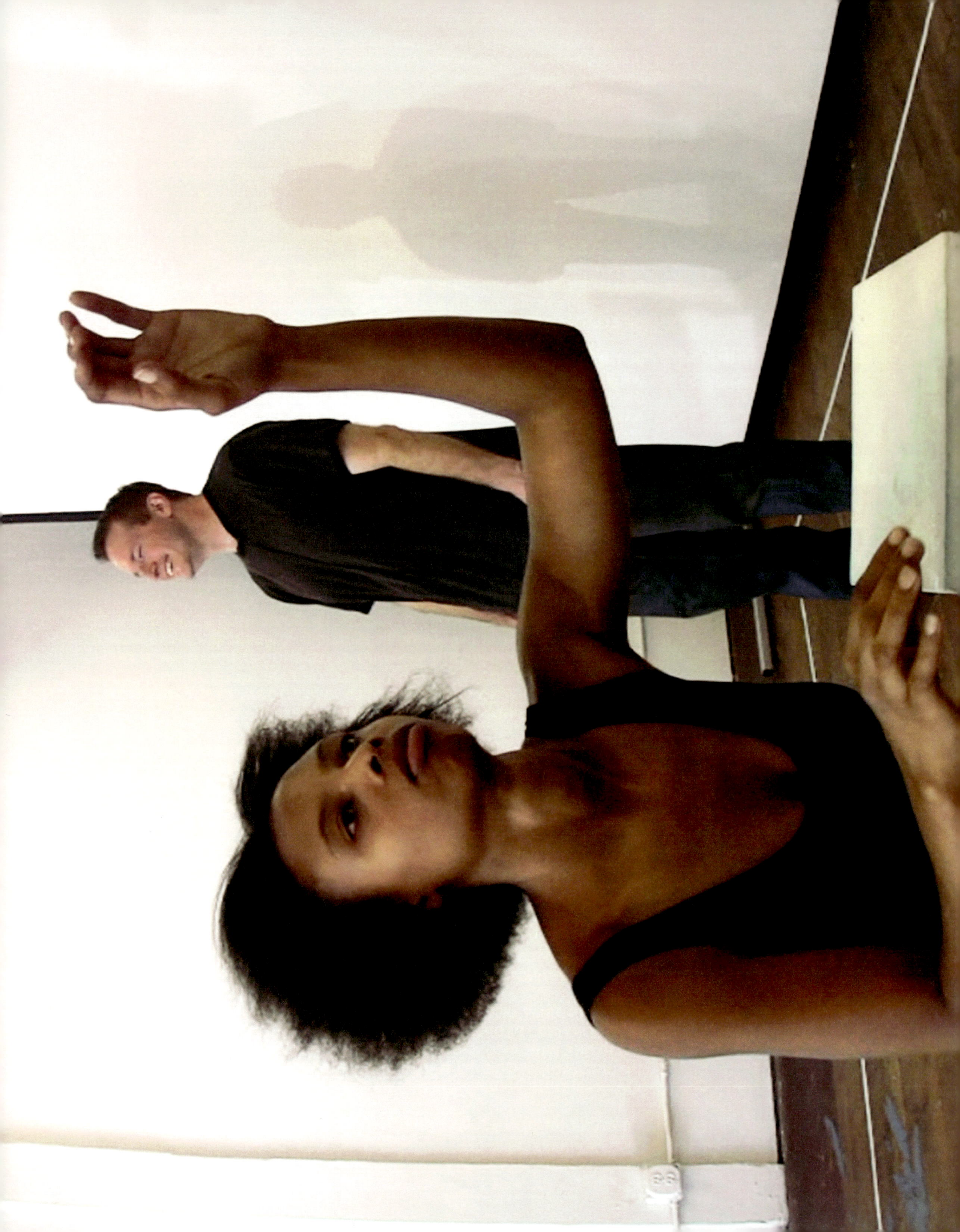

BRODY CONDON
by Alex Gartenfeld

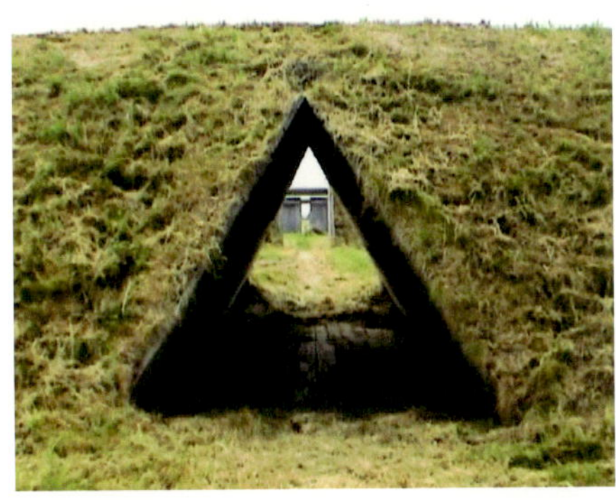

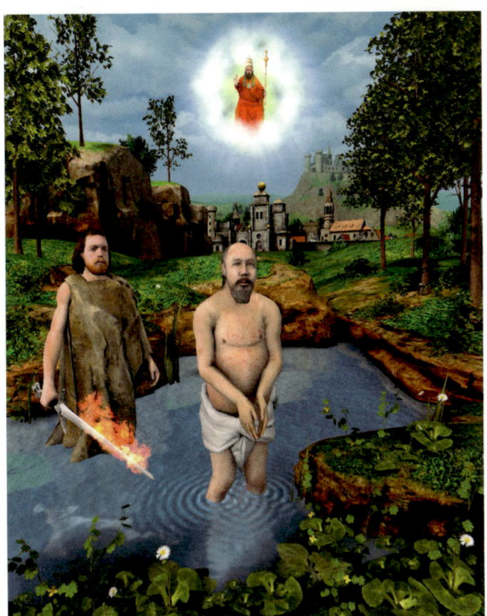

Like many people who grew up in the 80s and 90s, artist Brody Condon (b. 1974) grew up in a strict New Age household. That meant a rigid distrust of established culture, a dabbling interest in sub-cultures and archaic symbols, and a steady diet of video games.

This may be why Condon's videos, photographs, and performances articulate a disappointment in major histories, where the myths of High Renaissance painting and the consciousness-expanding experience of drugs are debunked as just one narrative among many, and put to new, less sacred use.

Condon's colorful digital photographs track a history from Northern Renaissance painting to the imagery of fantasy video games, thus combining two less-than-hegemonic visual vocabularies never quite removed or fashionable enough to qualify as alternative or sub-culture. One July 21st, the longest day of the year, Condon records an experience with a Robert Morris sculpture that drags visitors out of bed early in the morning, only to encounter a mistake. Still one is left wondering: what kind of culture is it, and what is it for the older, iconic artist to make a mistake?

ALEX GARTENFELD *So this section, Blog Cabin, is about the ways that the Internet, either through presentation or distribution, affects an art medium, photography. I thought we should start with your work* Without Sun, *because it originally existed in an online format, but you've also sponsored its re-enactment in physical space.*

BRODY CONDON First, the video is an edited collection of videos found online. The performance is a re-creation of that video with one dancer and one actor. The piece began as a collection of 'found performances', which I eventually trimmed down.

The edit features self-made web cam videos by people taking a drug, salvia, and reacting, mostly to a feeling of disembodiment brought on by the drug.

The reactions vary from person to person. I just started collecting. I would assume an artist with an Internet connection collects images related to what they do. It also allows me to cut different edits using a surplus of source material.

So the experience of the people being unable to inhabit their body, that was incidental?

It's a collection of people freaking out; I don't care what they are on, although I was interested in the fact that this specific psychedelic substance causes mental and physical dissociation. It has a tendency to incite performative actions as the users lose conscious control of their body.

Is it a drug you were interested in because of any personal experience?

I don't want to comment on any of that. The important thing is that they are documentation of found performances focused on the surface of their 'projection of self' into other spaces, like watching someone face while they play a game.

Do you think of the performances as native to the technology they're using to document?

It's a big question but yes, in that it intuitively allows the creators to record themselves. Would these performances happen if Youtube weren't there? Probably, but they wouldn't disseminate in the same way.

Do you have a favorite performer in your collection?

If there's a meme kid, one viral shot, it's the kid named Alex, because he's so self-conscious. He's trying to articulate his experience as it happens. He's not only trying to deconstruct his interior experience but also his relationship to the web cam and the space of online short form video that it represents.

You've performed the piece twice, once at the Portland Institute of Contemporary Art's TBA Festival, and again at Machine Project in LA. You have a third performance at MoMA this month. Each time an actor re-creates the voices, and a dancer mimics the on-screen performance. How have they been different thus far?
Well, I think I'll do it three times and then stop. Each time I've had a different dancer, which accounts for the differences. I work with them very intensely. They have to mimic 15 minutes from beginning to end, schizophrenically jumping between several different characters. We watch the video over and over for a month. The video functions as the script and the choreography document; I am not a choreographer. As we rehearse, I pretend I am working in a video editing and animation program, pulling the mover's arm here, a leg there, setting a key frame, then rewinding the scene and letting it run. Then we repeat until it is correct.

Without Sun is obviously named for the Chris Marker film of the same name. Literal art historical references move throughout your work, in the titles and in the very subject matter you approach. Most of your still images are religious images adapted to the visual vocabulary of a video game.
There are a few reasons for that. I don't feel any particular responsibility to religious imagery; there hasn't really been a comprehensive critical history of fantasy art visuals that influence computer games, which I have tried to trace. One of the places it led me to was the religious paintings of Late Medieval Northern European masters - particularly due to their odd use of perspective.

Coming out of a New Age family myself, I don't have a clear understanding of narrative of religious iconography. To me it looks and feels like a first-person shooter game, due to the scale of the characters, the immersive feeling.

How did video games become your primary mode of access for these images?
That's the primary visual material I consumed, from age 5 to 25. And then at a point in my art education I was able to enrich it with performance art strategies from the 60s and 70s. But standing in front of a Memling, I see it as fantasy, with zombies coming out of the ground; up top there are rogue hippies emerging from an extra-dimensional portal with flaming swords.

Do you think of these images as contemporary re-interpretations? That is, are the images you create put to a similar use as their source material? Is appropriation an accurate term for the types of strategies you pursue?
It's modification. A lot of the earlier work I made came out of game modificiation. Eventually I began to use that logic of modification not just on games, but other artworks.

How do you define modification, as opposed to a type of collage of separate vocabularies of imagery, or even pastiche?
It comes straight from the game modification community, hacking computer games and adding your own content. For me that term feels appropriate for the alteration of artworks, contemporary or historical, rather than sampling or appropriation. Appropriation is ubiquitous; every kid does it using Photoshop and the Internet. It has more to do with creative consumption of existing media - consuming, and in so doing, modifying.

Is kitsch a valid category for the images you're working with, or producing?

I'm not using fantasy imagery because I think it's kitsch. That's another difference between modification and pop art. I'm not in a place where I can objectively stand back and point from a position of cultural power at the pop culture industry, and say, 'This is interesting'. I'm blindly working myself out of my own patterns of consumption, which include video games.

You've spoken about your New Age parents, and about your early use of video games. Those seem like such an ironic, albeit culturally pervasive, combination. This brings me back to the un-ironic combination of high and low in your work, specifically in your Summer Solstice *piece (2006), about the eponymous Robert Morris earth work, which you've scored an amateur 'Stairway to Heaven' cover you found online.*
A friend and I made a pilgrimage to the Robert Morris piece at 4 or 5 in the morning, to pay homage to the summer solstice via this grand artwork. Then we got there, and this fucking thing was two weeks off. It summed up my whole relationship with the work from this period. This is my parents' generation, so not only do I get this New Age shit down my throat - it's in so much of the art of the era as well. Critical histories leave that out; they exclude the astral projections, clichés in a few of Nauman's videos, for instance. So I left the installation feeling tricked. And 'Stairway to Heaven' is this middle-aged, drug-addled rock'n'roll. The connections seem obvious.

Page 44 Without Sun (Performance), 2009
Page 45, top Summer Solstice, 2006
Page 45, bottom Default Properties ( ), 2006
All images courtesy of the artist

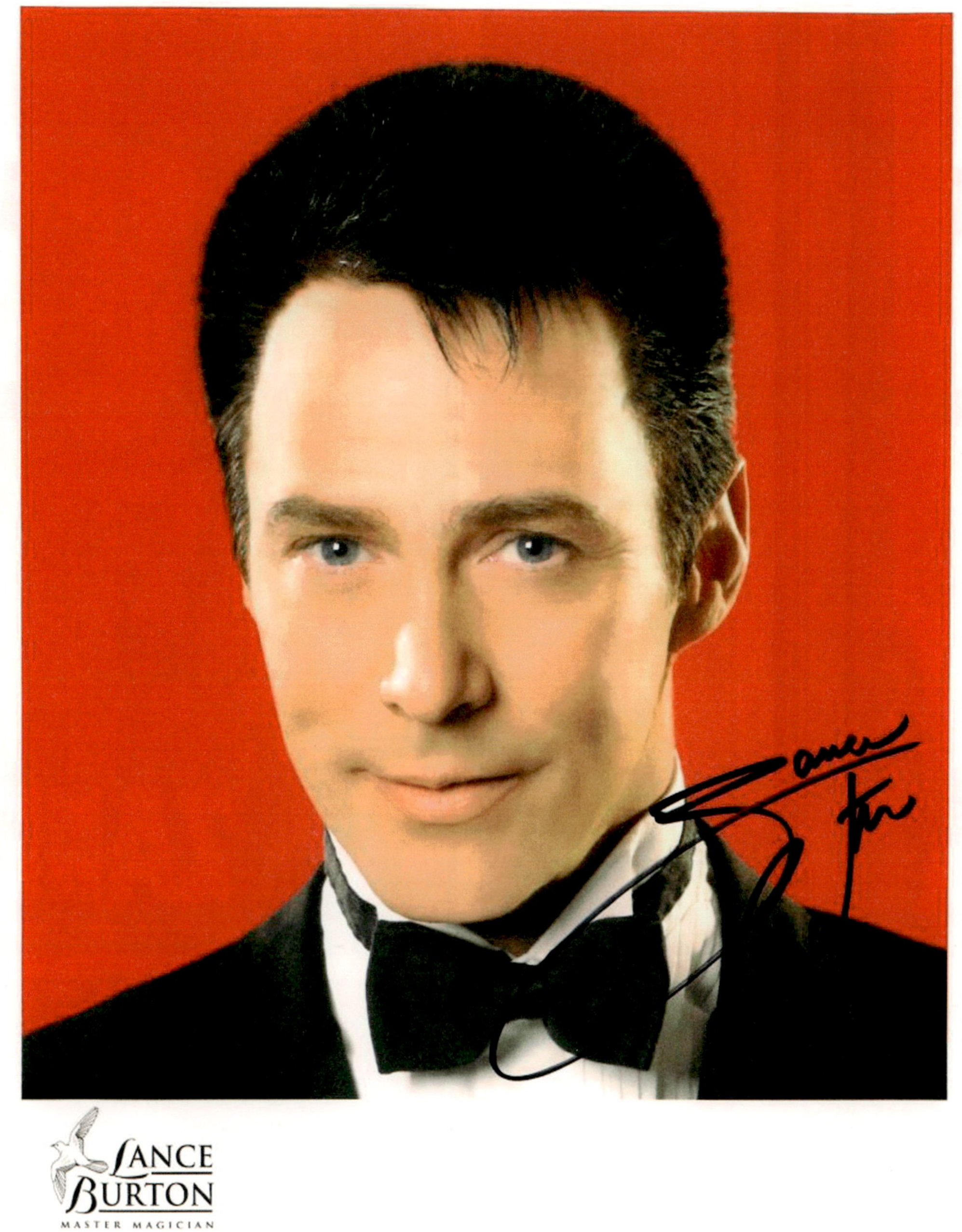

COUNTER-HEAVEN

TRUE, FALSE, FAKE; MAGICIANS, AS PHANTOMS AND PHOTOGRAPHY, MOVE ACROSS THESE LINES AND THEIR INTERPLAYS. THEY ARE THE GATEKEEPERS OF ANOTHER (DIS)ORDER, WHICH LET US ENTER A WORLD BLOWN BY THE SPIRITS OF SURPRISE, ASTONISHMENT, EERINESS, AND STYLE. WHERE WE ENJOY THE MOST DELIGHTFUL SUSPENSION OF DISBELIEF. A COUNTER-SKY THAT MAKES THOSE HEAVENS OF GODS AND MEN DISAPPEAR IN A FLASH. IN THE WHISPER OF AN ABRACADABRA. THIS SELECTION OF MAGICIAN FOUND ON AND AROUND THE INTERNET IS THE FIRST INSTALLMENT IN A SERIES ON THE AESTHETICS OF MAGIC.

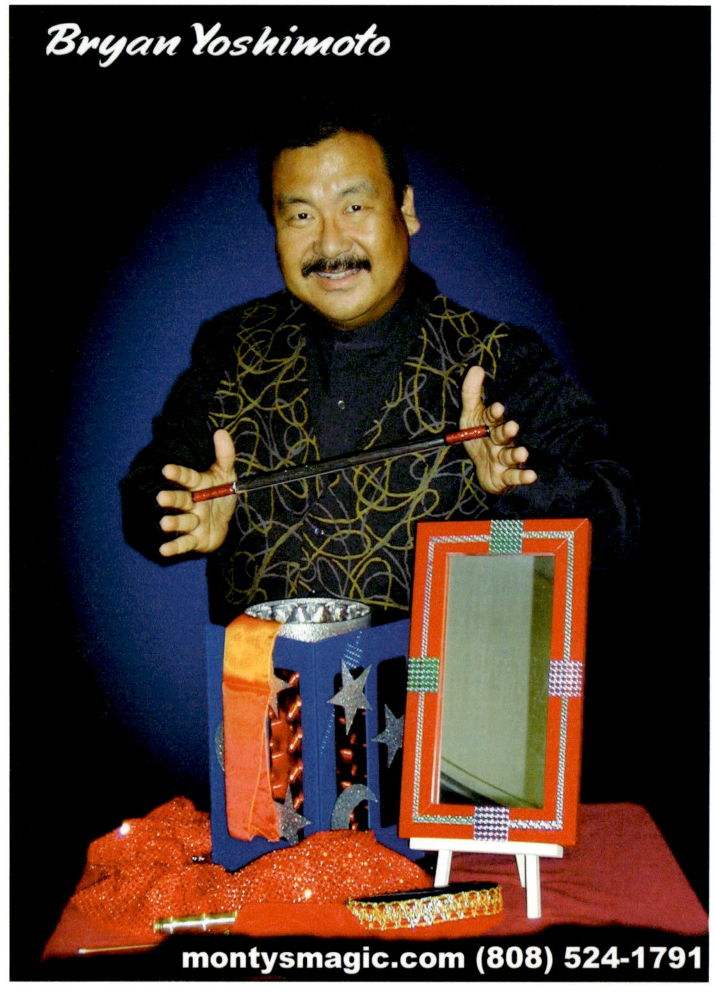

Bryan Yoshimoto
montysmagic.com (808) 524-1791

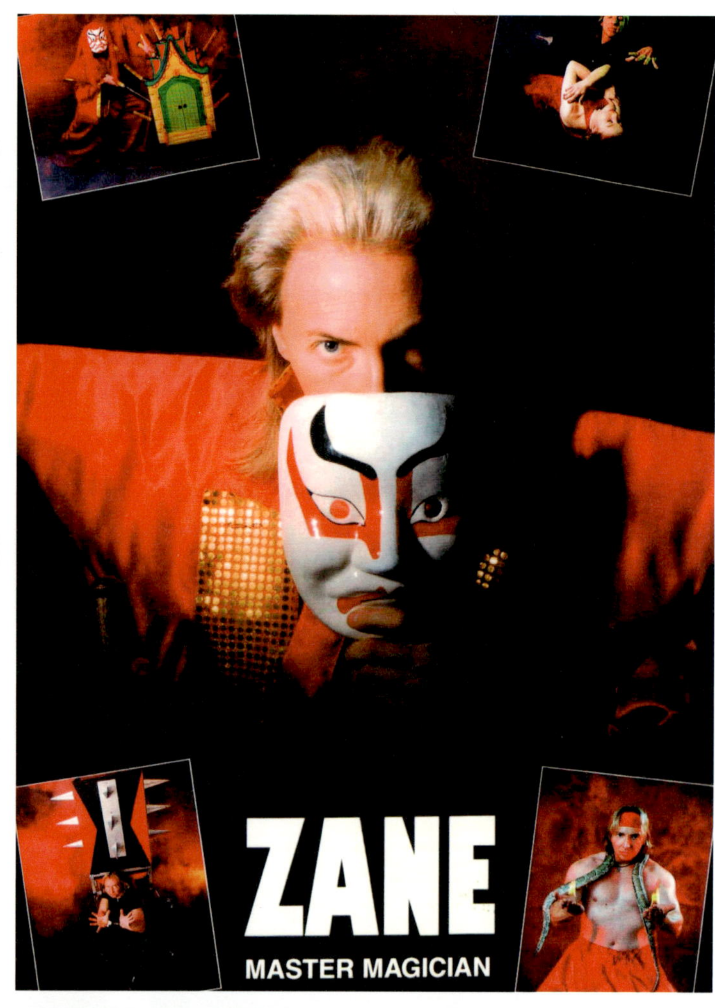

ZANE
MASTER MAGICIAN

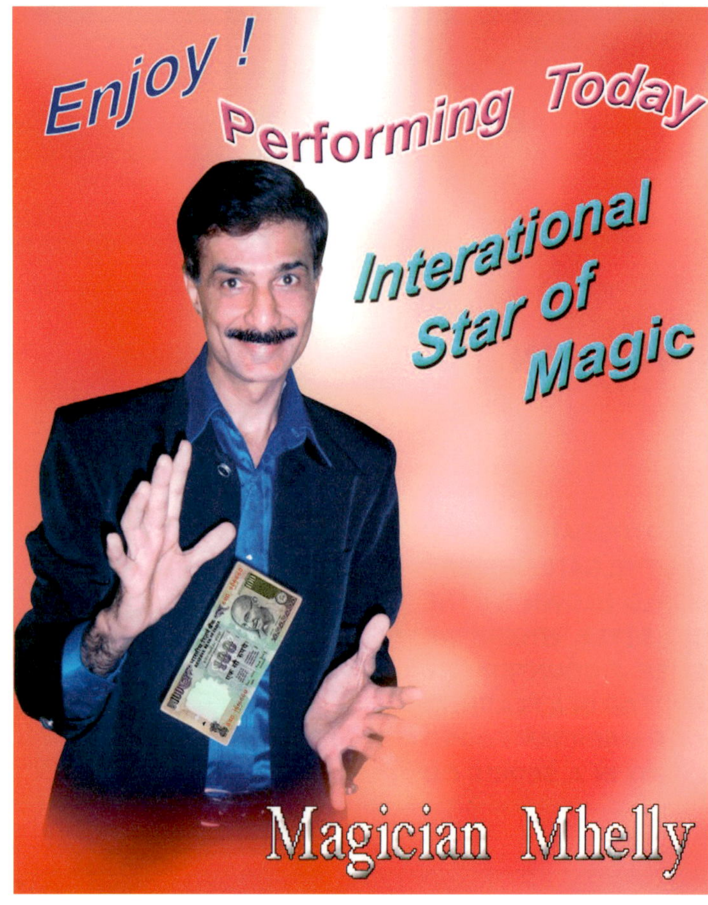

Enjoy !
Performing Today
Interational
Star of
Magic
Magician Mhelly

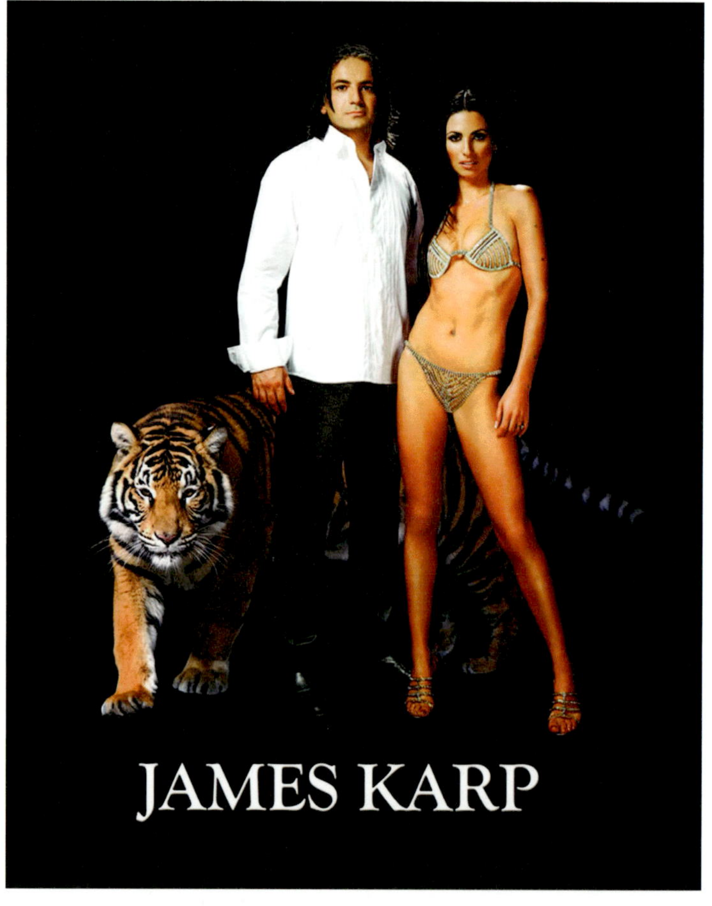

JAMES KARP

BRUNO RODRIGUES

PHOTOS & RÉALISATION ESPACE CRÉATION 06 11 48 79 31

Back to the future
and vice versa
ILIKEMYSTYLE.NET
sampled by Adriano Sack
and Judith Bahnham

These photos were taken from the 24'' screen of an Apple iMac with a Leica D-Lux 3 camera. They show images on *ilikemystyle.net*. This website was founded two years ago and is run independently by a group of journalists, designers, programmers and enthusiasts. The users of the website upload pictures of themselves, their friends, their clothes and their world. They comment on the pictures of others, starting discussions, debates or friendships. They also can pick their favourite pictures and put together a Toplist. All the images here are on the Toplist of Clark Parkin, username: Clark, a stylist and fashion editor based in Munich. They represent both the variety, beauty, vanity that you find on *ilikemystyle.net* as well as Clark's taste, humor and some very personal relations he has to the people on the photos.

To create a Sample Size we decided to photograph the images from the screen because we see the dynamics on *ilikemystyle.net* as a series of magnifying glasses. Before becoming active, the users of the website take a scrutinizing look in the mirror - both metaphorically and naturalistically speaking. They carefully chose how they want to expose themselves in the semi-public space of a social network. They look at other pictures, comment on them, rate them, add them to their toplist and by doing so they make the process of looking at someone (and judging her/him) visible to other users. By taking pictures of Clark's Toplist from the screen we make the process of 'looking at somebody looking' visible.

And so on. Users of *ilikemystyle.net* are under suspision of being uninhibited and self-obsessed, which we on the other hand regard as one of the key virtues of the digital age. Also we feel that the speed and insatiability of the Internet create anxiety because a lot of beauty, fun and creativity is swept away without being noticed. The next logical yet slightly ironic step for us is to create a printed magazine based on *ilikemystyle.net*. We all find ourselves in a constant search to figure out how different media will work. To create a user generated but printed style magazine seems a step back to the future.
· *ilikemystyle.net*

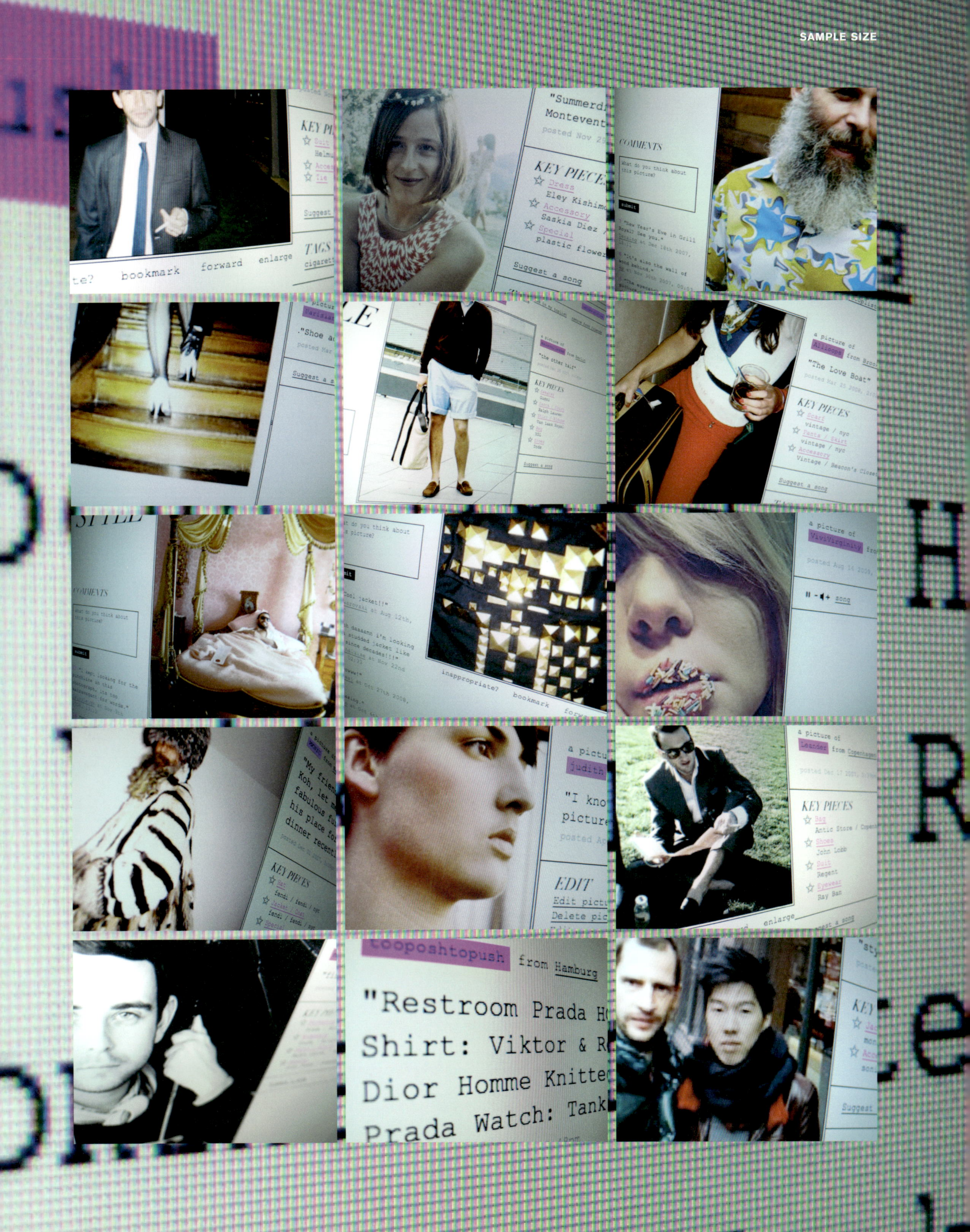

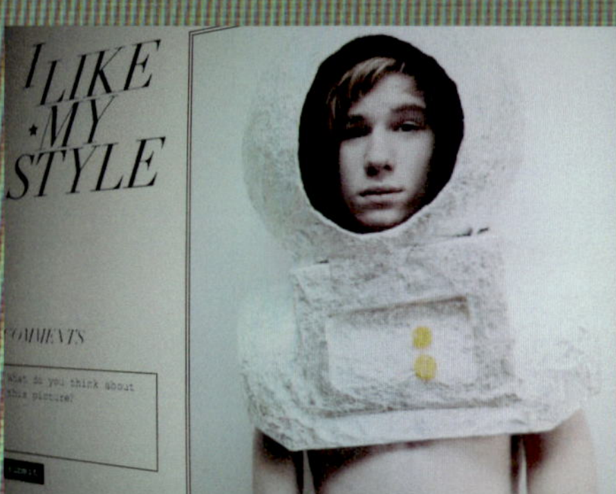
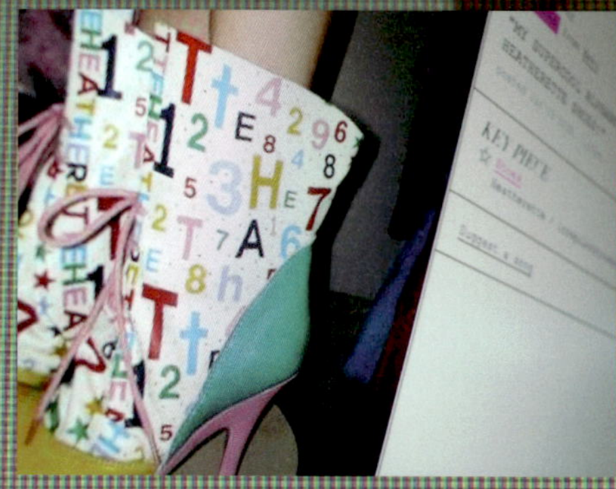
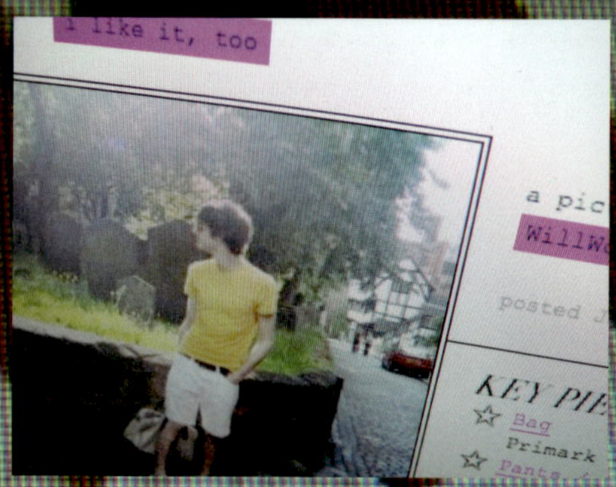
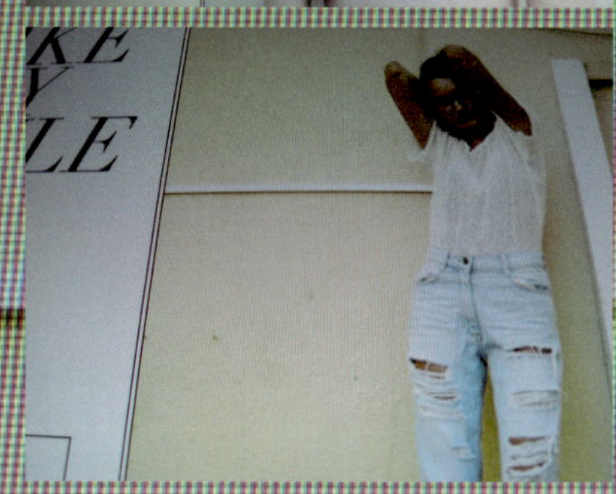
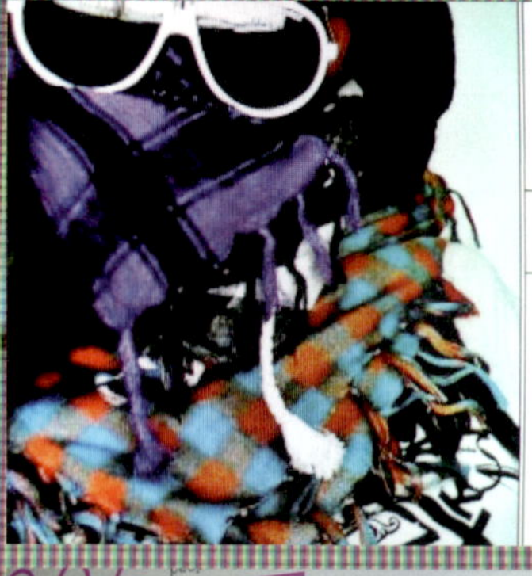
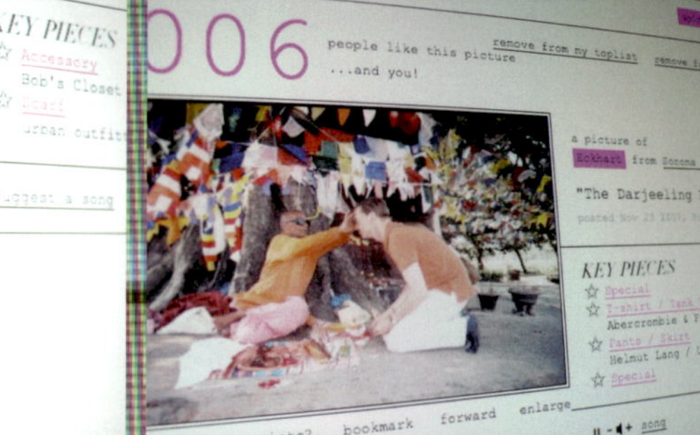
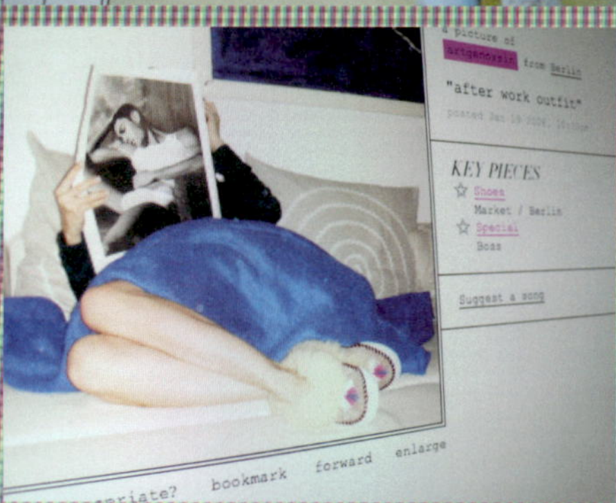
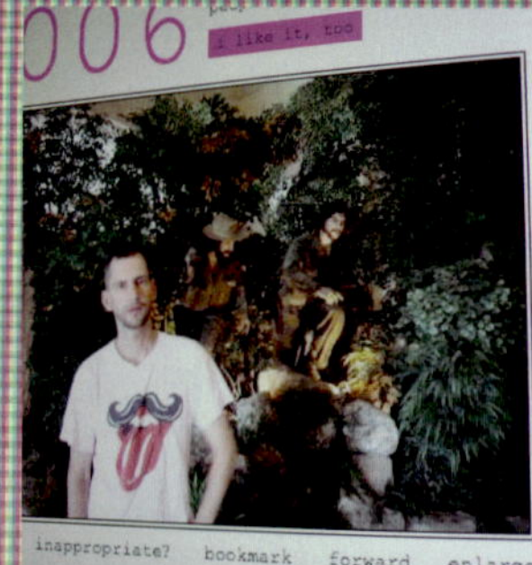
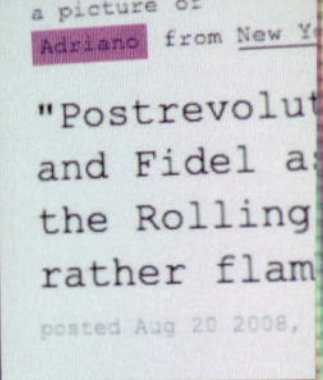
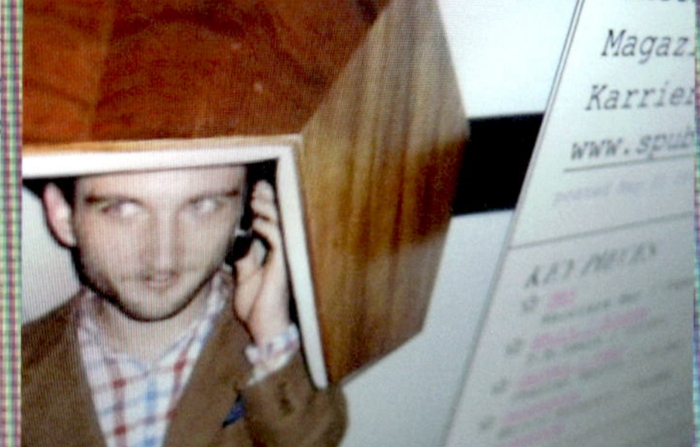
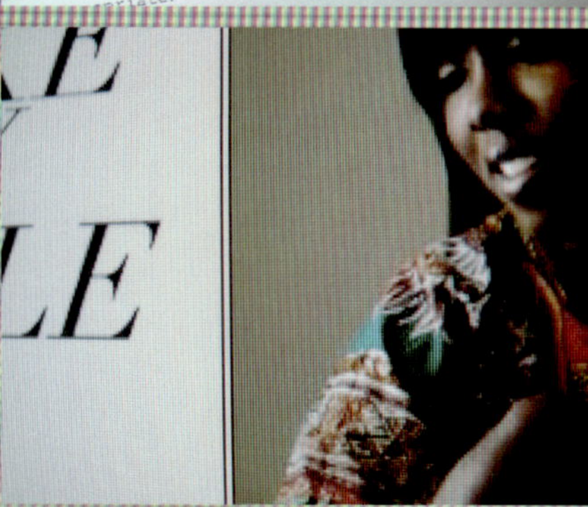
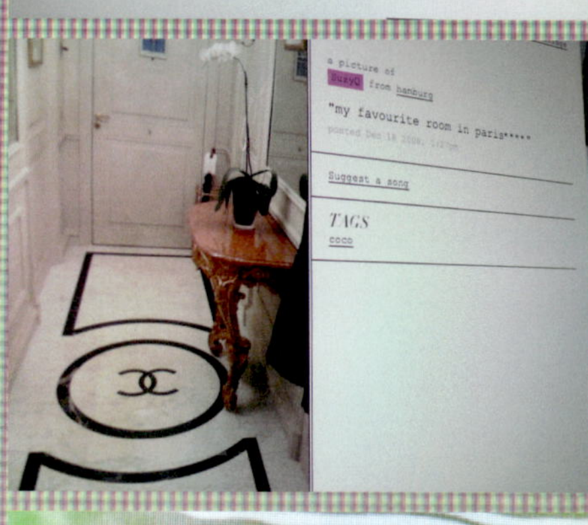
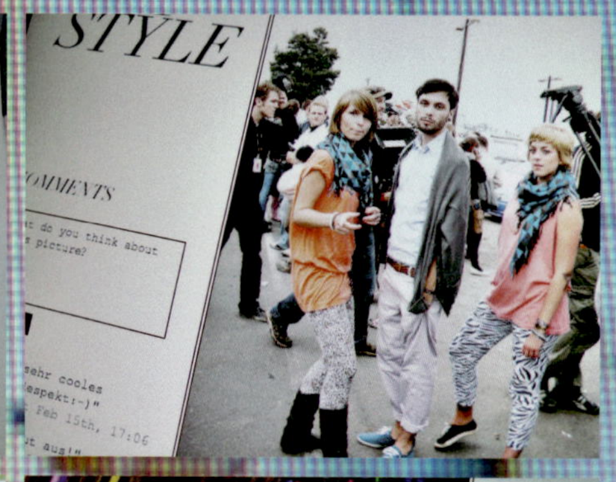
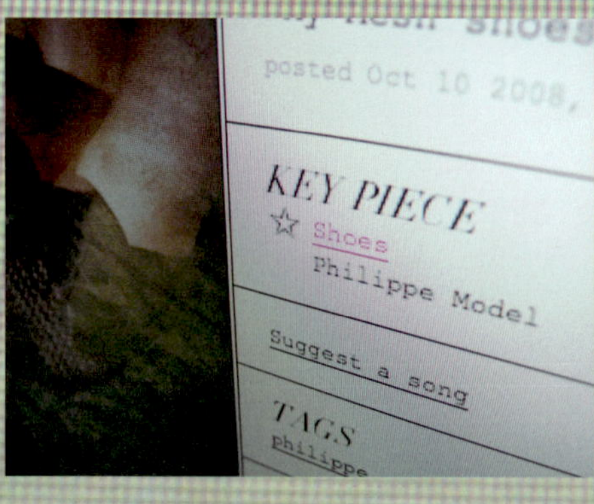
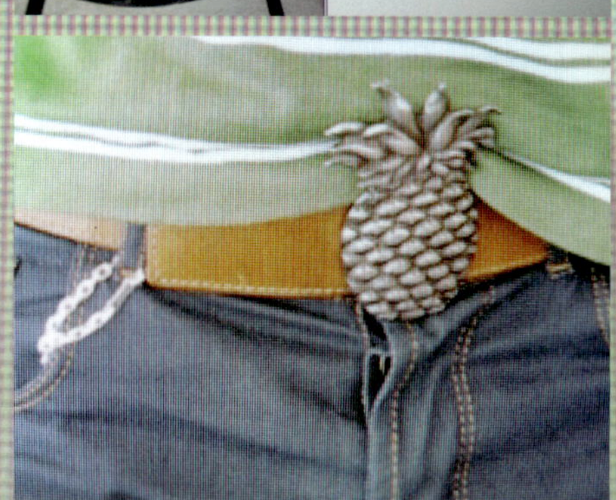
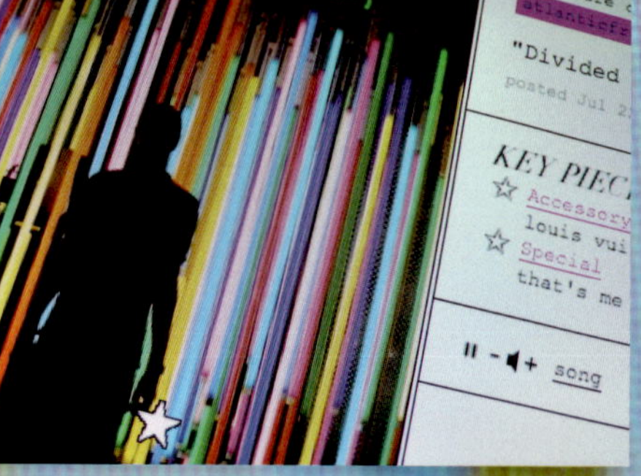

Lino Sabattini
EVERYONE SHOULD DO WHAT THEY KNOW HOW TO DO
told by Porzia Bergamasco
photography Sergio Ghetti

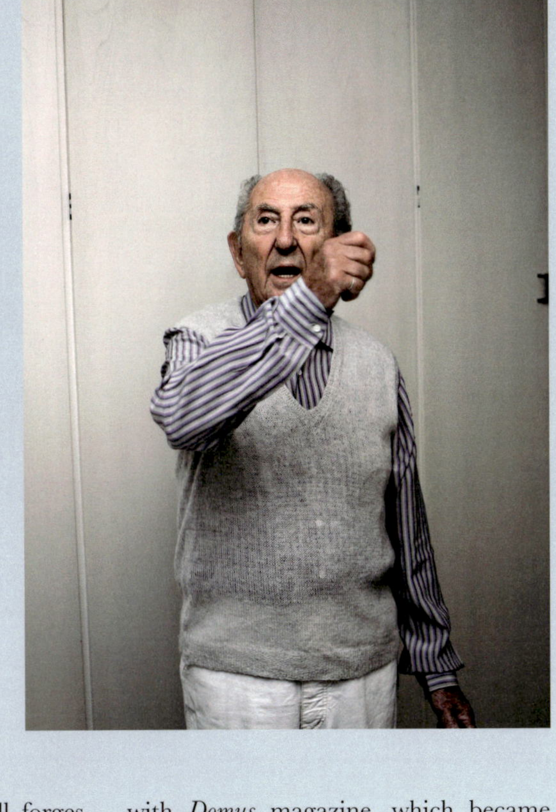

It is not difficult to understand what he does and what his primary tools are. All you need to do is watch his hands. While he talks they are always busy giving shape to his thoughts. Seeking in the air a three dimensionality which assumes a precise form every time. So, he is telling the truth when he says, almost thinking out loud, "I was lucky to be born an artisan. I was gifted with the talent to make things. I have been able to render other people's visions as well as produce my own". And he makes no attempt to hide the fact that, by using that innate ability to make and render, he has managed to fuse, even invent, cultural and aesthetic expressions which have denitively broken with tradition and the past.

Proposing a new "Arte in Tavola" and originating, at the peak of the industrial age of large-scale mass production, a form of rare, limited-edition, artistic craftsmanship. Resisting "useless objects" and "revival" and siding with the imagination, with the aim of depicting beauty and educating people about "free forms", which have their own lives, meeting functional needs with their material properties.

Lino Sabattini began his training working with metals in the dark days of the war. At the age of just seventeen he was working as an apprentice in Blevio, on Lake Como. At the same time he honed his talent drawing inspiration from nature and cultivating a taste for harmony, taming metal as though it were paper. And he has never looked back, letting himself be enticed by glass and ceramics in order to "imbue weak things with strength" and "seeking to endow all things with the most correct way of being and acting".

Now, at the age of 84, he still forges sculptures and creates and decorates ceramic vases. He does it for himself but leaves the mould for his friends at the oven "just in case someone else likes it". He has spent his life creating things. He has cupboards - which he also designed - that are crammed with prototypes. Some have remained so as they were made for the sheer pleasure of making them and in order to share his ideas with friends. Others are the result of working partnerships with various firms (Moser, Rosenthal, Zani…). And he still has many projects in the pipeline.

Yet he asks nothing of life and thanks - human beings and God - for all that he has had and built. Like the lovely house in Bregnano, in the province of Como, where he moved in 1964 and where I met him. He is fond of saying: "Things are born out of chance openings, you only have to know how to seize them". He created his own opening first and foremost by becoming fascinated

with *Domus* magazine, which became his ABC of aesthetics when he was still wearing short trousers. My chance to meet him came about through a friend, director Gianluca Migliarotti. He decided to make a documentary about Sabattini's life and invited me to come on this journey into the past. Fate and chance have meant that the name of Lino Sabattini will forever be linked to that of Giò Ponti. It was this architect, who introduced everyone to the modern age with his designs on the pages of the magazine Lino thirstily drank from, who turned up in the flesh in the Milanese workshop Lino had set up in the 50s. He commissioned him to produce the prototypes of his ideas. It was a lengthy partnership, which lasted until Ponti's death. The most wonderful opportunity? Putting his teachings into practice.

Because "you have to learn, and then make, and then learn by making". This partnership was founded on an understanding based on simplicity.

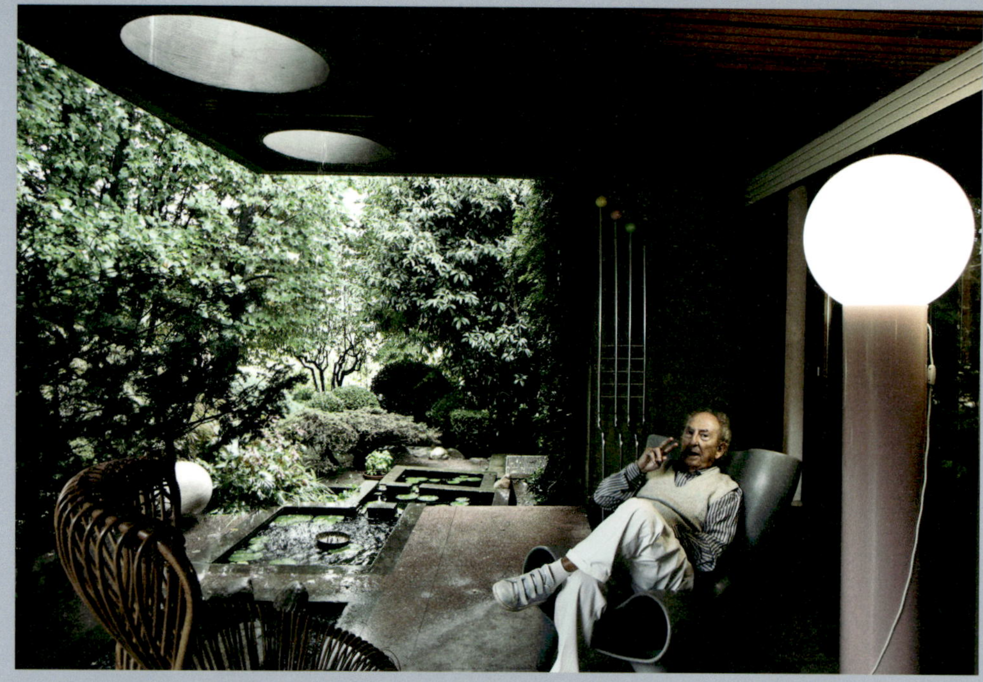

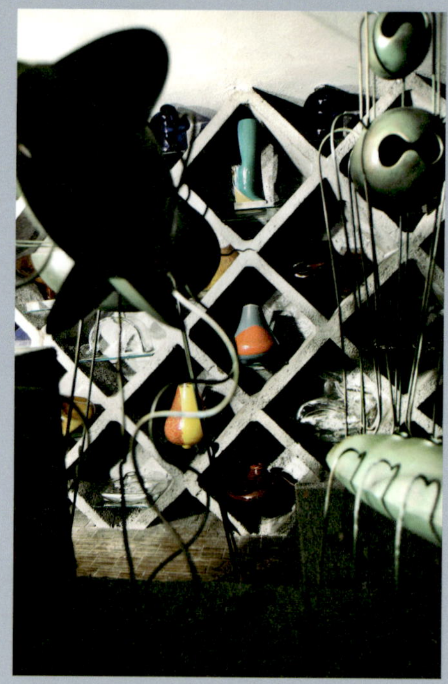

"You can only express simplicity if you feel it inside, otherwise you complicate it".

And there is nothing complicated in what they produced together. From masks to cutlery, from tea-sets to candlesticks… With immense satisfaction he points out the prototypes which belong - even now, many years later - to the collections of Christofle, the famous French house of silver, where he became art director in 1958, while creating the range for the Italian market. Separately he continued to work on his own objects - exhibited for the first time at the Triennale in Milan in 1954 and in Paris in 1956 at the exhibition *Formes et idées d'Italie*, eventually opening his own factory carrying his name in Bregnano in 1964. A factory founded on contemporary concepts: stages for overseas student, who could experiment with him, flexing and producing the solids and voids of the shapes of objects.

The factory is still there but no longer belongs to him. He began in the dark days and perhaps this is why he tried to illuminate his own, bursting to come alive again, with a gleaming metal alloy that challenged the silver tradition and democratised it. It kept its sheen and this helped to enliven in an abstract and functional way carafes, cutlery, teapots, vases, trays… which had a uniform, compact finish and were carefully soldered.

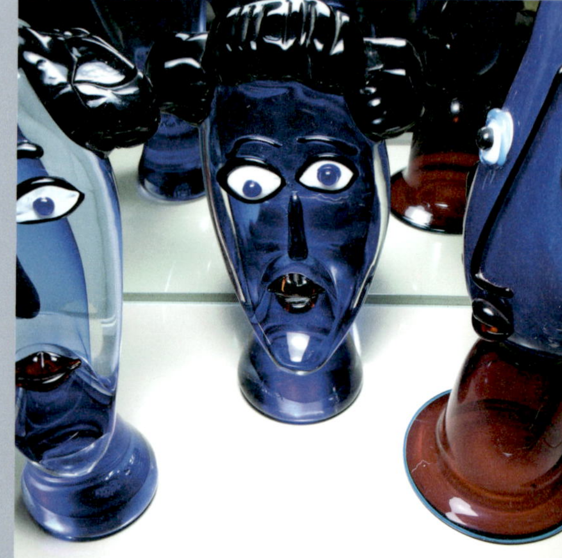

These handmade objects were all his own invention - about 30 people then worked on them - beginning with semi-finished articles which were subjected to various processes before emerging as "flawless pieces (...) which are also useful for looking at" as Giò Ponti said. This type of production was admired by his dear friend Bruno Munari "as an example of how imagination and technique, two components of design which many consider to be contradictory, can be successfully fused. (...) He is able to see in a semi-finished sheet or section of material, or in a conventional technique, that potential which leads to him creating new forms. He knows how materials behave and uses them without forcing them".

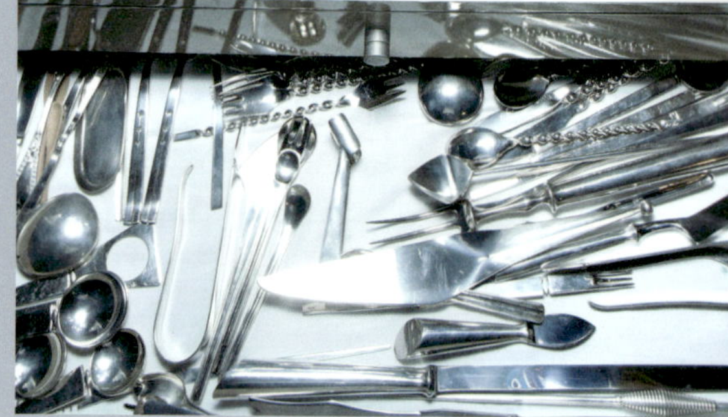

As for current techniques, Lino welcomes laser technologies, which allow one to produce hitherto inconceivable forms, although he regrets the disappearance of the artisan's method, which has eliminated an equal number of possibilities.

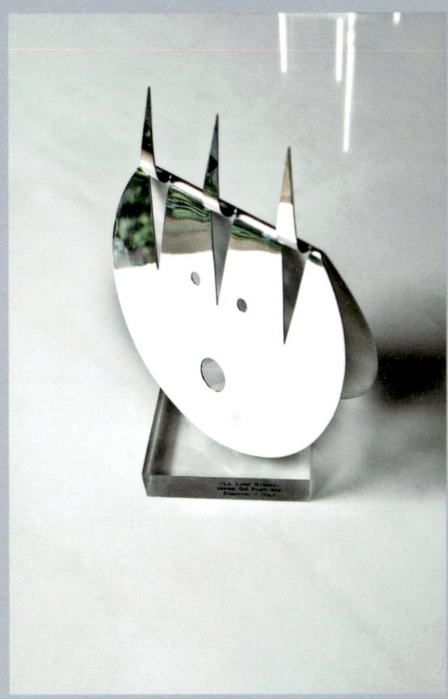

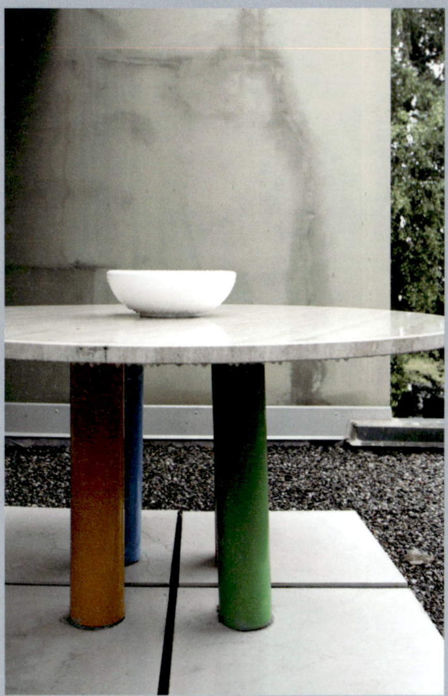

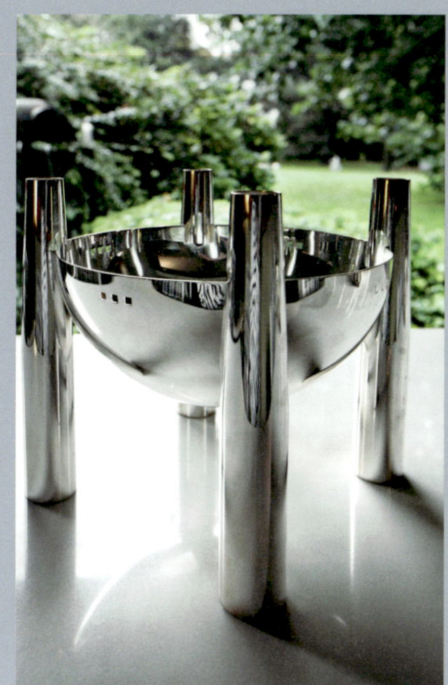

The story is not complete without mentioning the fact that, by applying his rare technique, he has also reproduced the pieces of Charles Rennie Mackintosh. Or without mentioning Japan and the oriental aesthetic which Lino espoused, in the true sense of the word, as his wife Sanae, a jewellery designer, was Japanese. They met during one of his frequent trips in the 60s but are now separated. This culture draws inspiration from nature, and harmony and is full of ceremony. From here, but perhaps also from having such a huge family - who lived in his large house - comes Lino's habit of having the table constantly laid, with an extra place set ready to welcome the chance visitor. Perhaps this is where his "Arte della Tavola" comes from.

Every time I return to see him with Gianluca for the documentary we are making, I discover new things to look at and to learn about. This last time too, for the *Fantom* photo call with Sergio Ghetti, he enthusiastically recalled more anecdotes and opened other cupboards. Happy to be able to add other pieces of the mosaic to ours and his experience. Time spent with him is a pleasure. He loves to talk and always cooks for everyone.

Lino's story is a story of encounters - "I have been lucky to make friends who have contributed to my own culture". One person he often mentions is Filippo Alison, with whom he has shared wonderful professional adventures. But there have also been battles and periods of isolation… above all when standardisation began to encroach and "cancelled the idea of educating people's tastes in order to merely give people what they wanted", he says with a bitter note of polemic.

It is a story which can be summed up in objects, books, magazines prints and paintings, a story which tells the tale of half a century of artists, designers and enlightened firms. In Italy, Europe, America and Asia. They peep out from shelves, they take up room on a table or in a bookcase, they fill drawers. They transform a wall. They exist in two workshops, each occupying a room. The whole expresses a sense of restraint and formal and compositional precision. A stark and communicative rigour. They are merely waiting for someone to keep the memory of them alive.
Lino likes to think that one day his house might be made open to the public or

students as a foundation-museum but for this to happen chance will have to bring a new encounter...

Previous page, left Sabattini in his porch, on Marc Newson's Orgone, bought on the closing day of an early 90s Frankfurt Mobelmesse. *Right* Concrete manholes used as shelves. *Bottom* Prototypes of cutlery by Christofle, Rosenthal… *Here, left* A prototype of Giò Ponti's La Luna Strega (1976) produced by Christofle in 2008. *Right* A 1903 C. R. Mackintosh's centerpiece produced in limited edition by Sabattini in 1984

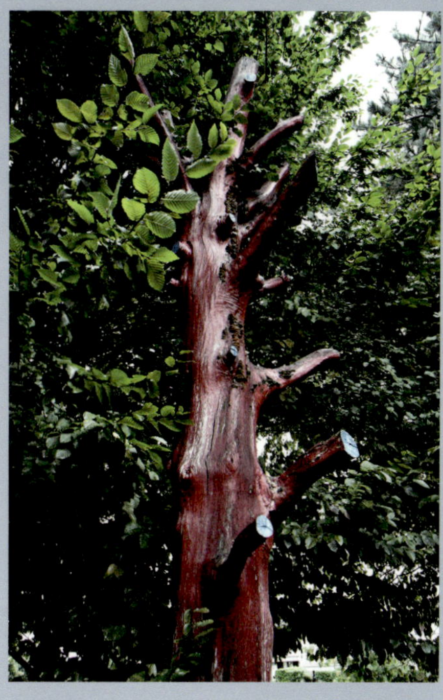

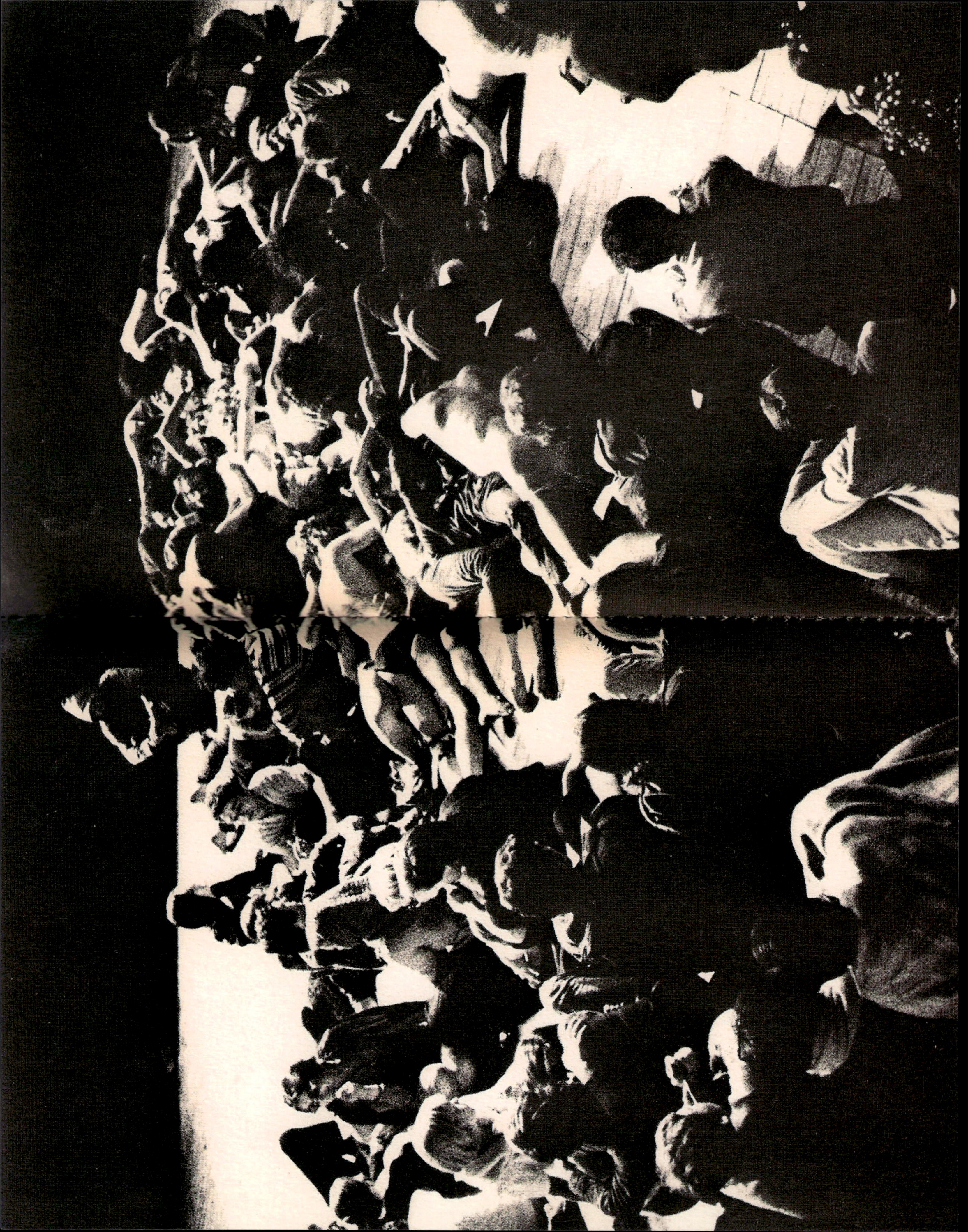

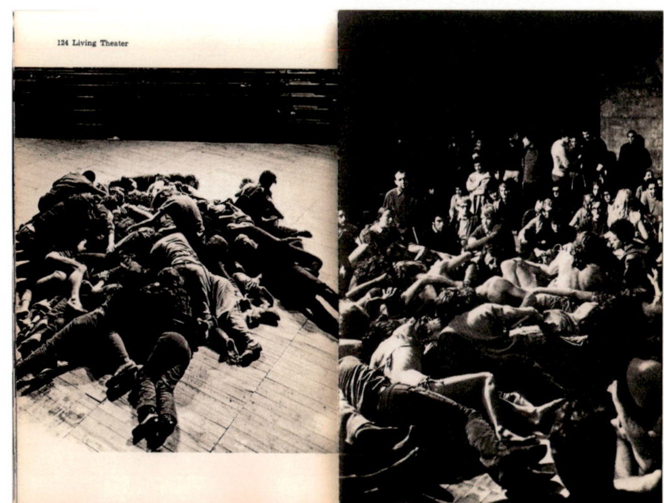

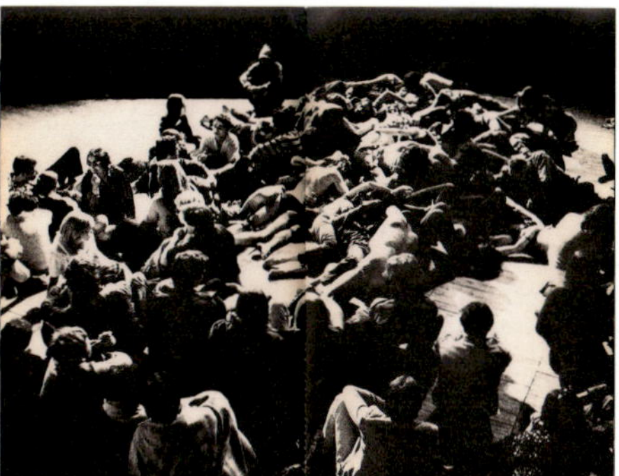

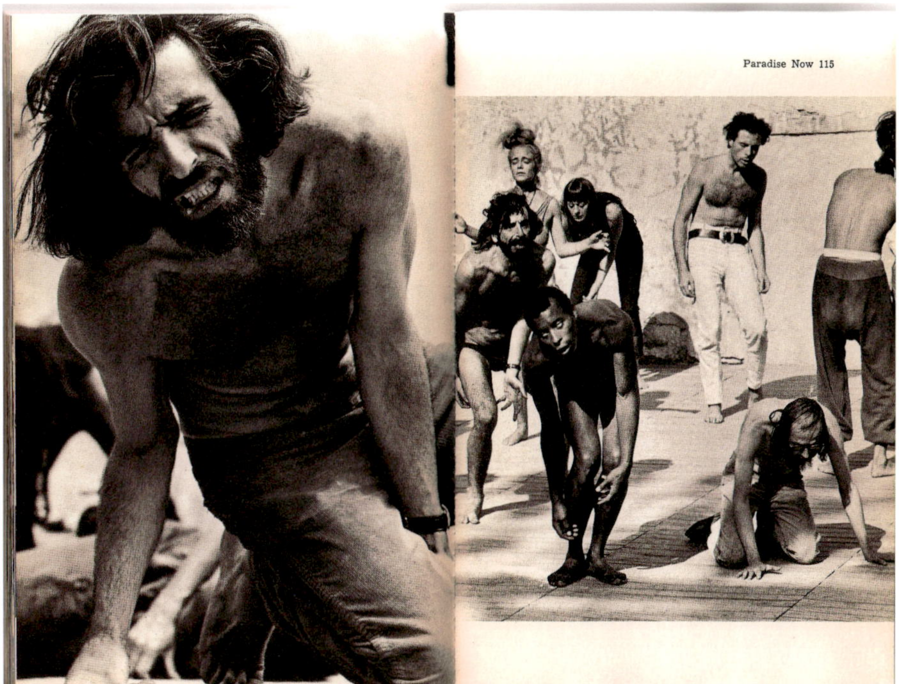

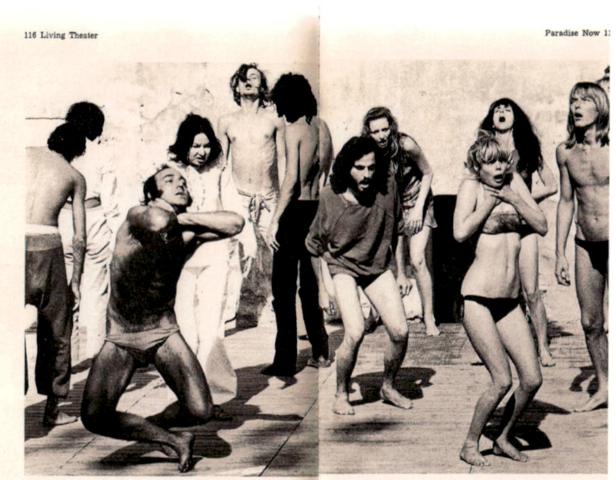

LIVING THEATRE
sampled by Spartacus Chetwynd

I am interested in trying to do performance that submerges into a mass of people already assembled, for example being in a club and suddenly performing a pre rehearsed dance, forming a spiral and tumbling on the floor in a heap, doing an elephant conga and then disappearing into the crowd again. I am into the physical contact and the idiocy of letting go to that extent.

I made up a dance called The Redundancy Dance and we did exactly this at a club a few times. I told my special art guru, he is a really serious and political artist that I ask advice about work and opportunities in the art world. He gave me the book to look at *Living Theatre, Paradise Now* by Paul Brand (Hilversum, 1969) as well as Brian De Palma's first feature film called *Hi Mom* (1970) that has a section on the New York based Wooster Group Versum, 1969.

DAYANITA SINGH Dream Villa

"Dream Villa is a landscape in my head. It's a world where nothing is quite as it seems to be. Dream Villa comes alive at night, when it is lit by artificial light. The moon is just ornamentation. So I suppose it is about darkness. But it is not a comfortable darkness. I go to many different cities, driving around without ever knowing where Dream Villa or its inhabitants will present themselves. It is a slow process as I cannot force it. There is no solace, no loss of the black and white. But I am possessed by it" - Dayanita Singh was born in 1961 in New Delhi, where she currently lives and works. She's one of the most renowned Indian photographers of all times and her black and white portraits of upper class families have been exhibited in galleries and museums worldwide. Her books are individual works of art where she distils images and a few words. In 2008 she was awarded the Robert Gardner Fellowship in Photography by Harvard University. *Dream Villa* is a collection of uninhabited scenarios originated in front of the photographer by the falling of Indian nights.

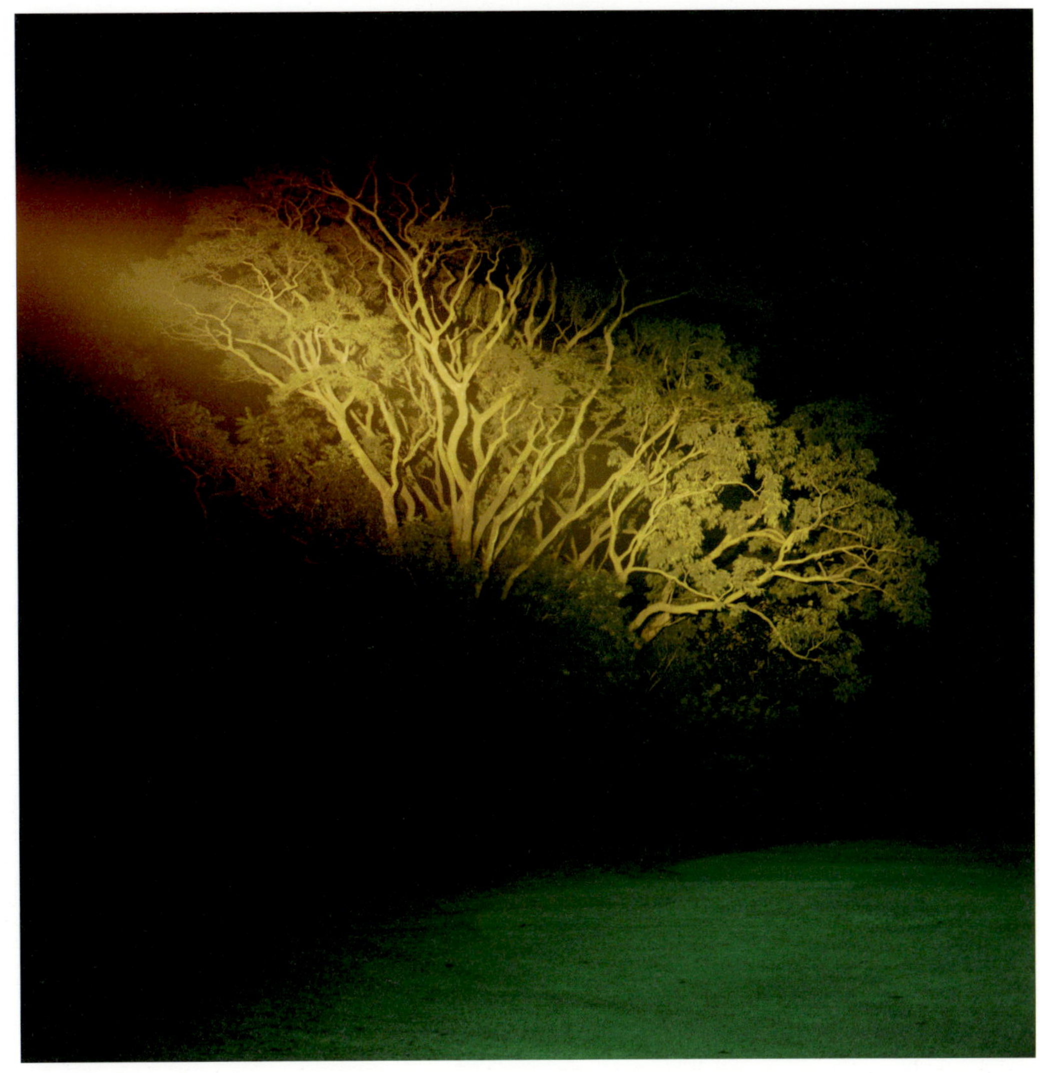

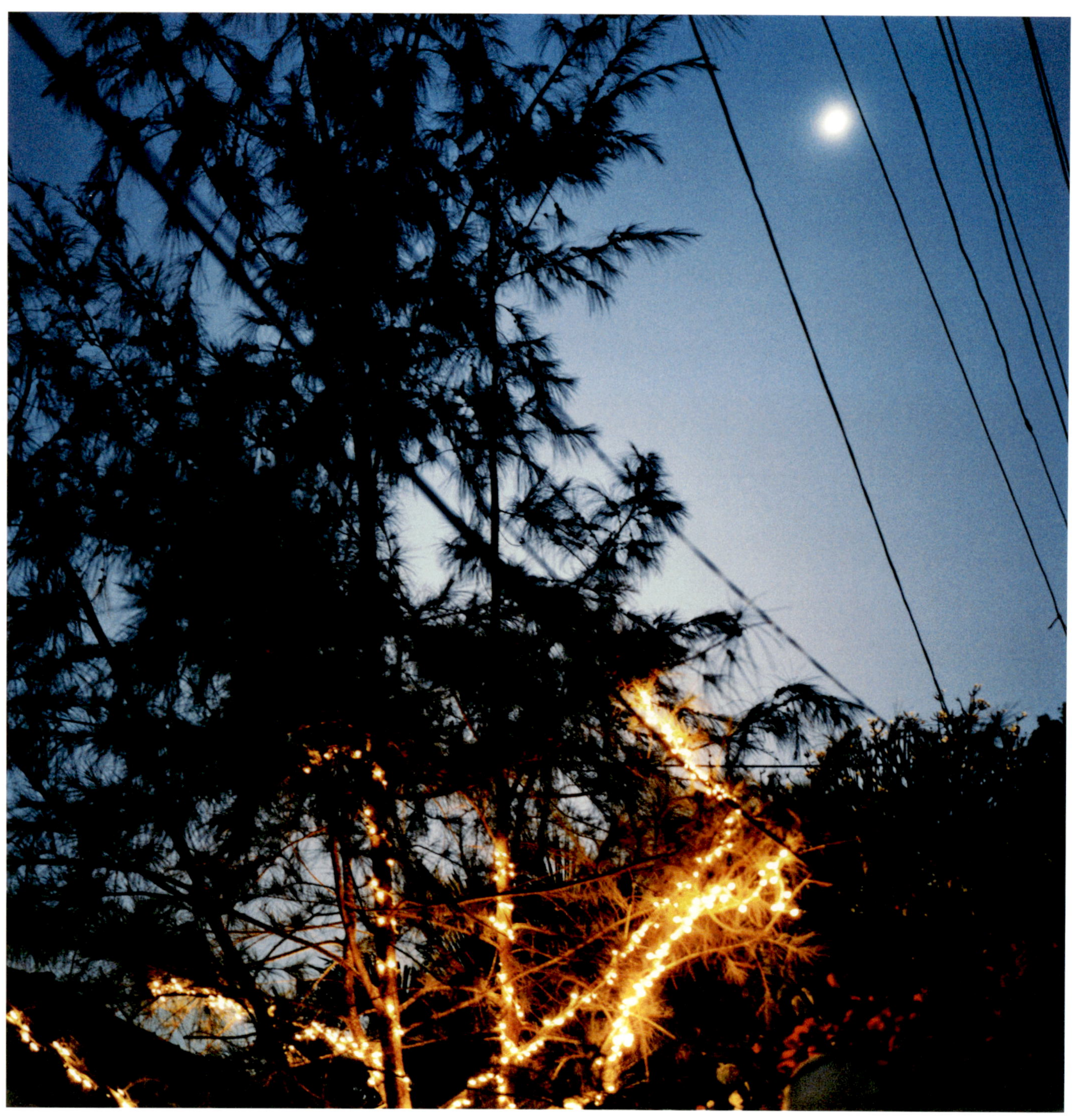

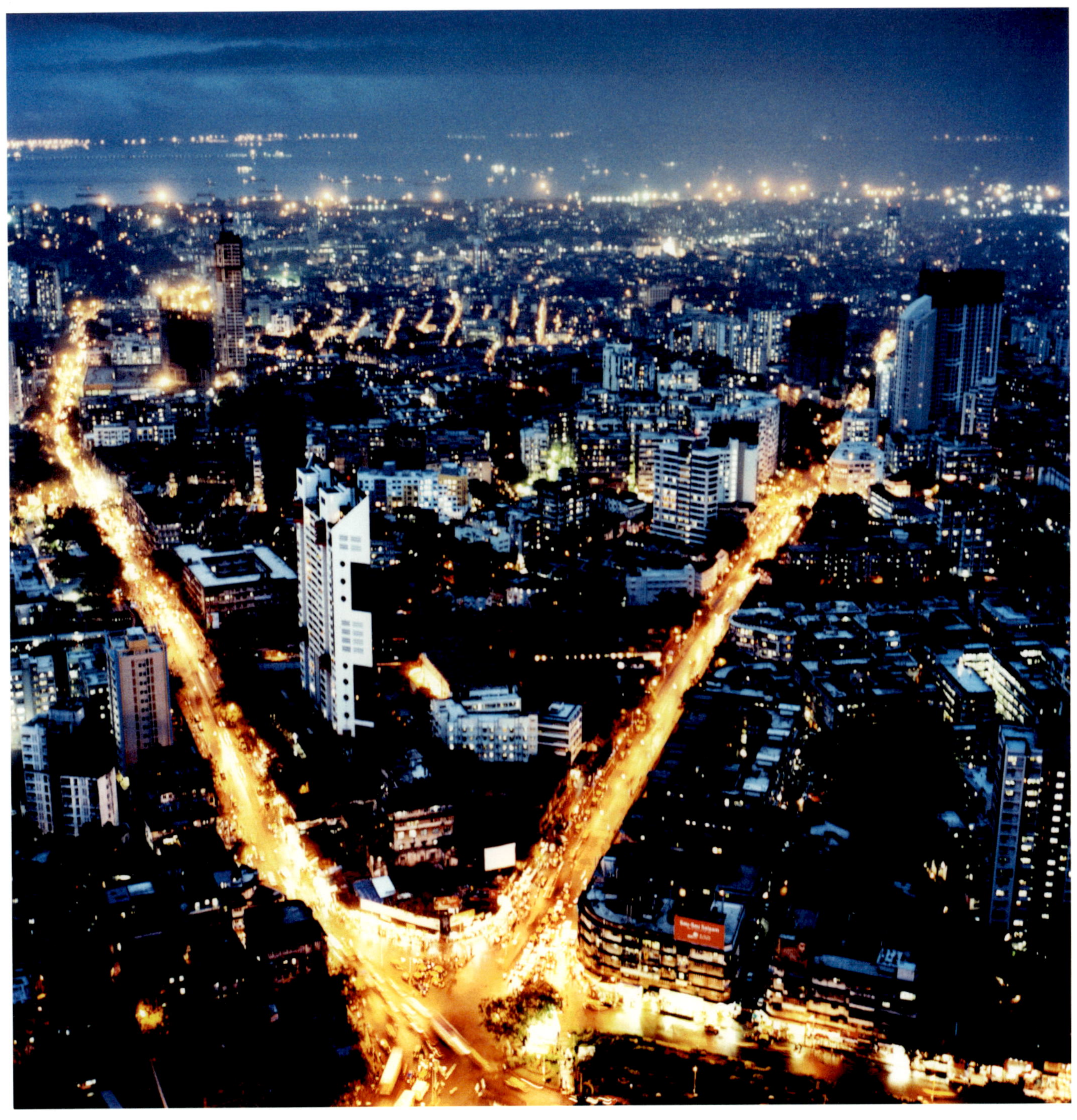

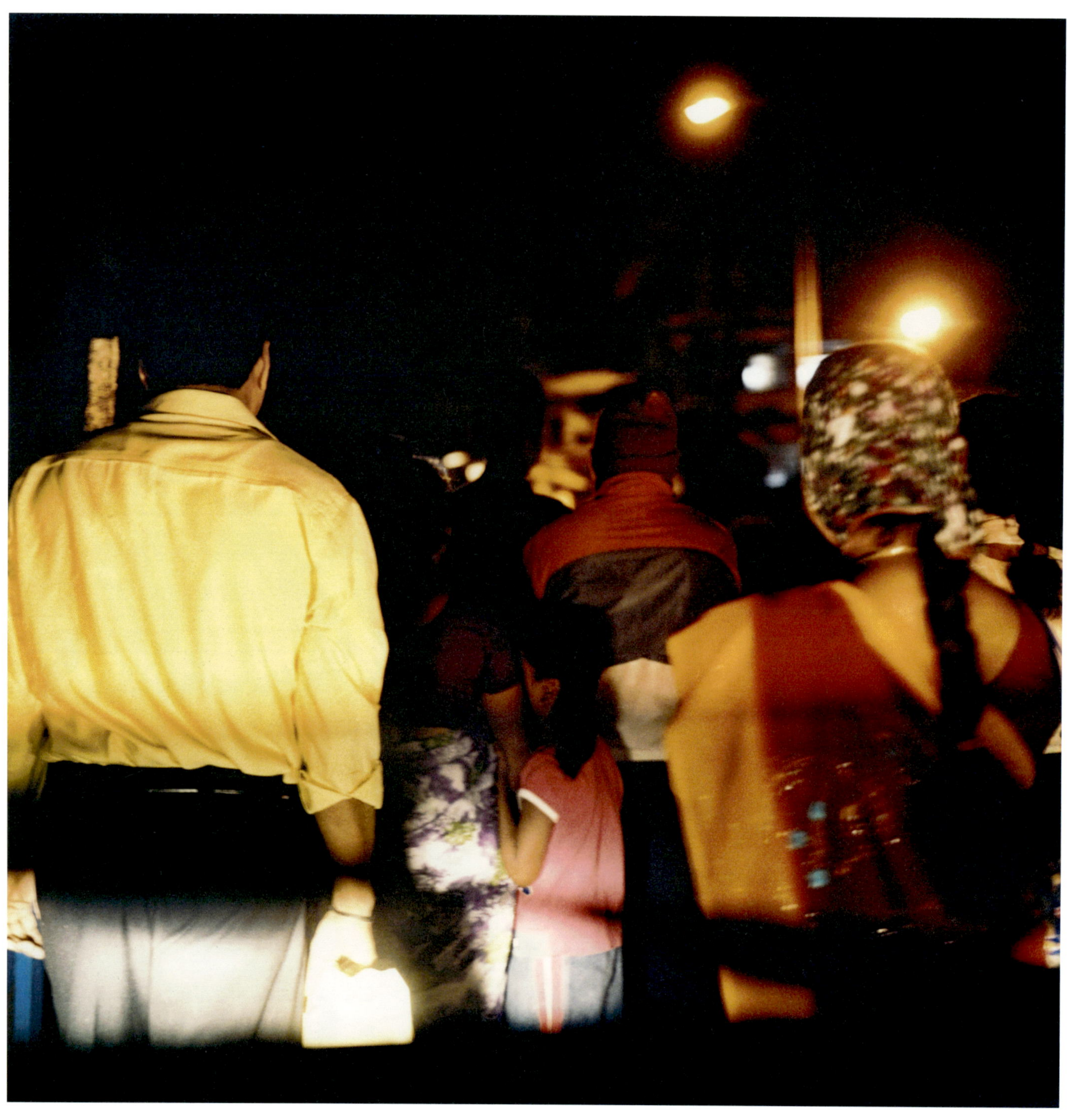

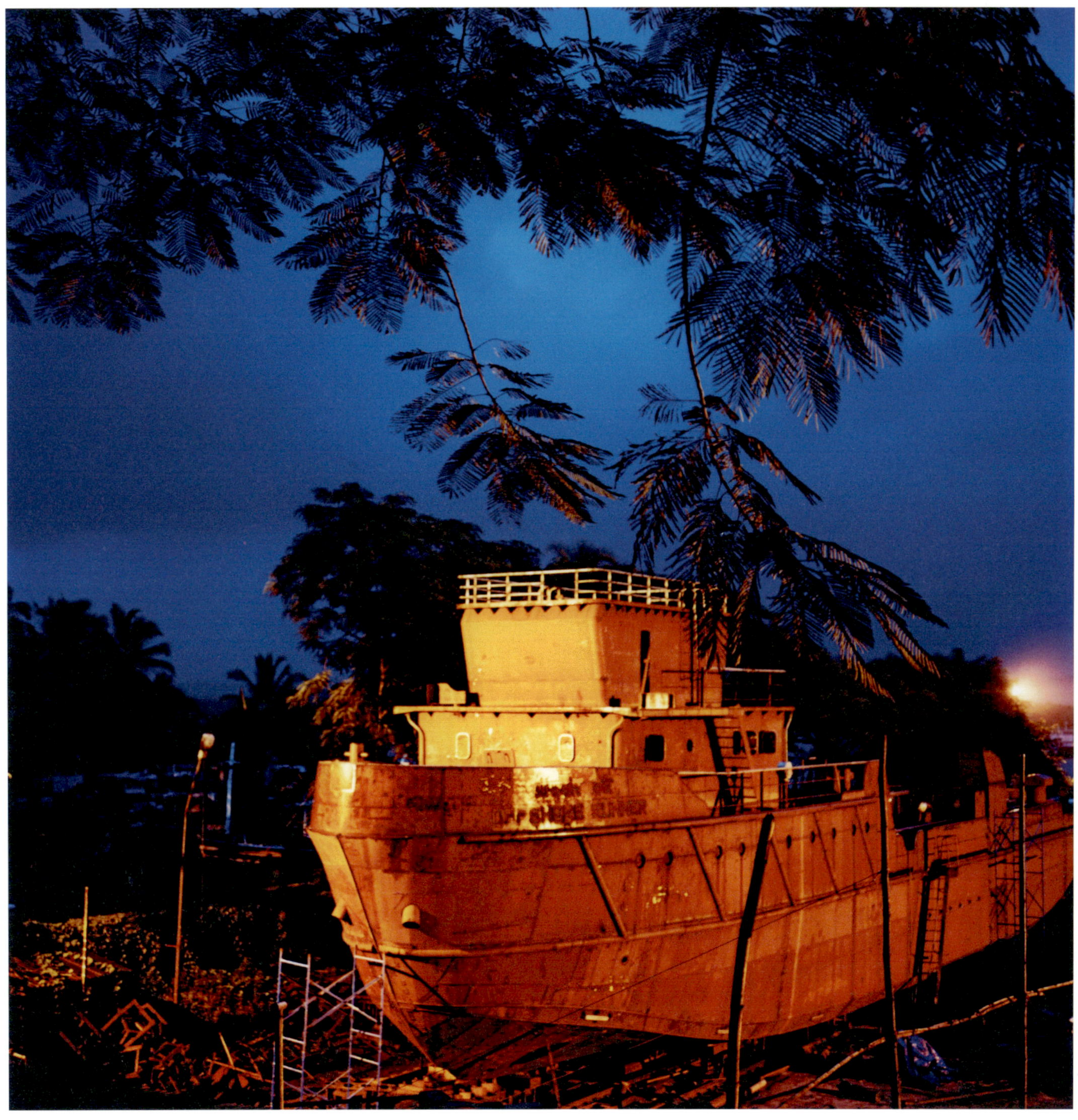

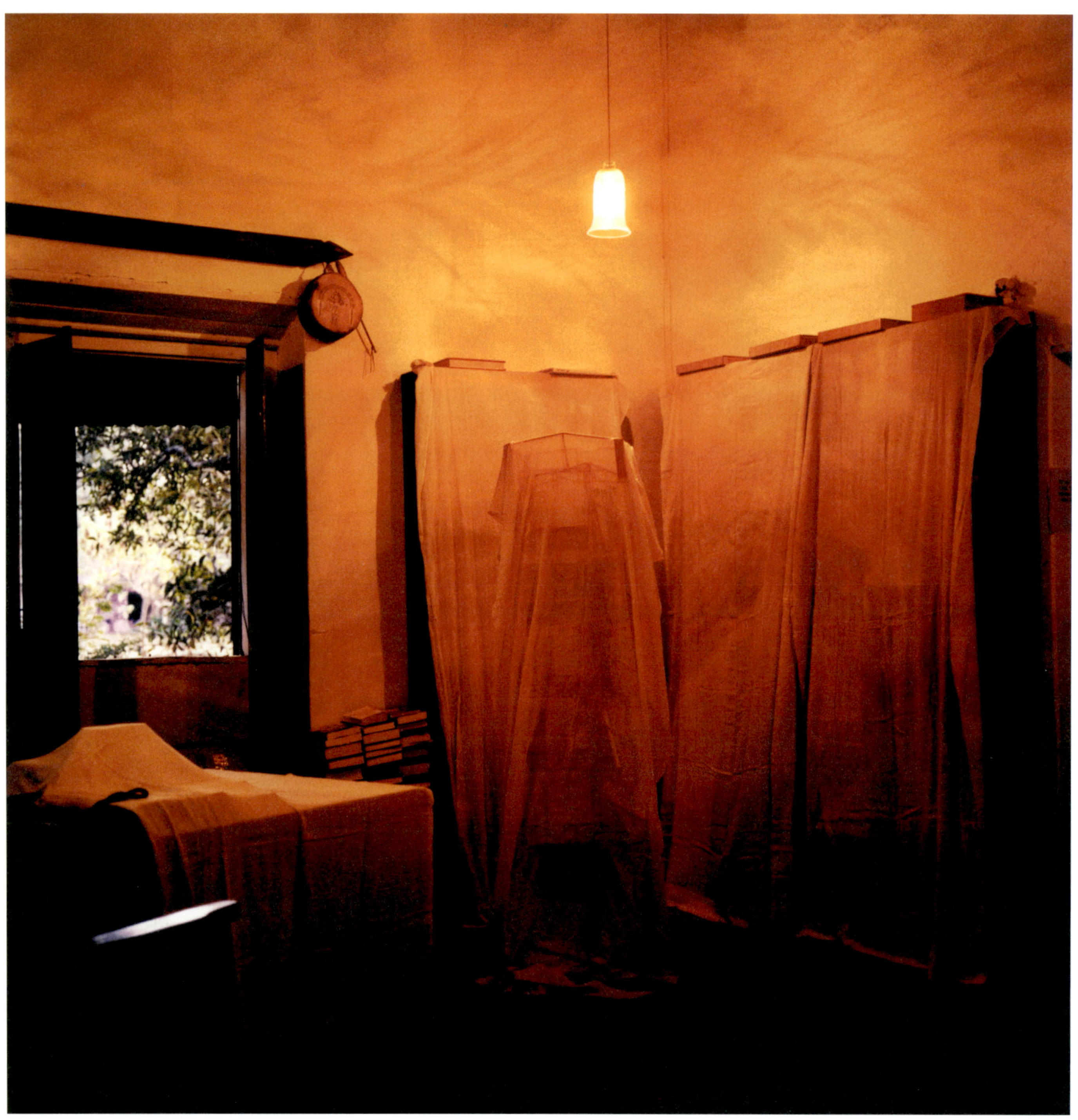

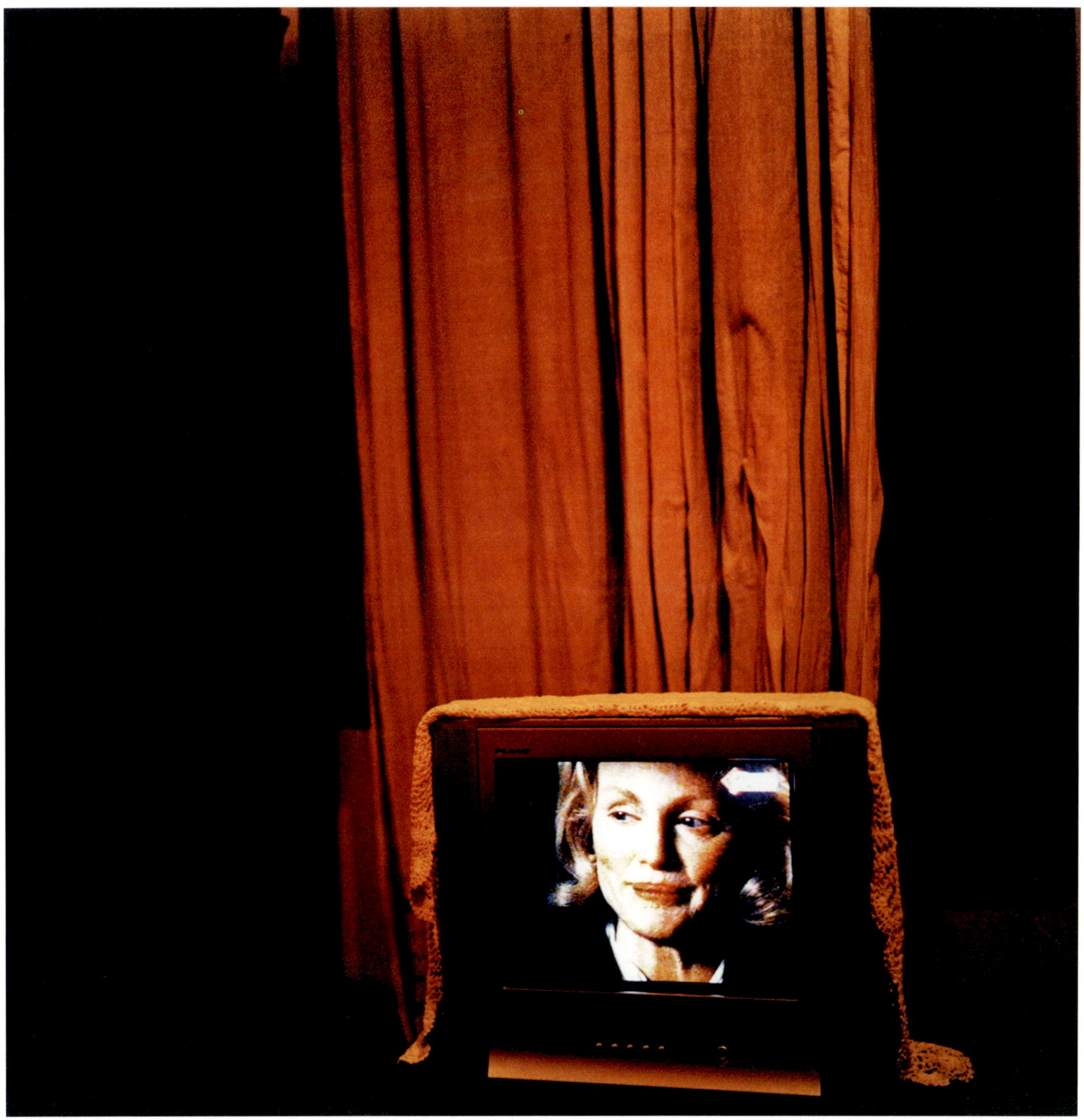

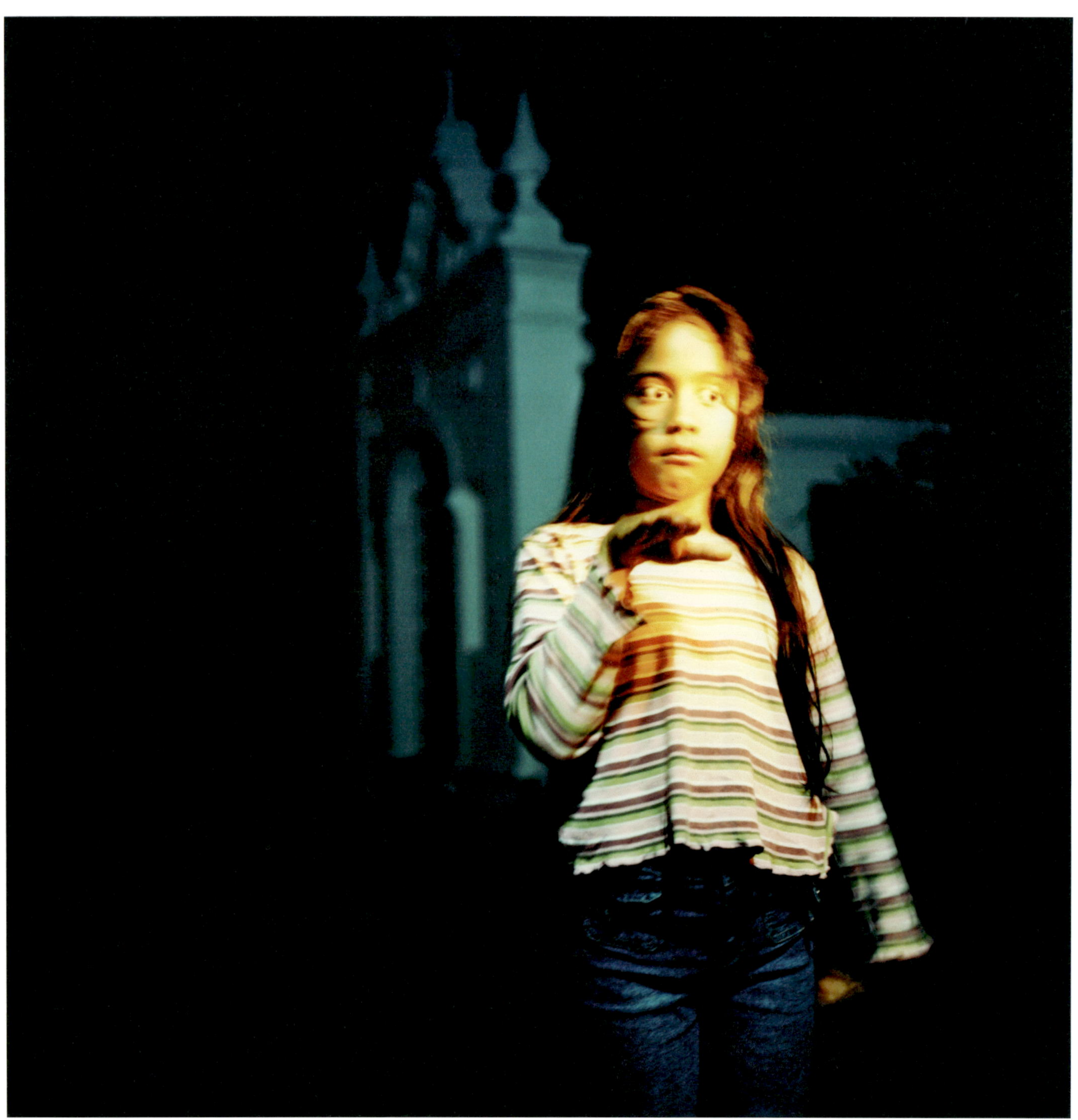

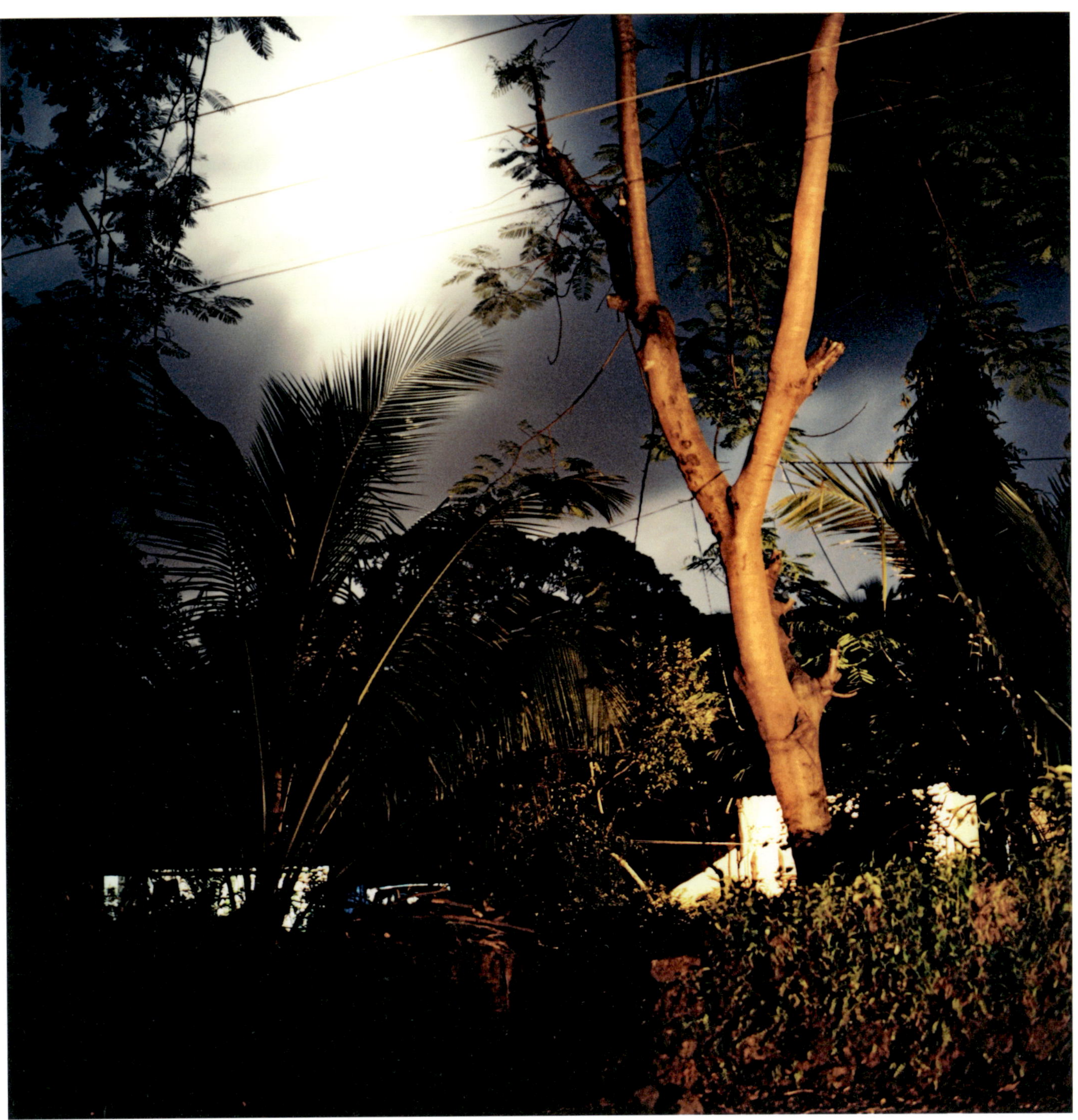

FRANCESCO ZANOT VISITS THE COLLECTION OF AKIYOSHI TANIGUCHI

1. SUBJECT - AKIHIDE TAMURA A photograph and its subject amount to two sides of the same coin. In referring to a photograph one must inevitably take into consideration the details of what it contains, whether or not they are interesting. This does not mean that there is a tangible connection between what one sees in front of the lens and its consequent portrayal. Not at all. While it is an accurate tool for observing reality, photography is at the same time a radical distortion of it. It allows us to take a ship, pull it out of the water and hold it in our hands, observing the tiniest details of what has been submerged below the threshold of the visible. *Untitled, circa 1970s, gelatin silver print, 35 x 35 cm.*

2. SUPERABUNDANCE - ISSEI SUDA Photography is a superabundant medium. It gives us many more answers than we are able to read. The result is a series of questions regarding what we are seeing, whose story we are unaware of. What, for instance, muddied the front hooves of this goat with her white skin and swollen udders? *From 'Fushi Kaden', 1970s, gelatin silver print, 16.5 x 16.5 cm.*

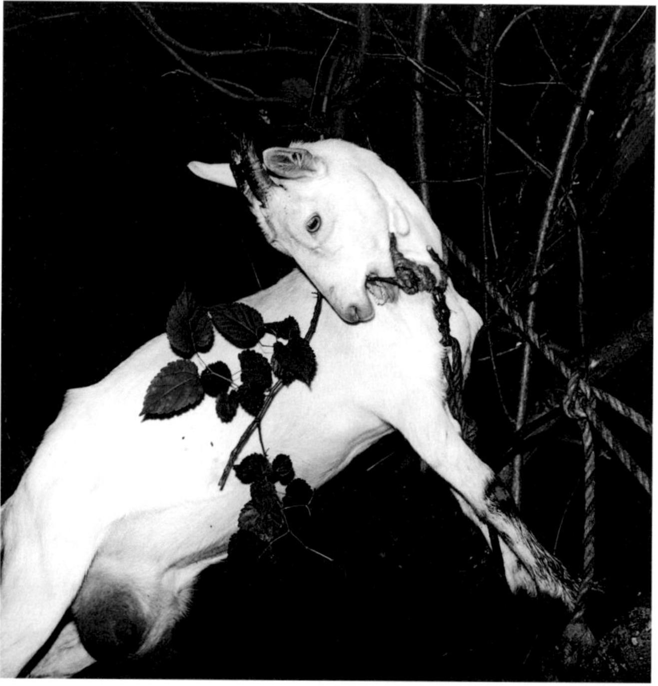

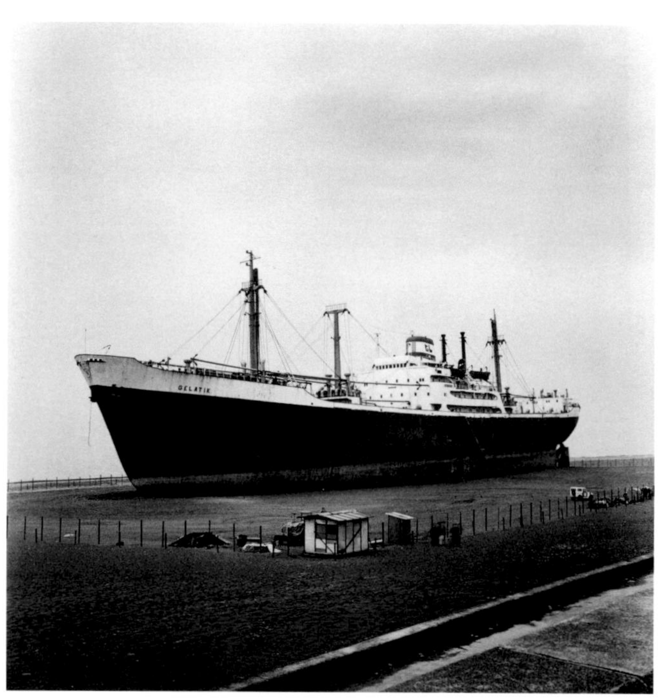

AKIYOSHI TANIGUCHI IS A PHOTOGRAPHER, COLLECTOR AND HEAD PRIEST AT CHOHOUIN BUDDHIST TEMPLE IN TOKYO, WHERE IN 2006 HE OPENED KURENBOH ART SPACE. WE VISITED TANIGUCHI'S COLLECTION OF 20TH CENTURY JAPANESE PHOTOGRAPHY IN AUGUST 2009. WHY DOES REV. TANIGUCHI COLLECT PHOTOGRAPHY? BECAUSE OF THE LIMINAL AND UNSTABLE NATURE OF PICTURES, WHICH INCESSANTLY REDISCUSS THE CONCEPTS OF TRUTH, REALITY AND EMPTINESS. "A PHOTOGRAPH IS JUST A PIECE OF PAPER AND A MASS OF CHEMICAL PARTICLES", HE SAYS, "BUT IT IS ALSO THE IMAGE OF SPIRIT". *Images © the artists, courtesy of Akiyoshi Taniguchi Collection*

3. SILENCE - NAOYA HATAKEYAMA Photography is silent. In bringing the tiniest details of reality to film it leaves all traces of sound behind it. All gestures and acts are deprived of sound effects. Sometimes quietness is a feature of the very scene that is being portrayed. At other times, there is a violent contradiction between what the image relates and the silence of the medium. In the latter case the ideal condition for observation is the total absence of sound. Then what you see achieves a new balance and alters the relationships between subjects. In this photograph by Naoya Hatakeyama, it is as though the violence of the explosion was mostly due to its rumble while its visual results are perfectly juxtaposed with the outline of a bird in flight. *From 'A Bird', 2007, c-print, 150 x 100 cm.*

4. BACKING - AKIKO TOBU When it is printed the photograph adheres to its backing. At this point the word 'photograph' designates the entire format of the image as well as the material on which it rests. Due to this process, the photograph acquires the status of an object (you hold it in your hand, you paste it into an album, you hang it on a wall, you swap it) and, as such, in some cases, it can even substitute the object it represents. This is the reason why Shirin Neshat writes on the bodies she portrays and why some people keep a photograph of their loved ones in their wallets: the concrete presence of the subject impregnates the paper from which it emerges. *From the 'Hotel Upstairs', 1999, c-print, 30.5 x 20.5 cm.*

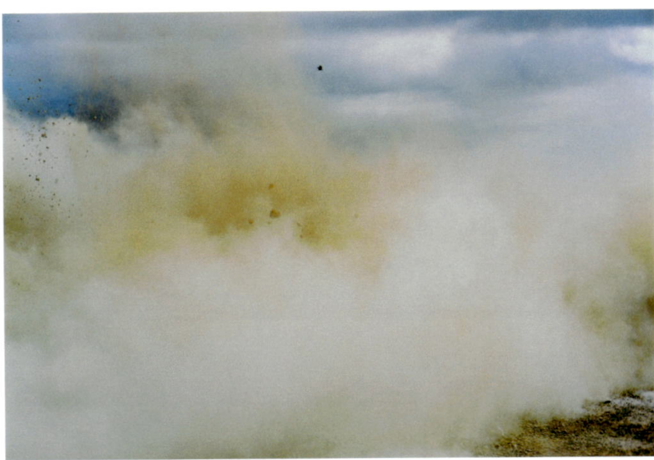

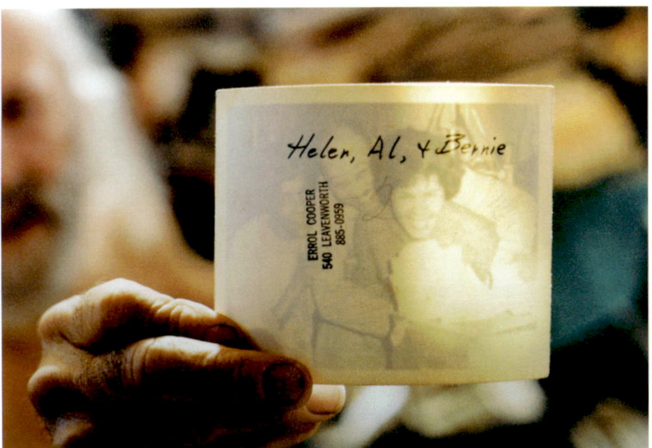

5. DESCRIPTION - DAIDO MORIYAMA Daido Moriyama took this photograph two years after the 1968 publication of *The Bikeriders* by Danny Lyon. Taken during the course of an extended stay with the motorcycling community Chicago Outlaws, Lyon's work is decisive in inaugurating a new strain of photojournalism, where the photographer is personnally involved in the events he is describing. The shortening of distances theoretically leads to an increase in the level of authenticity. This echoes the logic of participative observation in the field of ethnographical research, which is based on integrating the researcher into the social group that is being studied. But what degree of authenticity can the photograph guarantee when the faces of all its subjects are erased with a single blow? Maintaining that the photograph shows what is captured on the film is clearly correct. Yet, the photograph does many things at the same time: it describes, interprets, encodes, decodes and - at the peak of its expansion in American culture - it transfigures the bodies of ten Yokohama motorcyclists making them almost indistinguishable from their overseas counterparts. *Bikeriders, Yokohama, 1970, gelatin silver print, 30 x 21.5 cm.*

6. DISTANCE - ASAKO NARAHASHI By representing the infinitely small (filmed through a microscope) and the infinitely huge (the earth seen from the moon), photography has taught us that objects and facts are transformed in proportion to the distance from which we observe them. From a few centimeters the ocean mutates into a dense, jet black magma that engulfs everything, including the reflected sunlight and the planes flying overhead. *From 'Half Awake and Half Asleep in the Water', 2002, c-print, 55 x 37 cm.*

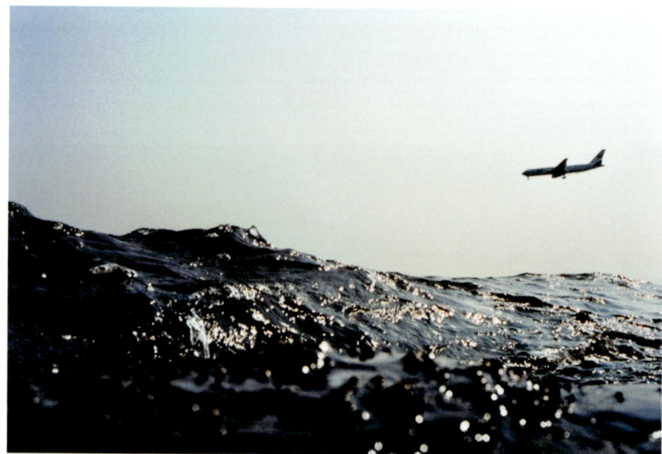

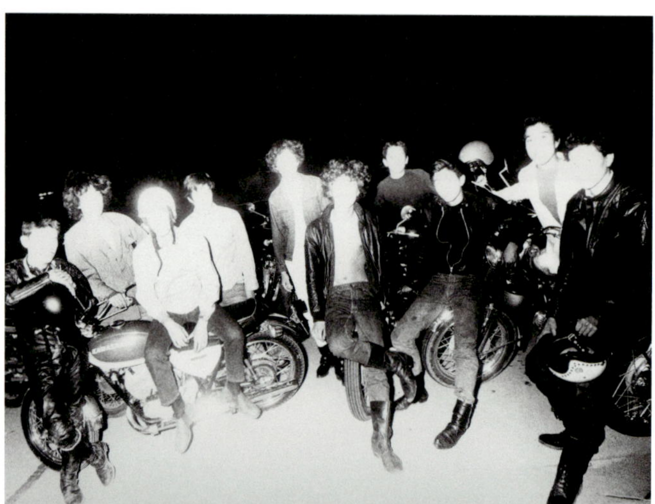

7. THE TILTED HORIZON - MIYAKO ISHIUCHI Photography has a perpendicular history. For many years, beginning with its invention, photographers held their cameras straight out in front of them, making sure that the line of the horizon ran parallel to the upper and lower edges of the frame. Then came the Wright brothers, the first World War and, subsequently, the experimentalism of Alexander Rodchenko and Ralph Steiner, Cartier-Bresson and Robert Frank's snapshots, and, eventually, William Klein, Garry Winogrand, Shomei Tomatsu, Daido Moriyama. Sometimes the world in front of them bows as though it were being observed from the cockpit of a banking airplane. Tilting the frame means pulling the rug from underneath the spectators' feet. Every photographed subject slumps, runs over the edges, slips outside of the camera range. *Yokosuka Again* is the title of the series that Miyako Ishiuchi dedicated in the 80s to the memory of his city, the home of the largest American military port in the eastern Pacific since 1945.

From 'Yokosuka Again 1980-1990', 1980s, gelatin silver print, 42 x 29 cm.

8. CENTRALITY - KIYOJI OTSUJI Placing the subject head on and in the center of the frame means abandoning the composition of the latter. A formal structure of this type is equivalent to pointing a finger at what you find in front of the lens. Some photographers have used it to prove their own neutrality and to stress the authoritative cataloguing nature of photography. As in every imperative affirmation, the interest first concentrates on the focus and only then moves outwards towards the edges. In this photograph by Kiyoji Otsuji, you can glimpse, on one side of a tumbledown brick building, a doorway that leads to a shrine and, on the other, a city street with overhanging signs and electricity cables. In the light of this, what remains in the middle takes the form of a cumbersome separating device.

Untitled, 1950s, gelatin silver print, 27 x 20.5 cm.

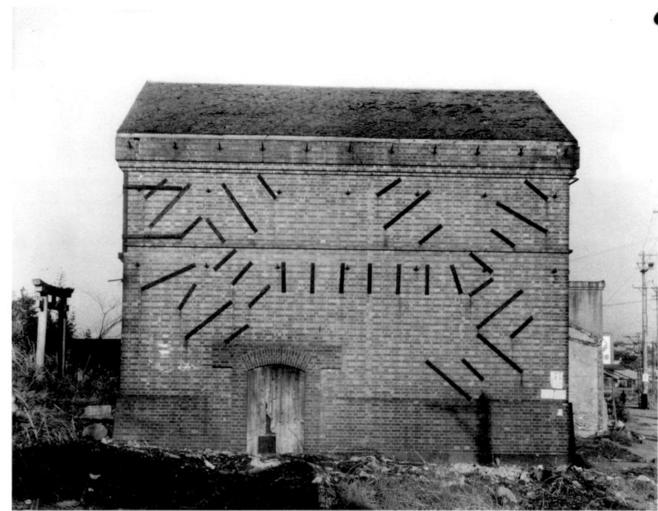

9. THE PUNCTUM - SHOJI UEDA "A photograph's *punctum* is that accident which pricks me (but also bruises me, is poignant to me)". Roland Barthes wrote this in 1980 in his last essay, *Camera Lucida*, in which a series of reflections on the nature, the rules and the exponents of this medium merge with the distress caused by his mother's death. This comparison highlights the intimate and diary-like perspective that informs Barthes' treatise, which examines his own individual relationship with photographs and photography, as well as his relationship with his beloved mother, without desiring or seeking intercessions. He hastens to exclude the photographer (the Operator) himself from the question of the *punctum*. "Certain details may 'prick' me. If they do not, it is doubtless because the photographer has put them there intentionally". We do not know if Shoji Ueda in some way orchestrated the emergence of a flash of light from behind the dark foliage of an enormous tree in his photograph. In any case when we see it there is no doubt that that point of light, exploding into the shape of star, pierces us. *Untitled, 1970s, gelatin silver print, 21.5 x 14 cm.*

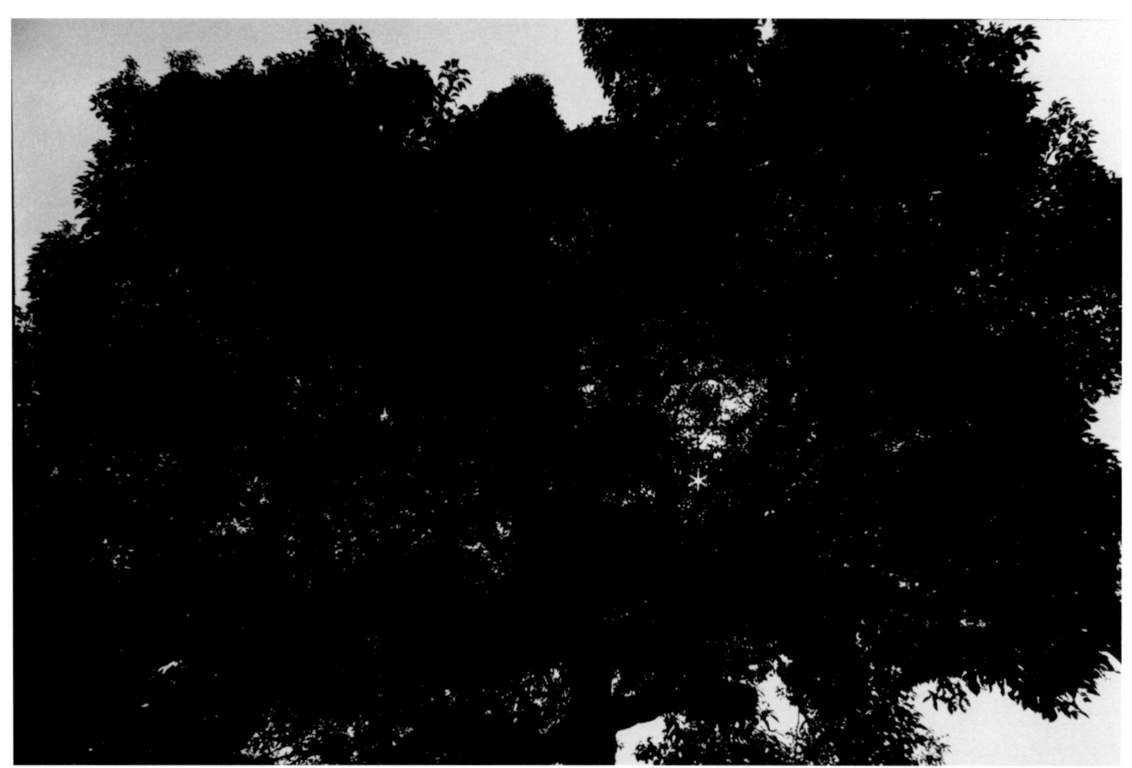

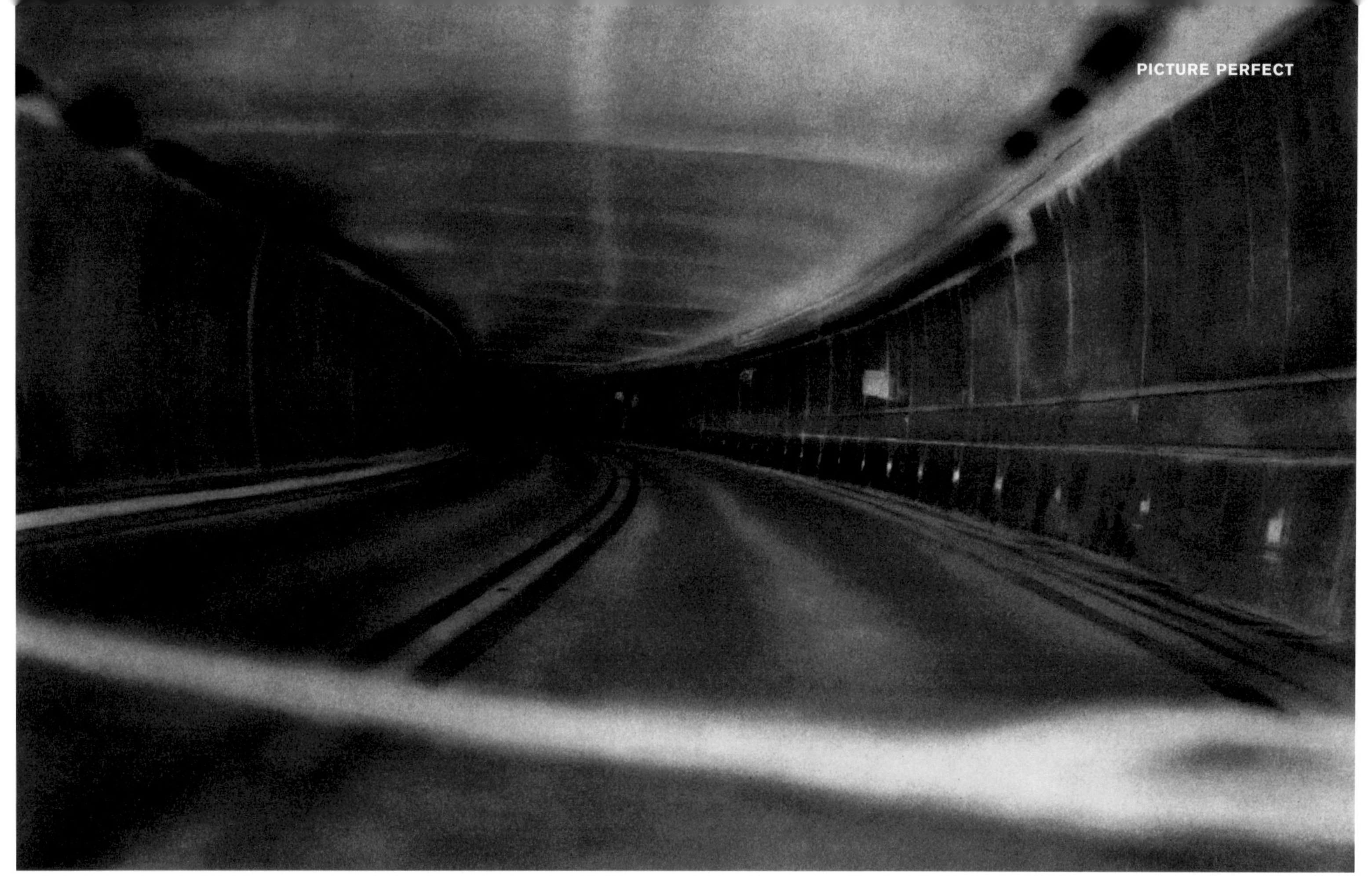

MARINA BERIO

Berio's photographic work often deals with physicality, surface and space. She has avoided overt narrative and declamation to favor quiet, open-ended imagery, which defies simple classification and signals an existential and meditative frame of mind. Her recent works on paper comment upon the physical and formal imperatives of the photographic medium by reproducing in drawings the visual traces of shutter speed, focus, glare and the way light behaves when it traverses the negative. Charcoal, a dusty, burned substance, echoes the chemically transformed molecules of silver that make up a photographic image.

Roads, tunnels, and the countryside viewed from a car window refer to traveling and passage, but the darker reversed tonalities convey mystery and the unknown. Sources of light conserve their association with creativity and celebration, but simultaneously allude to burning, decay and destruction. As Berio explains, "in this process what is not there is just as important as what is, what is black is just as important as what is white. Blackness and shadows become foreground, and highlights become absence".

Marina Berio was born in Boston in 1966. She grew up in New York City and in Italy. Berio has been granted the Aaron Siskind Foundation Award and a Pollock/Krasner Grant, and has resided at MacDowell Colony, Yaddo, and Schloss Plüschow in Germany. She has exhibited at various galleries and art spaces, including Michael Steinberg Fine Arts, New York; Smack Mellon in Brooklyn; Les Rencontres d'Arles in France; and Acta International in Rome. Berio earned her Master of Fine Arts degree in Photography at Bard College, and is Acting Chair of the General Studies Program at the International Center of Photography in New York City.

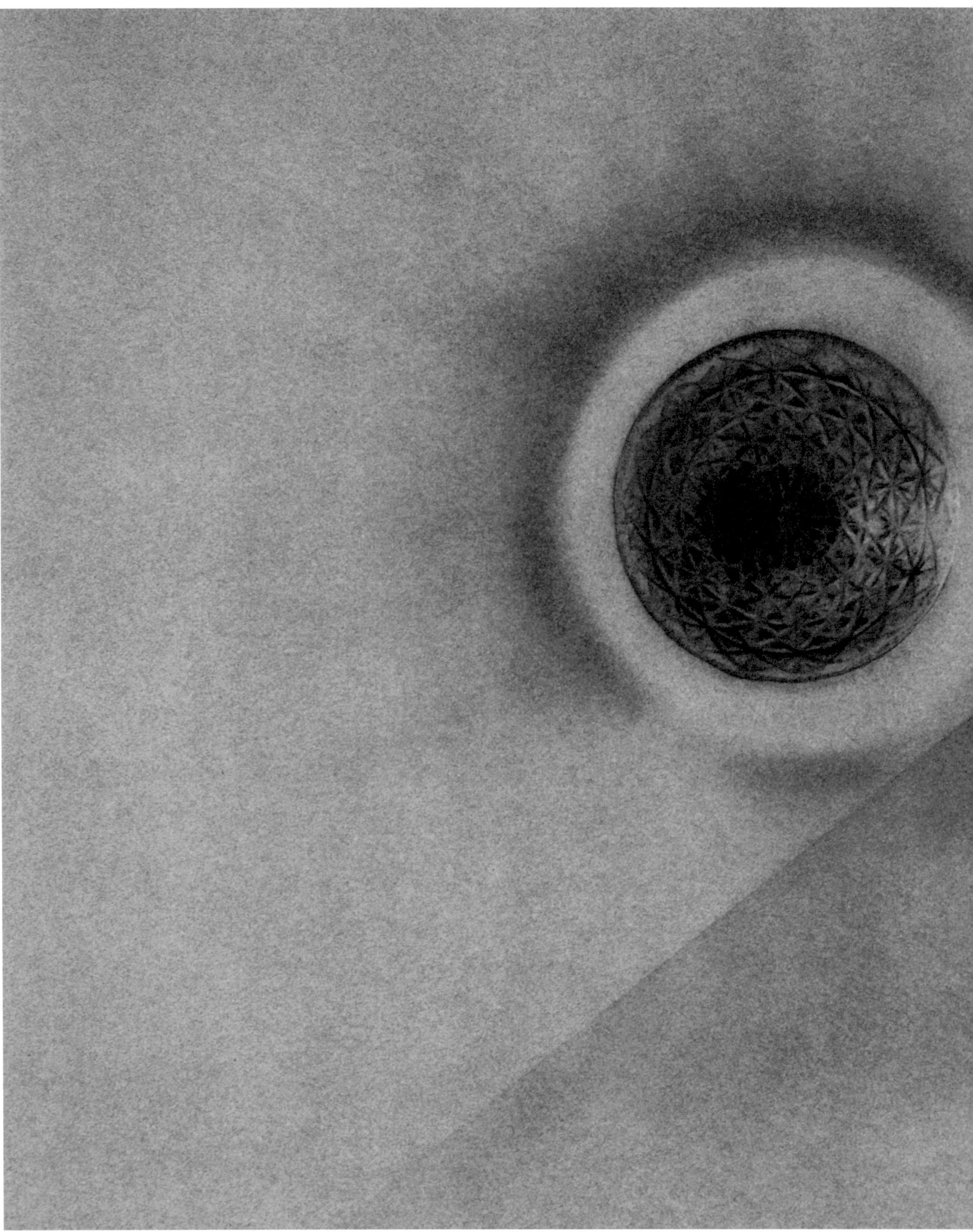

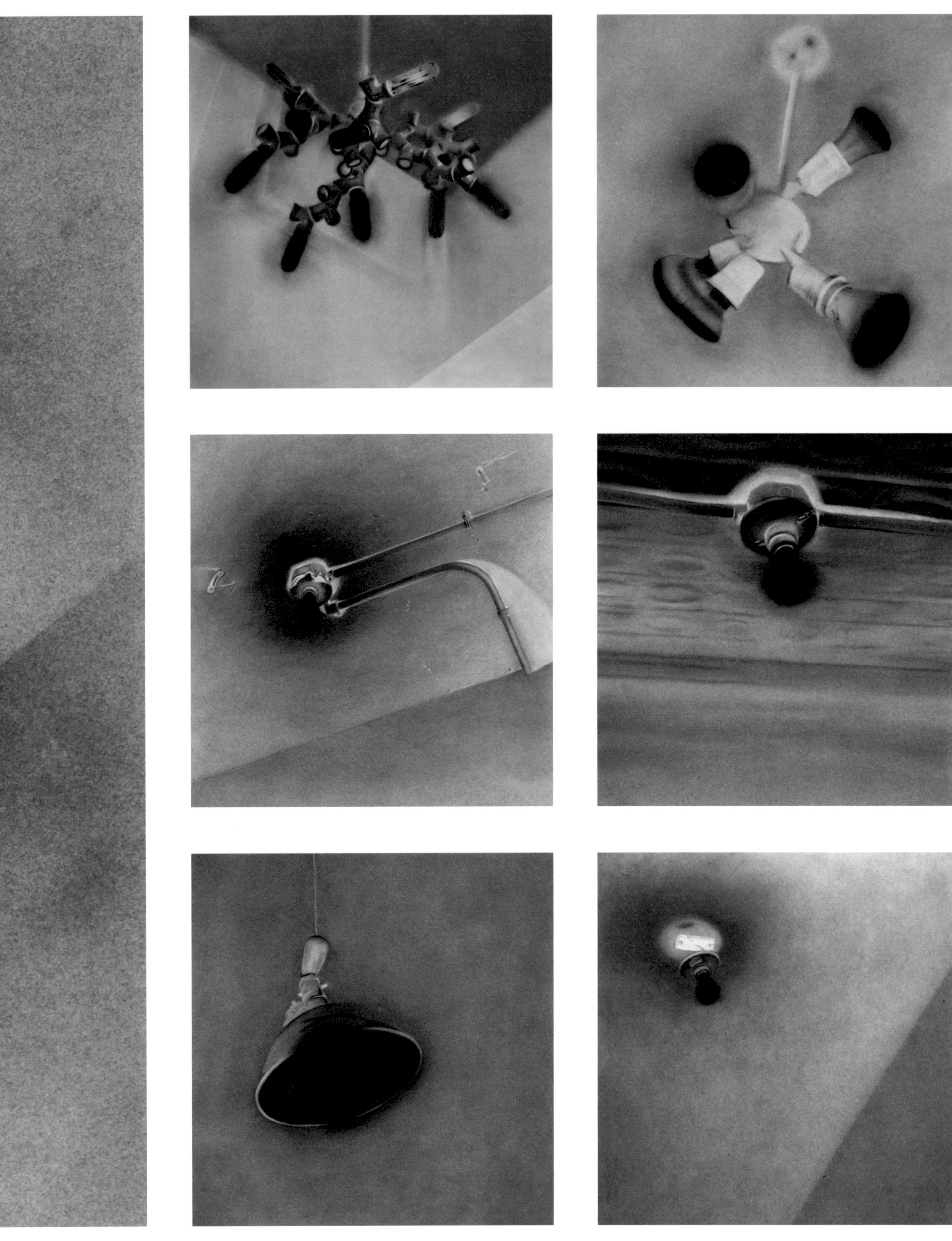

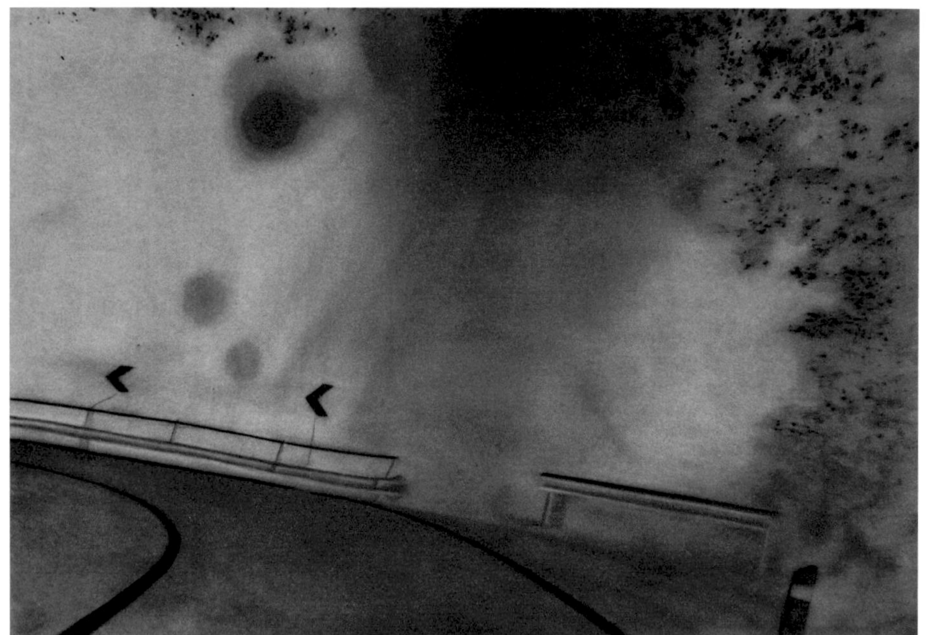

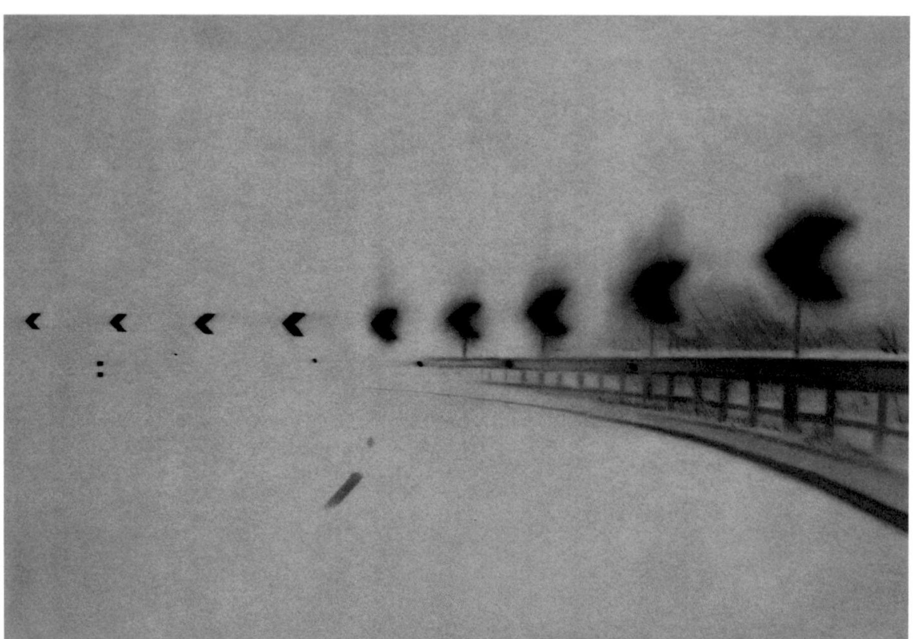

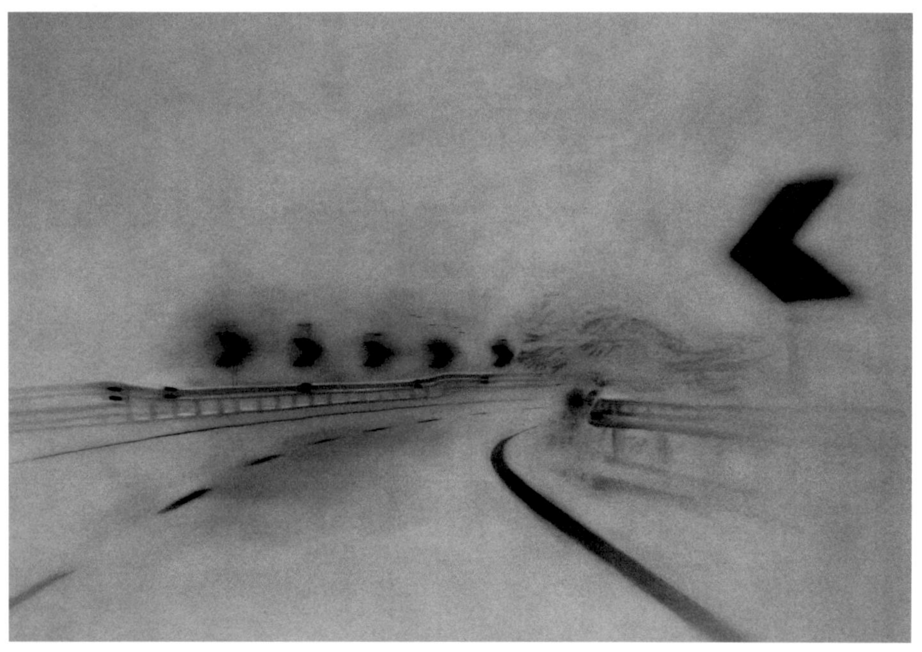

Opening page Through and Not 53, 2008, 102 x 152 cm.
Page 74 Burn Breathe Marina 5, 2008, 51 x 51cm. *Page 75,
top left* Burn Breathe Penelope 2, 2009, 91 x 91 cm. *Top right* Burn
Breathe Penelope 3, 2009, 51 x 51 cm. *All courtesy Michael
Steinberg Fine Art, New York. Center left* Burn Breathe Nan 3,
2007, 51 x 51 cm. *Center right* Burn Breathe Marina 5, 2008,
51 x 51cm. *Bottom left* Burn Breathe Alisha 2, 2008, 51 x 51cm.
Bottom right Burn Breathe Marco 1, 2008, 51 x 51cm. *All courtesy Otto Zoo Gallery, Milan. This page, top* Through and Not 50,
2007, 71 x 107 cm., *collection of Mike Kelley, New York. Center*
Through and Not 58, 2009, 71 x 107 cm., *courtesy Michael
Steinberg Fine Art, New York Bottom* Through and Not 59, 2009,
71 x 107 cm., *courtesy Michael Steinberg Fine Art, New York. Opposite
top* Through and Not 48b, 2006, 102 x 150 cm., *collection Bost-
Chambon, Bordeaux. Opposite, bottom* Through and Not 60, 2009,
71 x 107 cm., *courtesy Michael Steinberg Fine Art, New York.
All images © the artist*

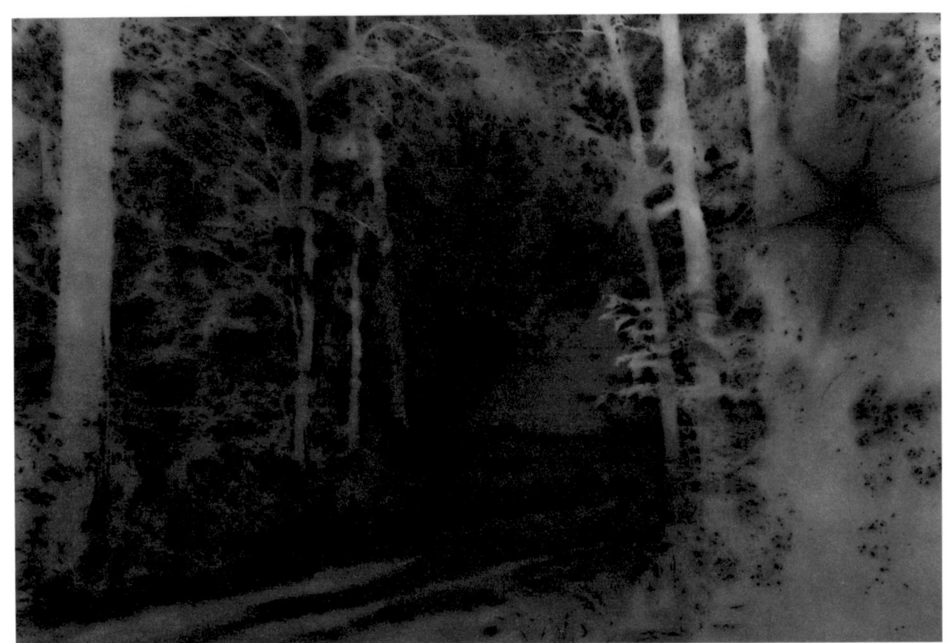

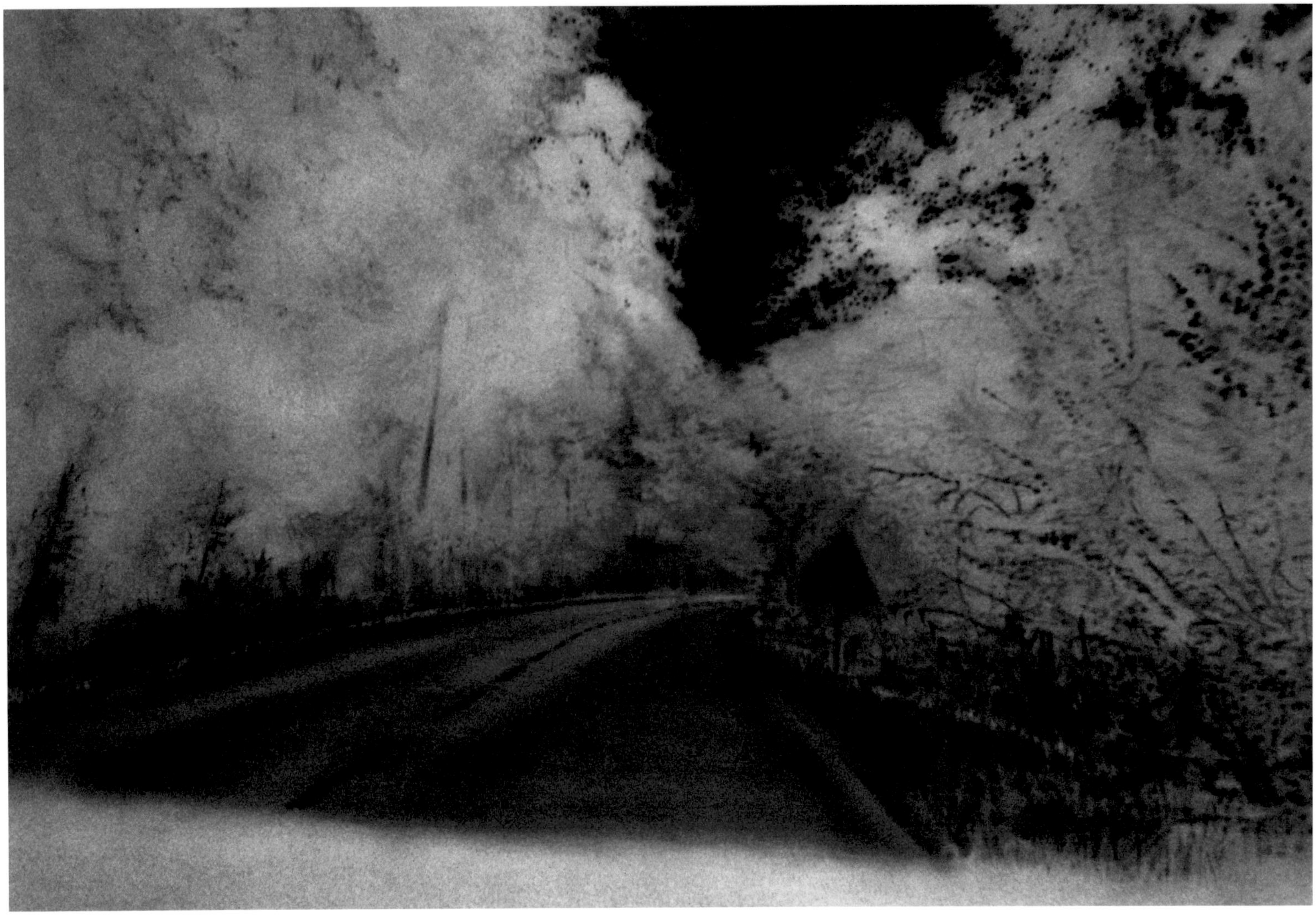

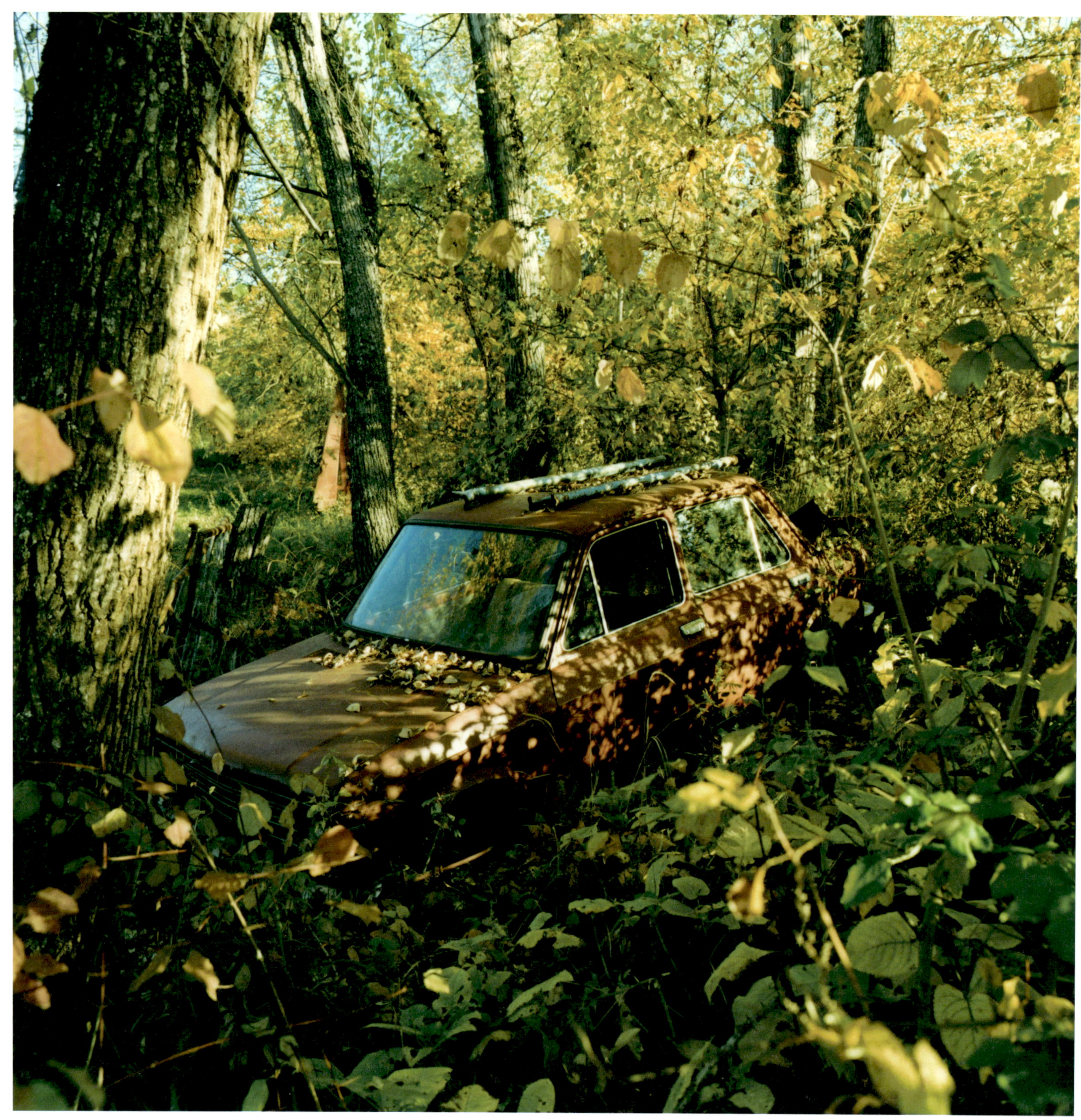

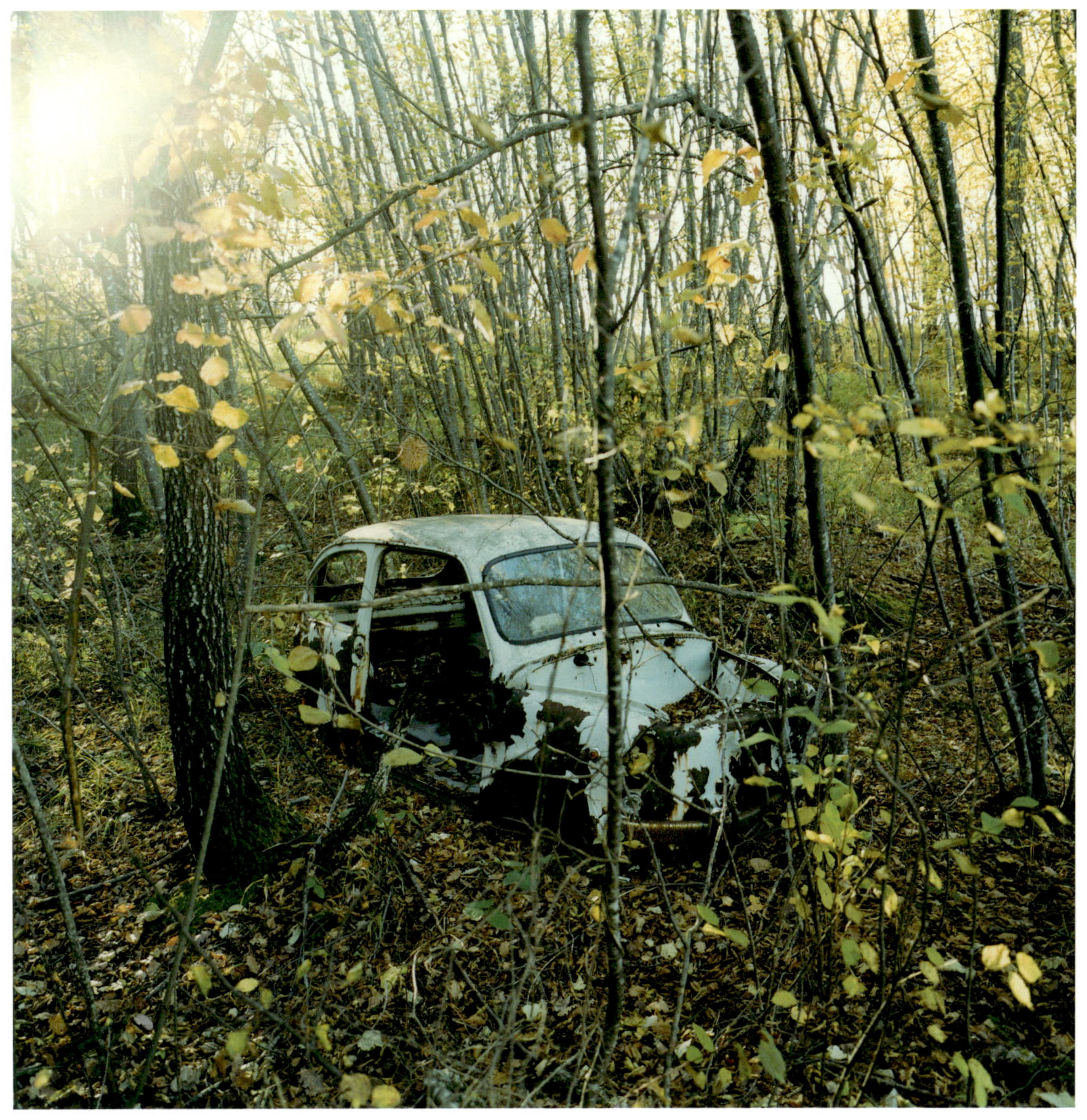

EMANUELE COLOMBO Giardini Auto Immobili

He defines himself "a landscape photographer", although his sceneries are always contaminated by human traces and focus mostly (and lyrically) on abandoned objects and places. As a teenager, Colombo started taking pictures of a derelict factory with his grandfather's camera, a 1940s Kodak. Since then, he has kept shooting on film with the detachment and fervor (and snobbishness) of the amateur; bringing his camera everywhere and considering his images more relevant to himself than others. Primarily maintaining an anarchic take on life, touring on his bike around his favorite countries (Australia, France, Ireland…), going about places with a peculiar sense of observation. In this car carcasses series the center of attention is on trees and plants growing inside and around the vehicles, transforming them into unintentional gardens. We are intrigued by the shade that branches and leaves cast on the automobiles, by the melancholy emphasized by the fog. We are amused by the tragicomic condition of life seeping from the image of a truck, dead, in the attempt to drag another car out of the quicksand in the Australian desert - Emanuele Colombo (Forlì, Italy, 1969) lives and works between Cremona and Milan and travels around the world.

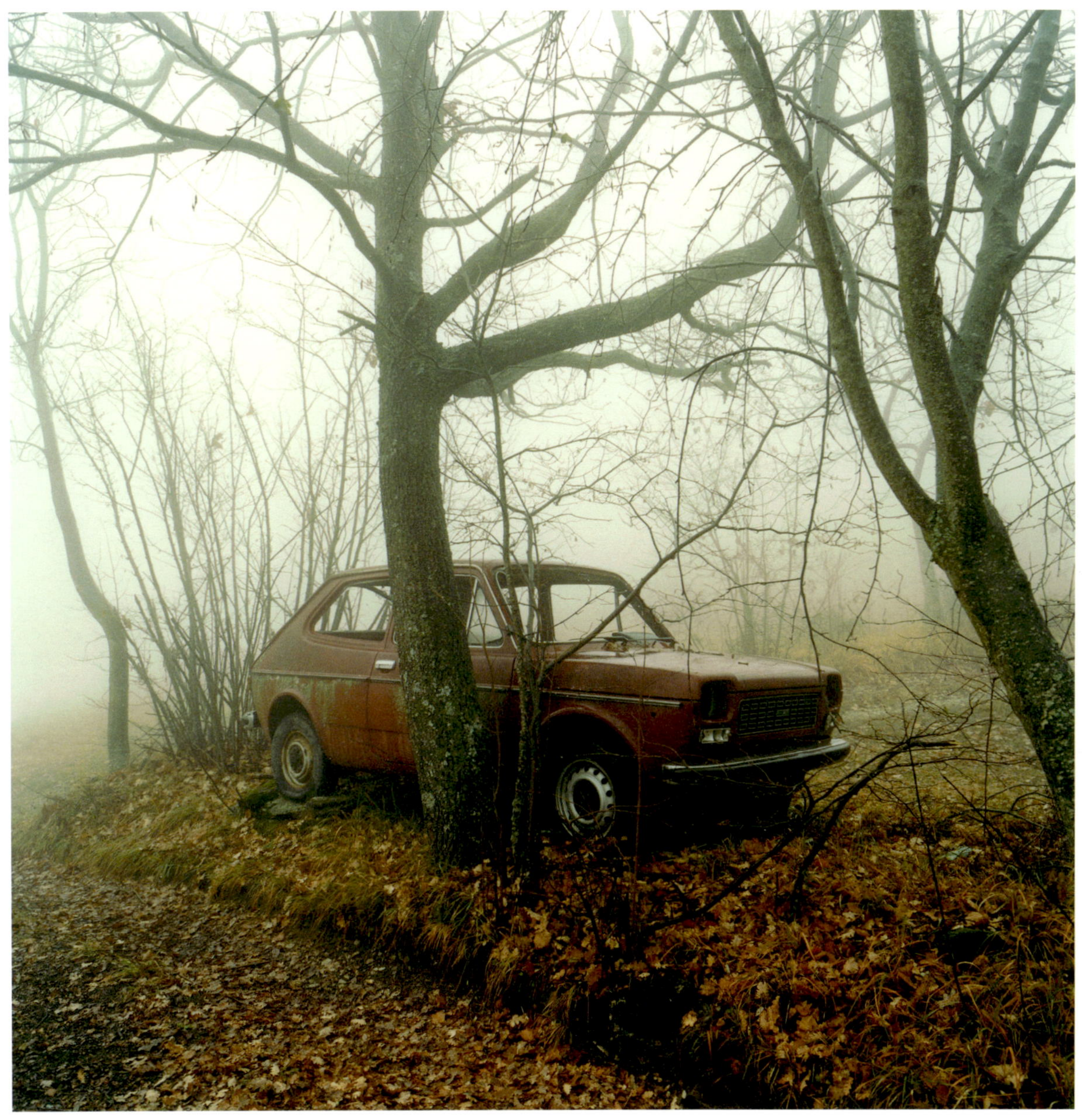

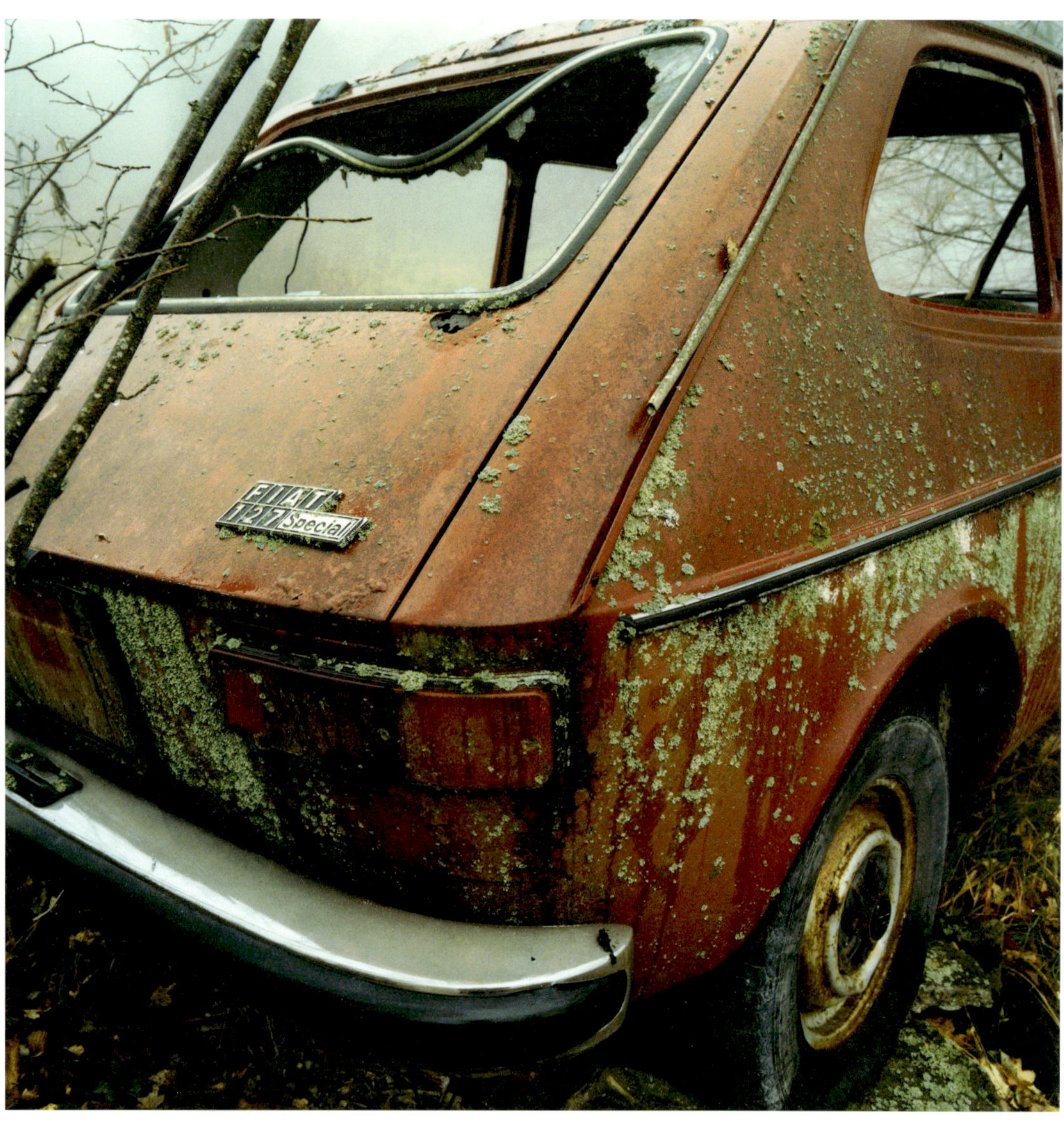

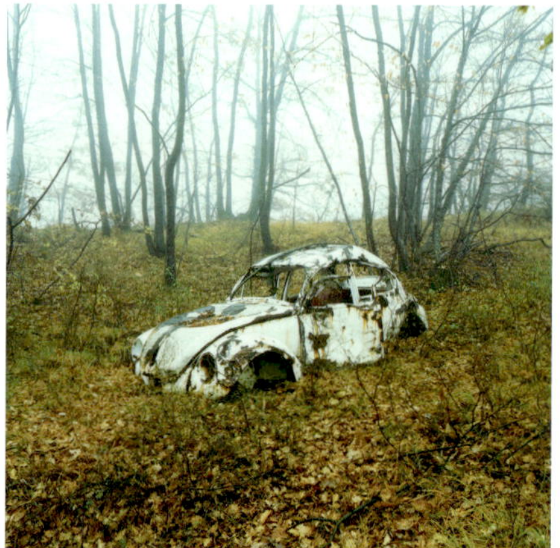

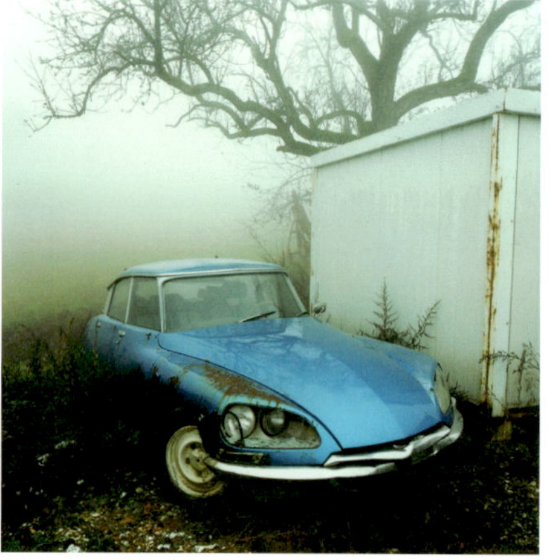

In this page, top left Fiat 127, Verogna (PC, Italy) 2007. *Top right* Volkswagen Käfer, Malvezzi (PC, Italy) 2007. *Bottom right* Citroen DS, Bobbio (PC, Italy) 2008 *Opposite page* Renault 20, Monticelli d'Ongina (PC, Italy) 2007. *Page 84* Fiat 127, Ebbio (PC, Italy) 2007. *Page 85* Renault 4 Van, Plateau de Millevaches (Limoges, France) 2007

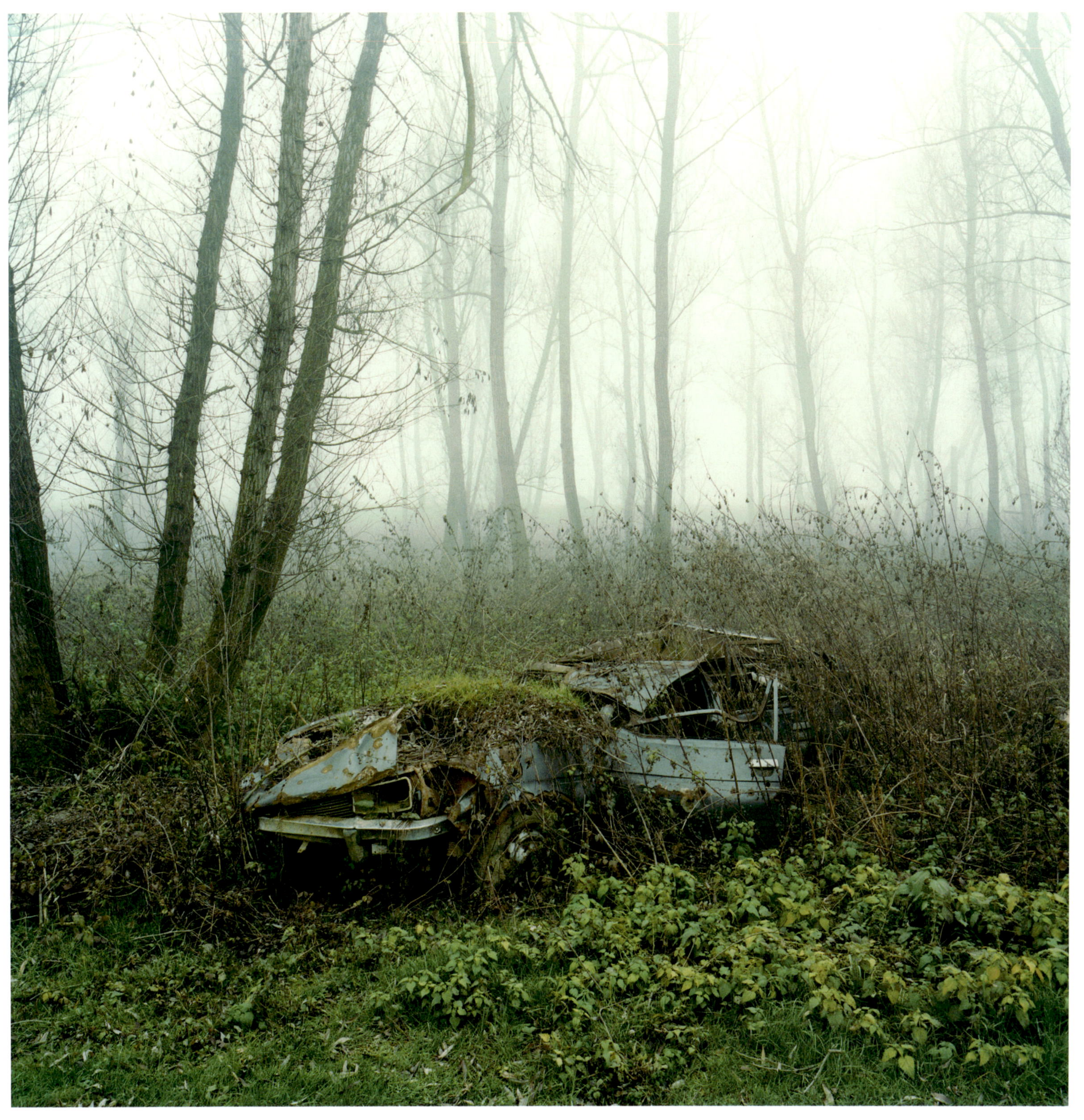

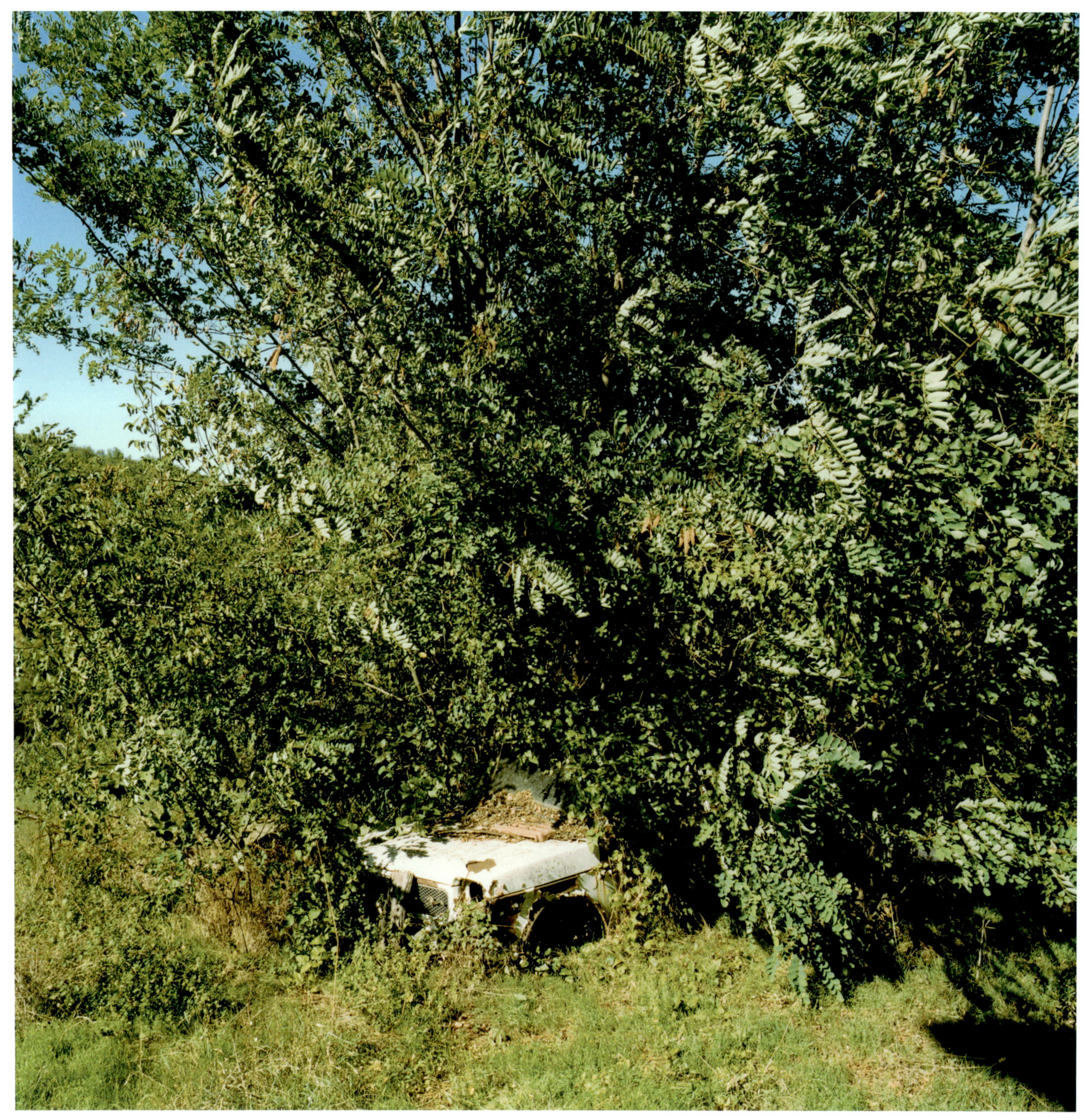

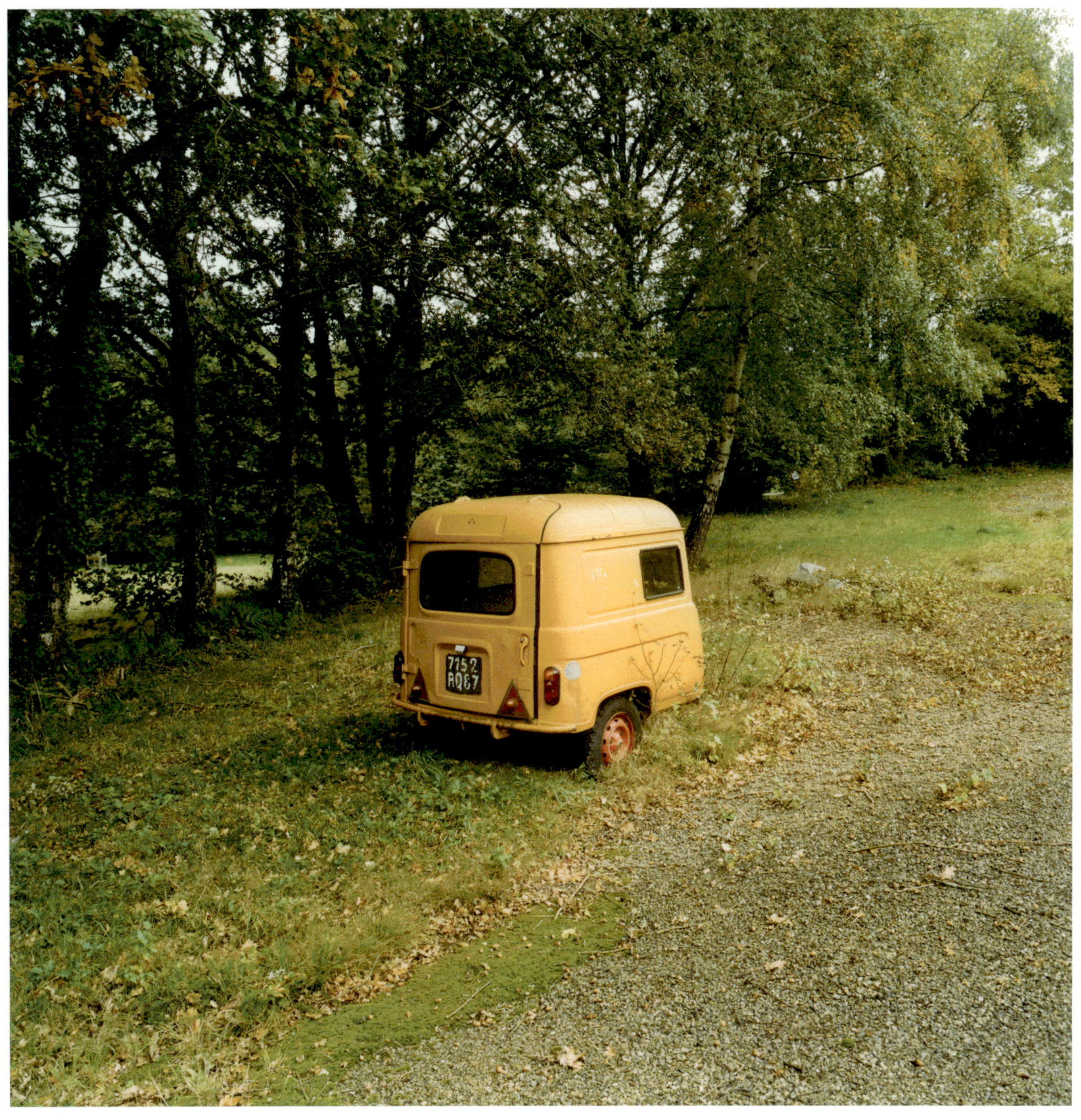

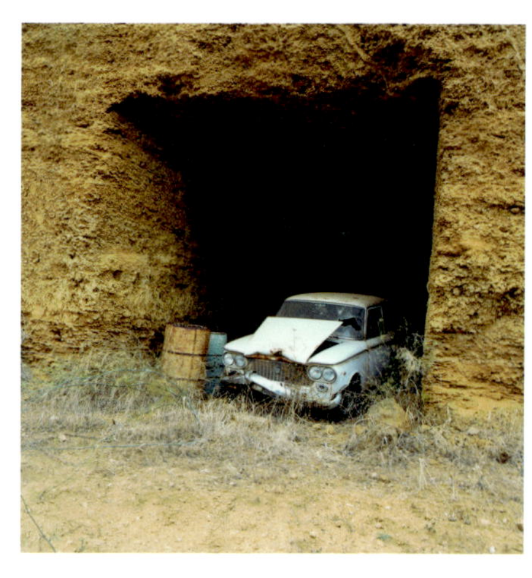

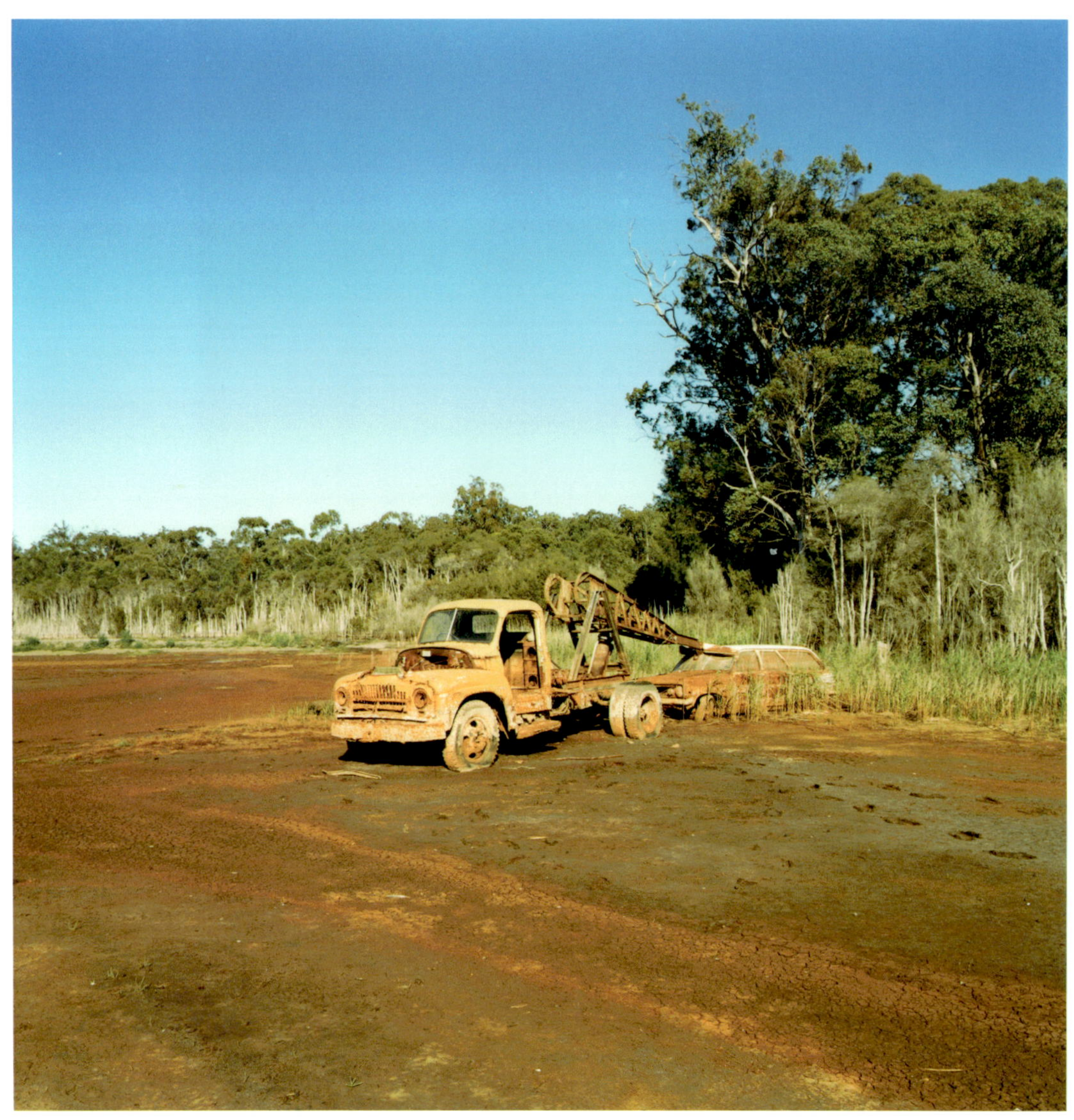

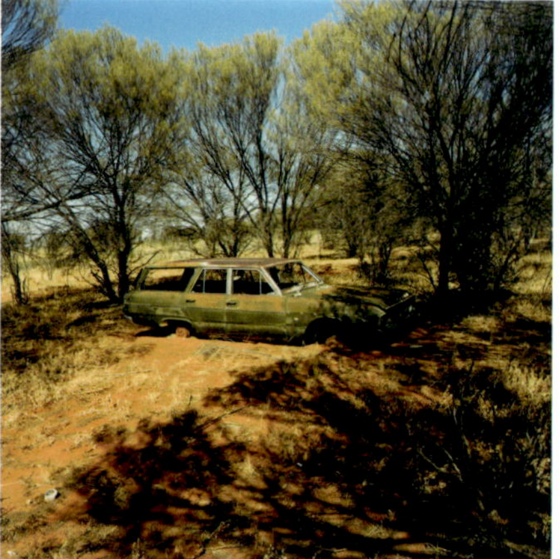

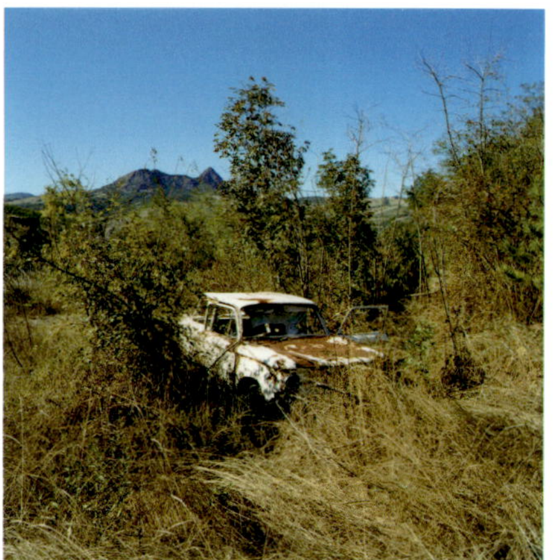

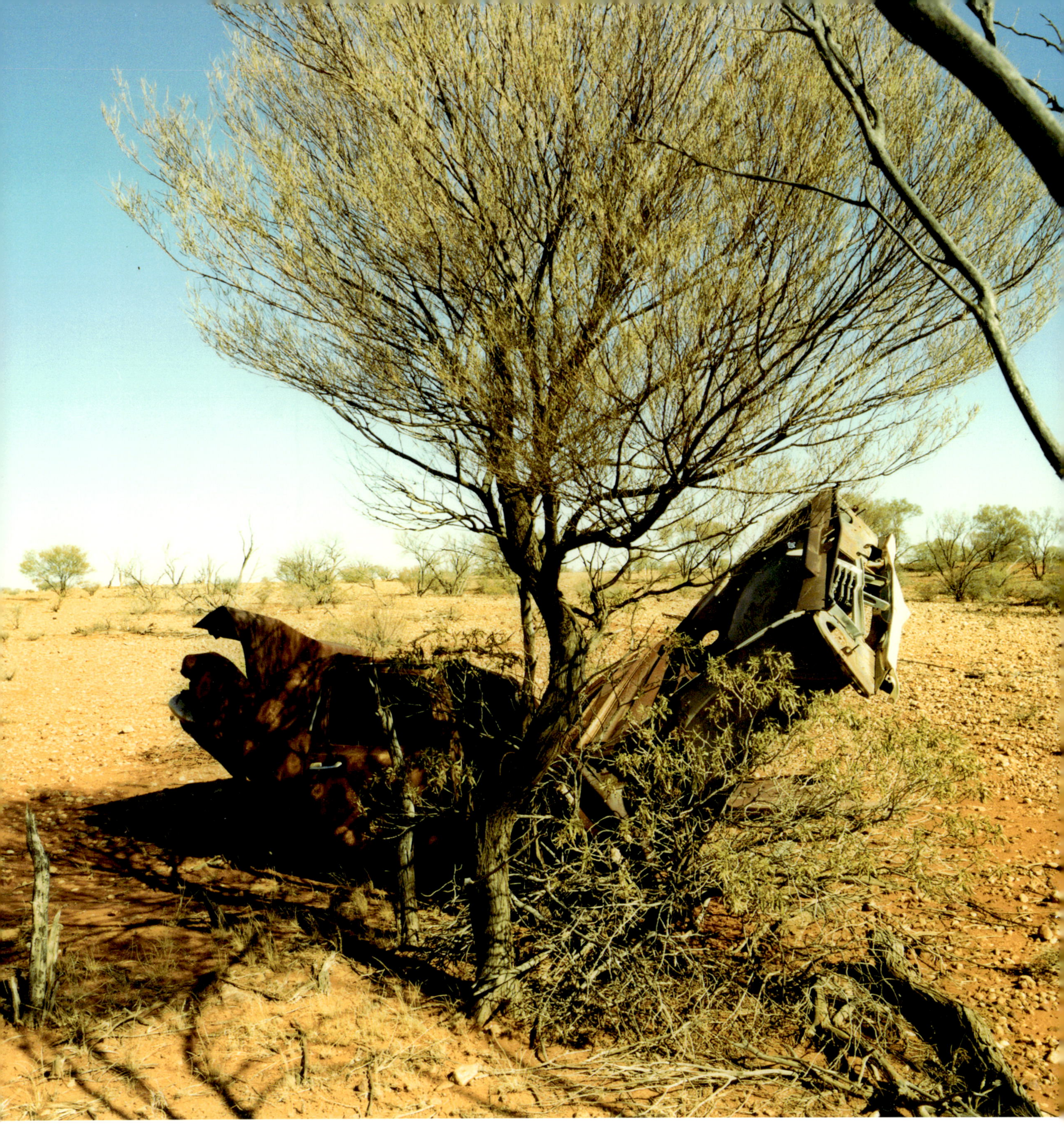

Opposite page, left Unknown car models, Nowa Nowa (Victoria, Australia) 2008. *Opposite, top* Fiat 1500, Selinunte (TP, Italy) 2007. *Opposite, center* Plymouth Valiant, Woomera Prohibited Area (Northern Territory, Australia) 2009. *Opposite, bottom* NSU Prinz, Perino (PC, Italy) 2007. *Here* Unrecognisable car, Coober Pedy (Northern Territory, Australia) 2009

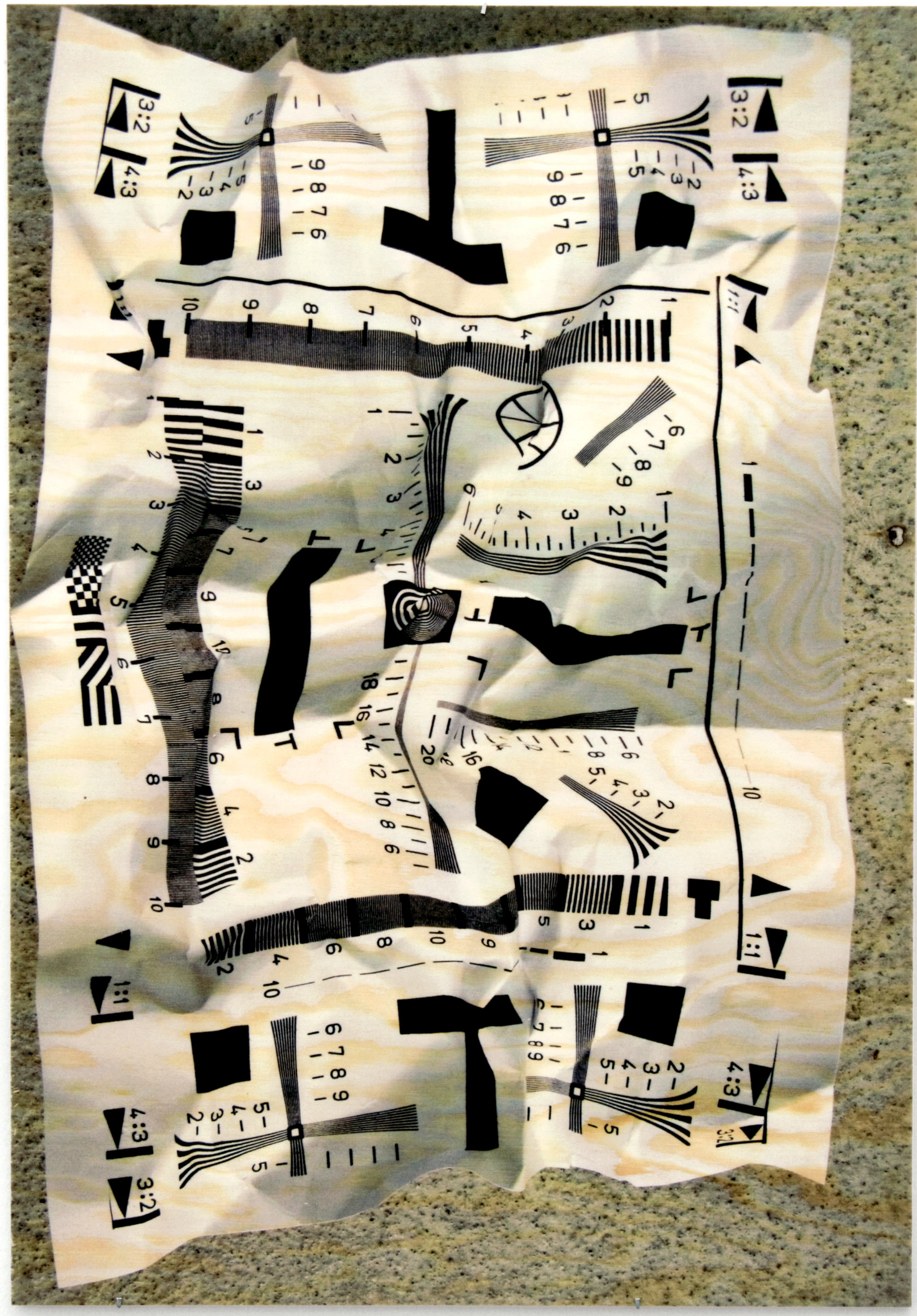

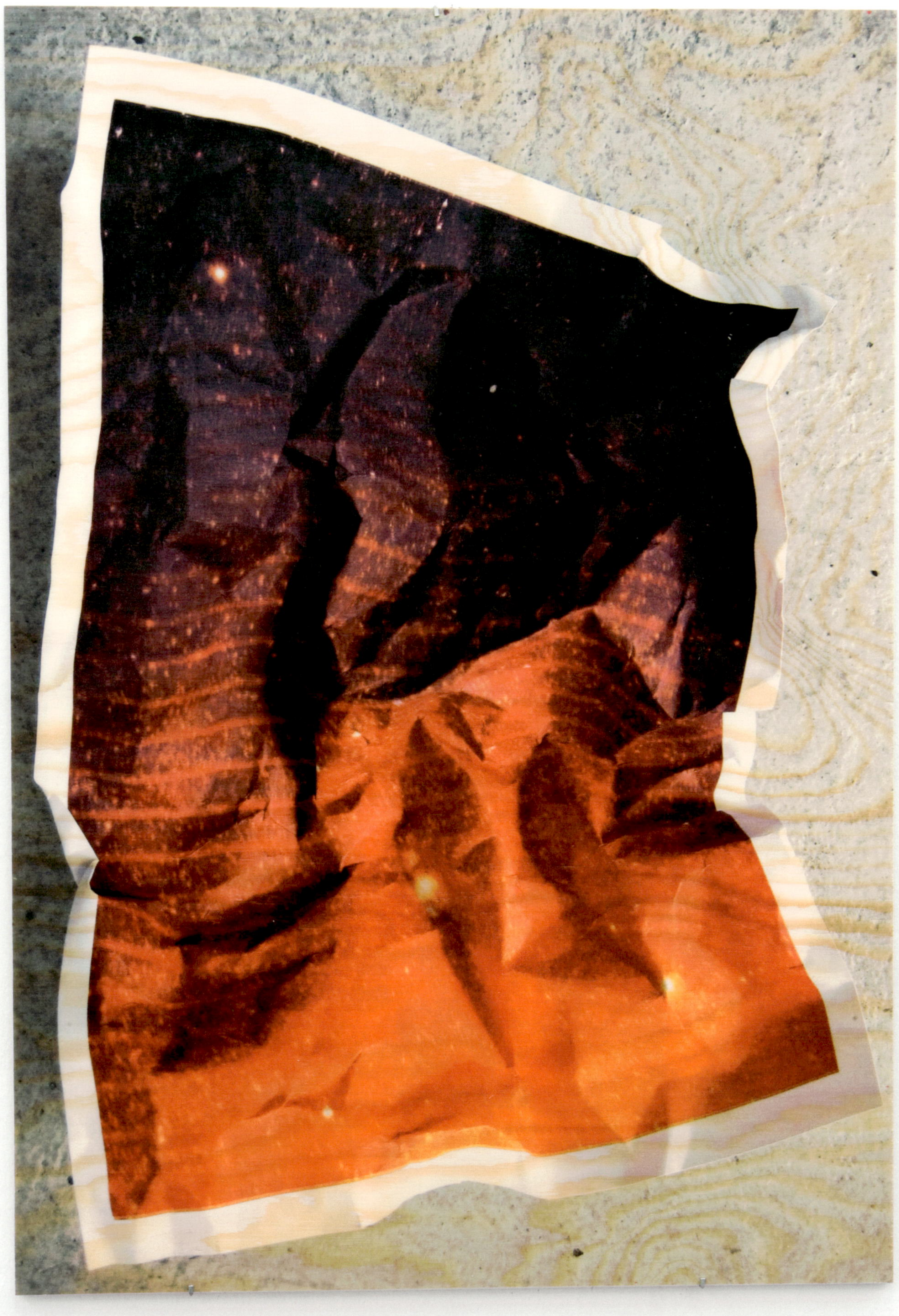

Beniamino Marini in conversation with
ERBOL MELDIBEKOV

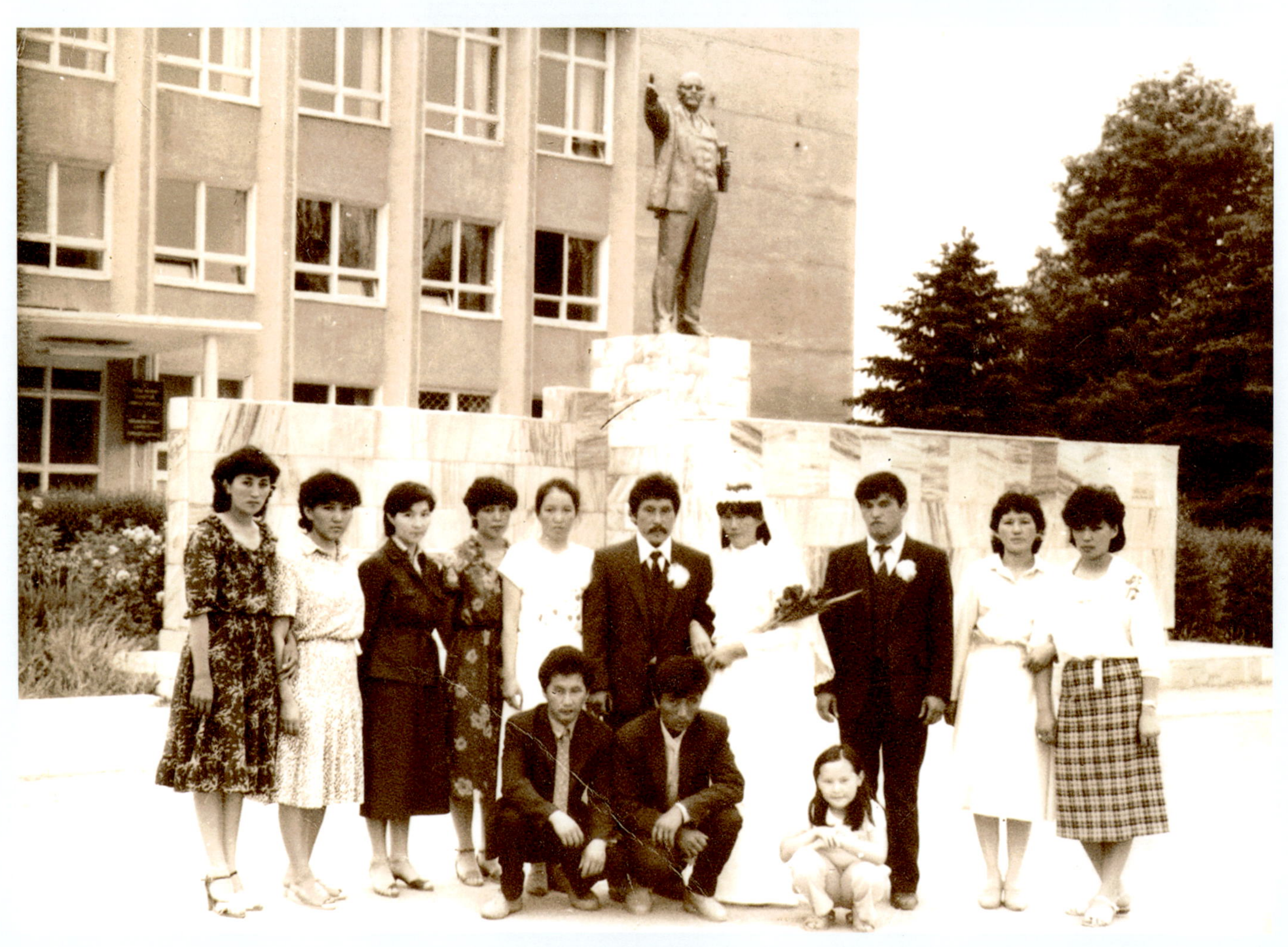

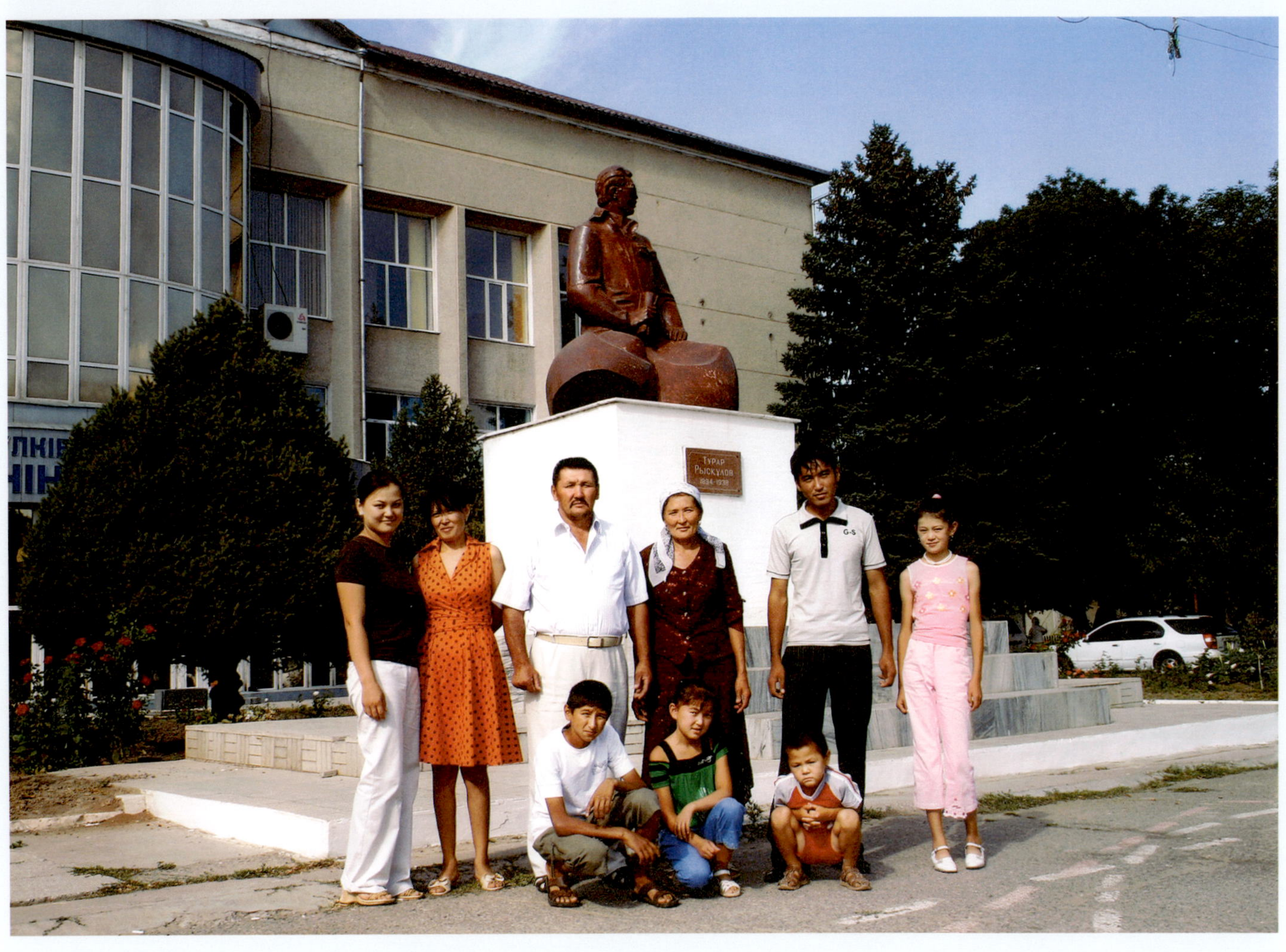

Talking with Erbol Meldibekov, sculptor, video and photo artist born in 1964 in Almaty, Kazakhstan, about his recent project *Family Album* - realized with his brother Nurbossyn Oris - is a pure wander through his imaginative take on the relationships between east and west, history and intimate life. Meldibekov studied at Almaty Theater and Fine Arts Institute and at Vermont Studio Center for visual arts. His works, including the well-known picture 'My Brother, My Enemy', symbolizing political turmoils between brother countries in the ex Soviet Empire, bring to the international art scene a new Central Asiatic perspective.

BENIAMINO MARINI *Some people say a photograph cannot lie, because - once it leaves the darkroom - it is fixed, immutable. Whereas oral tradition can change, be interpreted, can even turn into a lie. It seems that the* Family Album *project wants to demonstrate the opposite: photography only tells an instant of reality. Change, revolution are always possible. Putting together two different shots of the same people, in the same location many years later, you showed the effects of time on people and monuments, and prompted us to include geopolitics in our aesthetical observation. Did you want to denounce an untruth? Or just report a new state of things in your homeland?*

ERBOL MELDIBEKOV When I was a boy, my idea of God was connected to both Lenin and Communism. Everywhere from public offices to streets or buildings, the word-of-God was that of Communism. Therefore I thought of it as something eternal, compared to us mortal human beings. My brother Nurbossyn and I came to think of this *Family Album* project after we heard an absurd story about a public park in Tashkent, Uzbekistan. There, in a hundred years, 5 different monuments were changed after political turnovers: Russian general Kaufman (1913), monument to Revolution (1920), Stalin's statue (1940), a monument to Karl Marx (1969) and eventually an equestrian statue dedicated to Amir Timur, also known as Tamerlan. We can easily understand how even the Communist system itself was not that monolithic: everything depended upon

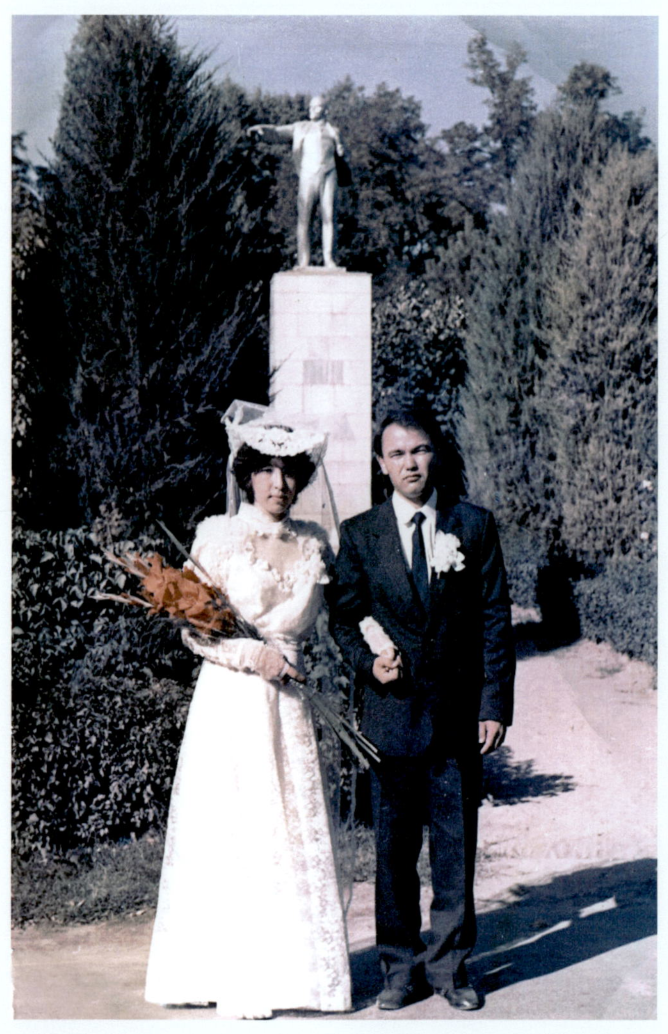

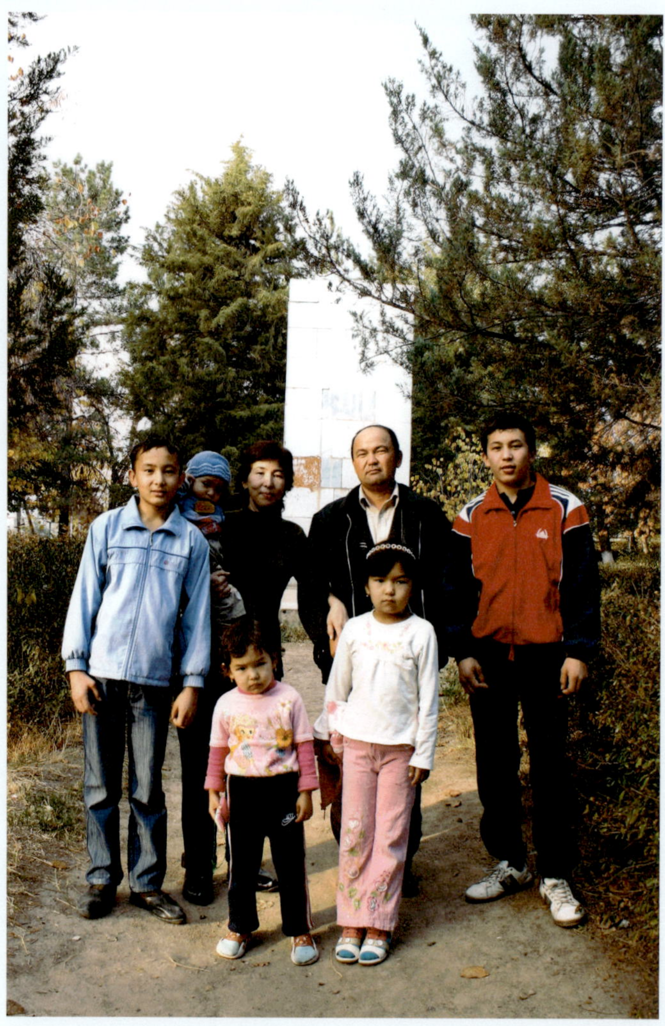

personal ambitions of each new dictator or party secretary. I think my mission as a Central Asian artist is that of researching amongst archive materials and demonstrating how present times are just a repetition of mechanisms from the past. As some critics underlined, all my works are connected to utopia. After 70 years of Communist utopia, a new utopia is being born in Central Asia (*or Pastan, as he ironically calls his area of provenance, ed.*). We used to be portrayed beside our monuments to get a souvenir and now they're all gone like an old vinyl record, even though they told us it was all going to be forever. So those monuments are not landscape anymore: their change becomes the subject to portray and human beings become the new landscape.

The subjects of these pictures are your relatives. A chance? Or also, as I think, is there a will of re-living an emotional past, adding some intimacy to a project that would otherwise be of simple chronicle?
Everything is family over here nowadays. In the past, Communist leaders were faithful to an idea and to an ideology.

Now leaders surround themselves with their relatives. Their families get all the power. By showing the artists' family, while embodying this issue, we want to show the change and tell a 'boring' artist's biography.

How come so many family portraits in front of monuments? Was it a common practice in your country at that time?
We used to live in an ideologized space. Every social activity used to happen around a leader's monument. It was typical to get your portrait done in front of those statues, especially because we had low quality cameras and professional photographers used to be found there. People could be proud of their 'monument portraits'.

Where are those places? Is there any particular monument or building that you would like to mention?
Most of them are in the south of Kazakhstan. There is a particular place where Kalinin and Stalin gave place to Gengis Khan's right arm. Another one in which Lenin was

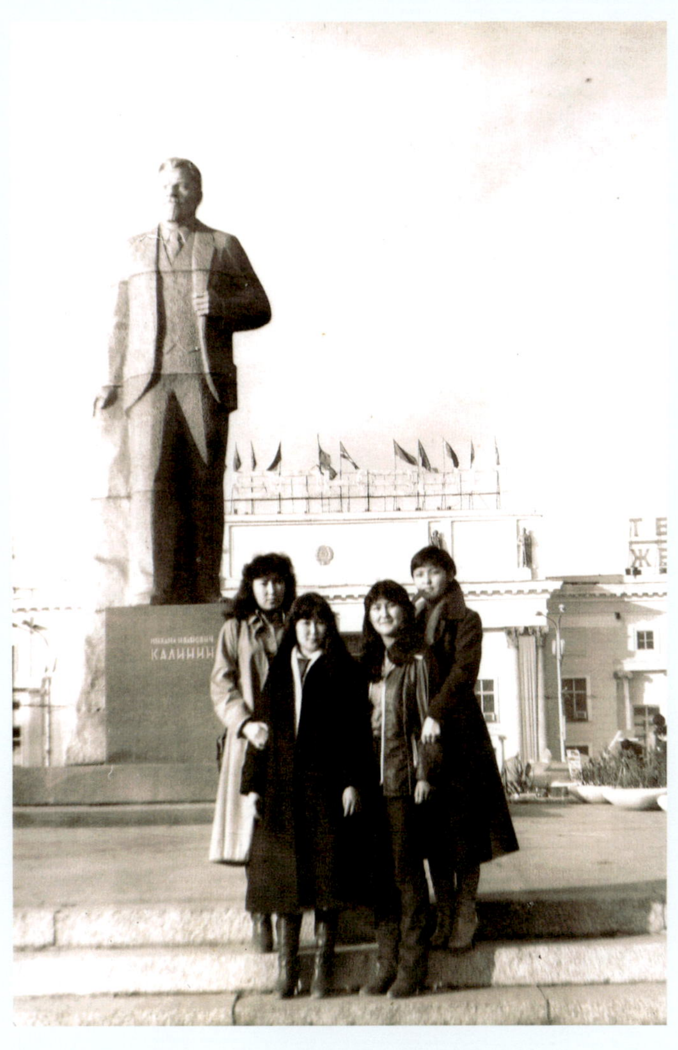

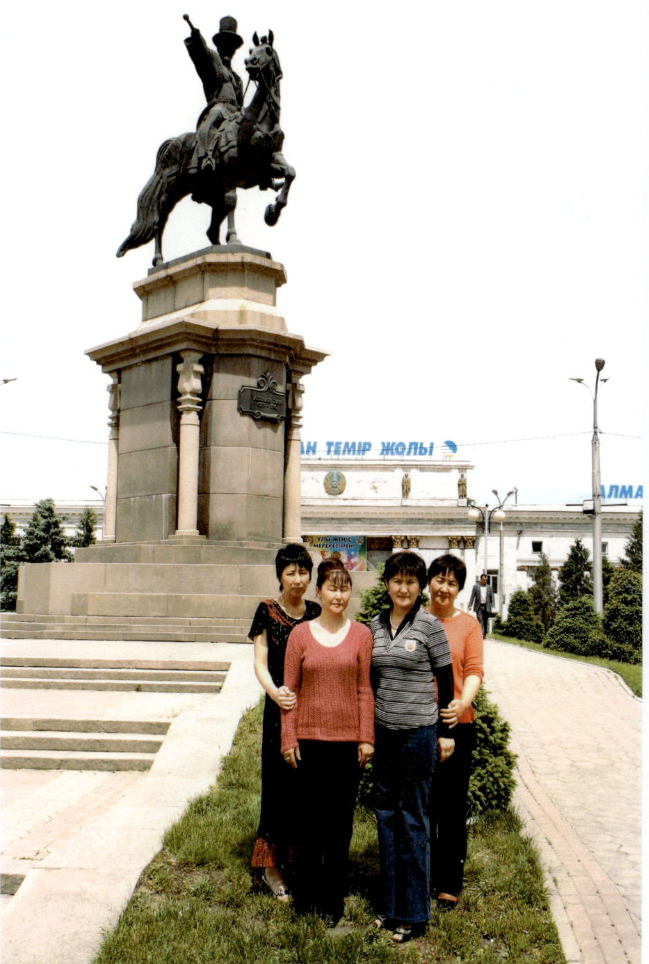

replaced by one of 'our' Communists, Riskulov, who worked with Lenin in Moscow. I am always interested in learning how much the choice of a new hero is so emblematic.

What was your relatives' reaction to your proposal of going along this photo album path again?
At the beginning, they didn't understand what we meant to do. Then they joined with pleasure in our project because basically we still love to get our portraits done in front of those monuments, whatever they represent.

What is their and your reaction to such a radical change in places, buildings, monuments, etc.? And what is your audience's reaction?
I think we live in a very strange moment. I want to answer by telling you about a new project I am working on. In Central Asia there are some towns (like Abai or Kentau) established in the 1930s that are going to be destroyed. It's called *A city, a life, a dream*; about cities that last only for one generation. It is a trauma for those who were born when those cities were built. I am collecting materials about all this. You know, most people would like to preserve their past. They get rid of Lenin and Stalin but then they look for people that look like them. There was a system of power in Eurasia at the times of Gengis Khan and it's still the same today.

It is common opinion that anonymous photography (not only that) has a fatal destiny: that of disappearing into oblivion. A risk that unfortunately is also borne by photographic prints that were intended for publication or for the art market, a chemical/physical hazard. Adding the magic of making photography, some people talk about a ghostly nature of photographical product (and the very name of this magazine, Fantom, *apparently reminds us of it). Retrieving your family album, a typical form of anonymous photography, you surely made its life much longer. What do you think about it?*
Well, yes! I think we have actualized old archive photos and we told an old and boring story. But we turned it into a myth.

Images © E. Meldibekov and Nurbossyn Oris, courtesy Galleria Nina Lumer, Milan

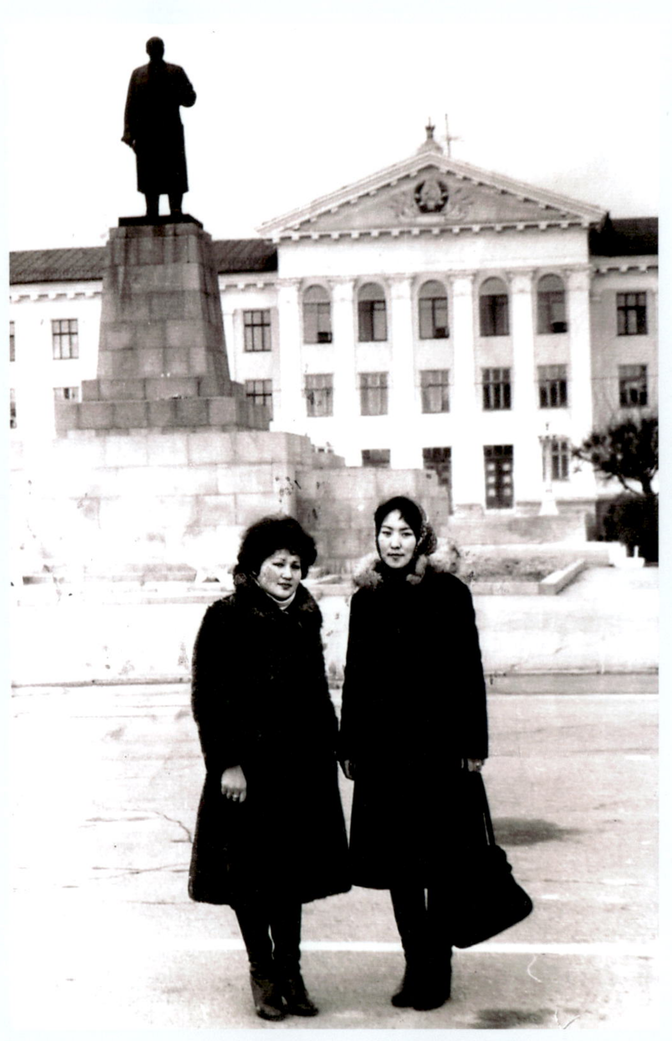

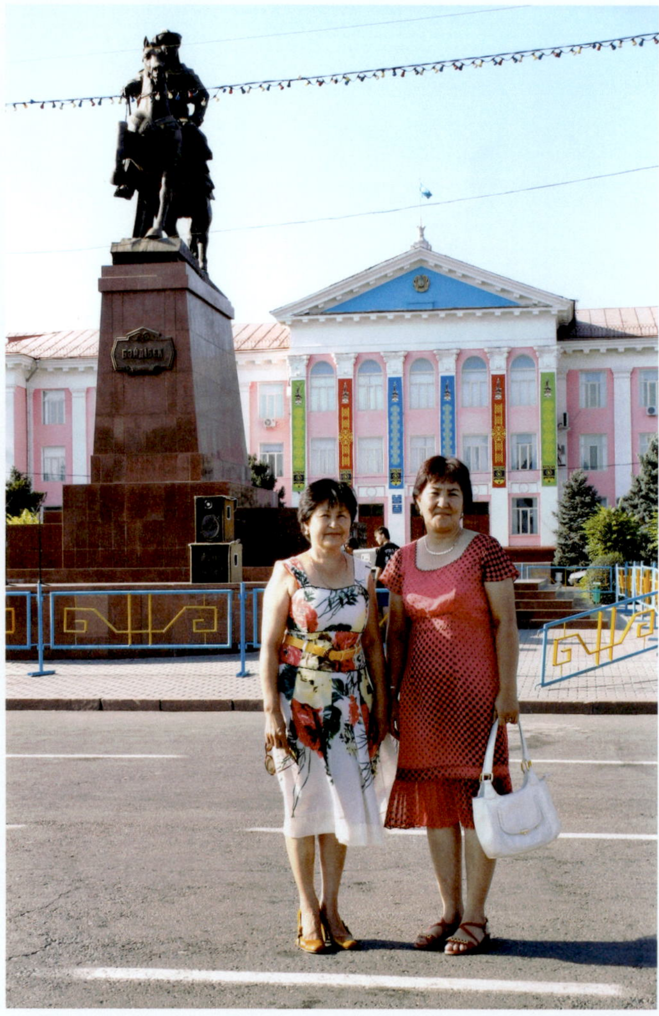

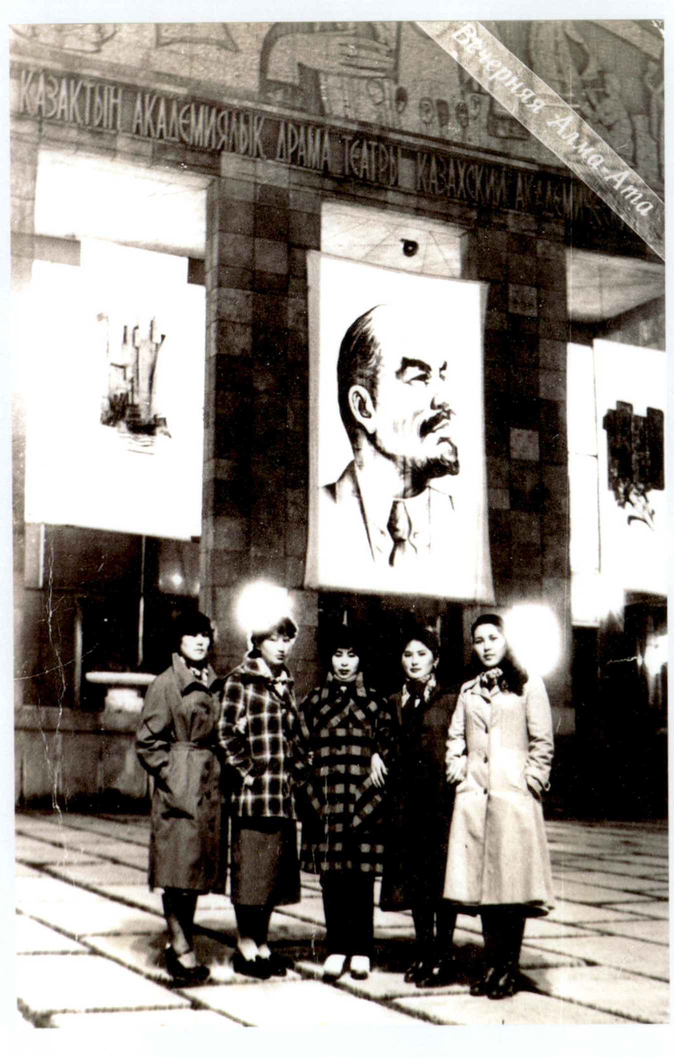
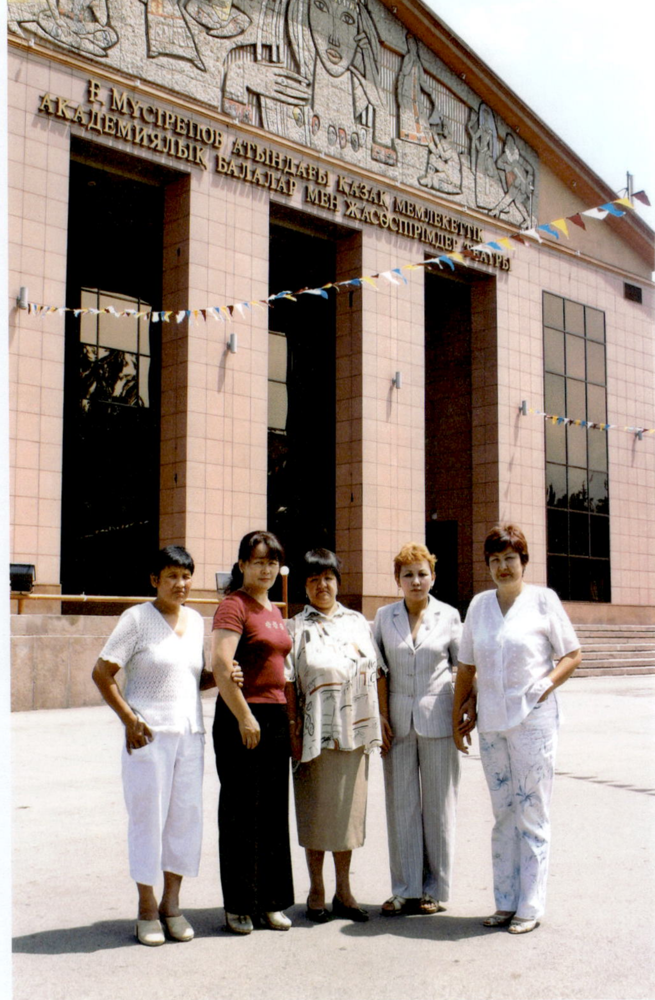

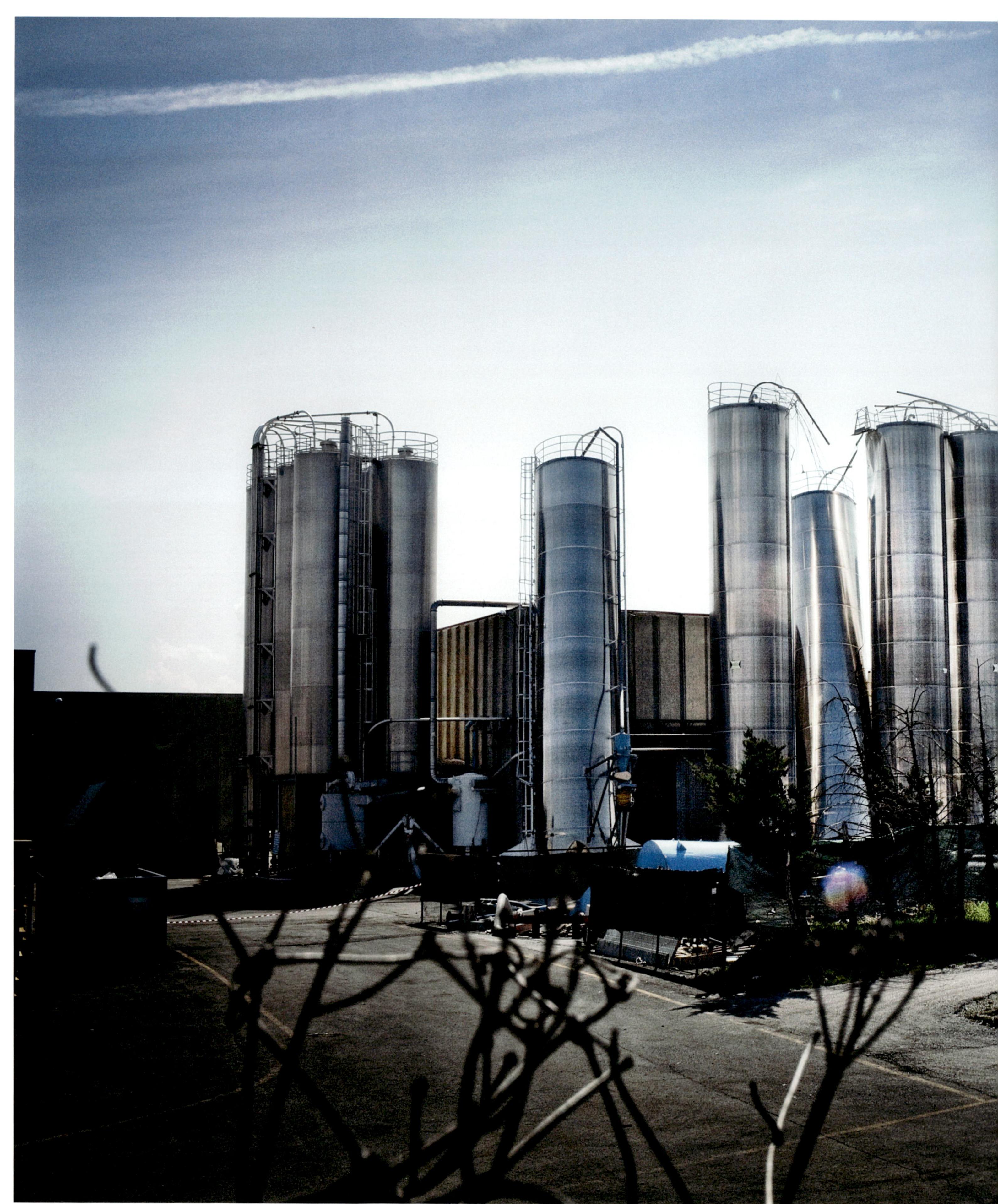

A factory near the village of Fossa

GUIDO GAZZILLI 6 APRILE 2009

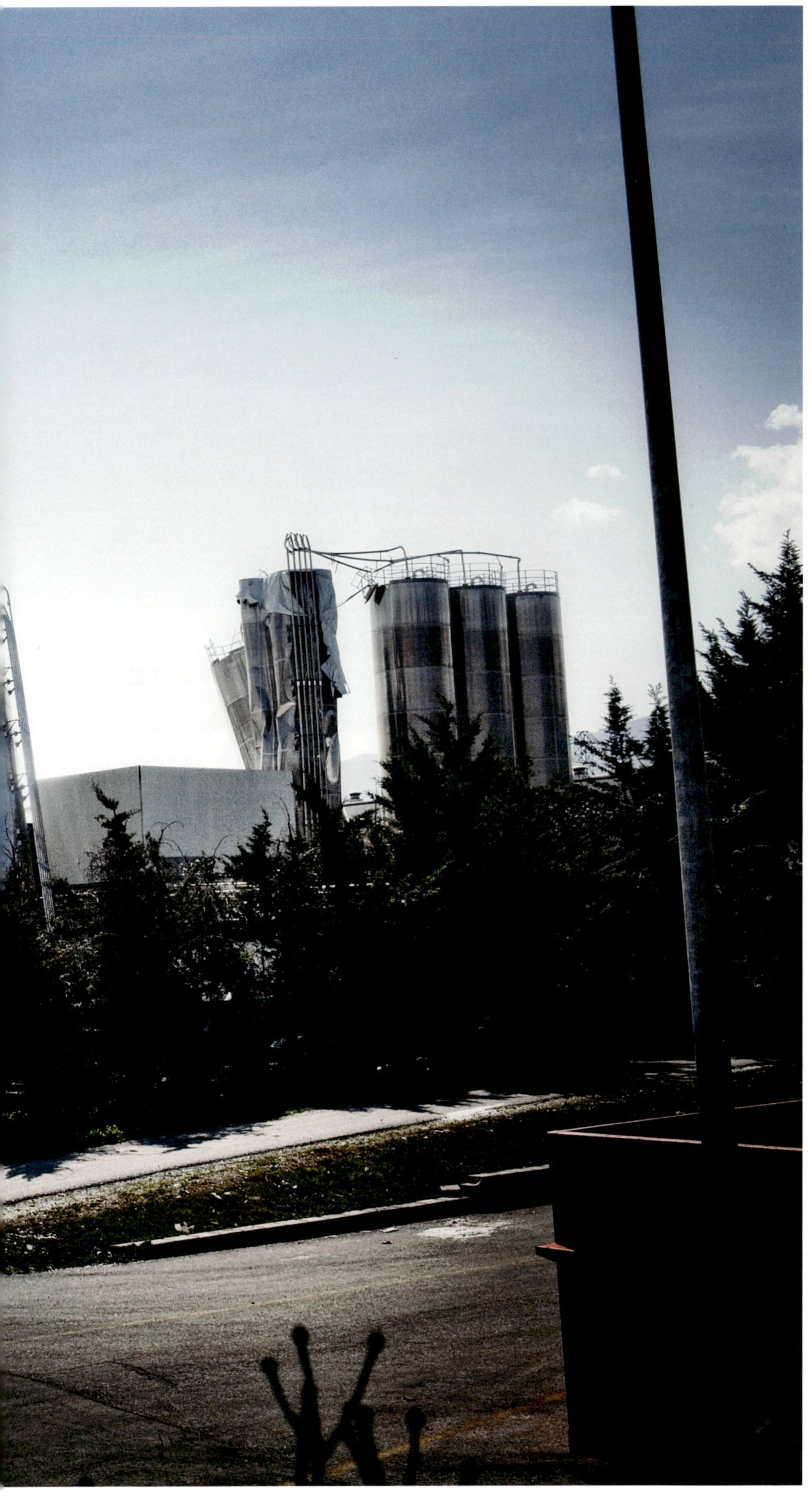

The earthquake of L'Aquila, in the Italian region of Abruzzo, was rated 5.8 on the Richter scale. After the earth swallowed entire towns and destroyed lives and cities, photographer Guido Gazzilli traveled to that scarred land and documented the aftermath of one of those occasions when death maps its existence on physical space.

The resulting photographs, presented here, with their complete exclusion of the human agent, achieve the rare effect of stimulating the formal nature of viewing while hitting you in the gut, of catering to your eyeballs with their luscious beauty while making you think.

The total absence of human presence in the frame somehow enhances the humanity of the tragedy they depict, invoking loss without showing its banality, grief without the voyeurism of grief.

The barren, destroyed landscapes remind me of the humans that should be - and were - living in those precise spots, and their disappearance, all the more powerful, speaks volumes about their despair, awe and helplessness. It could not be told more effectively. They make me 'feel' 'indignant' and 'angry' and 'powerless'.

The earthquake of L'Aquila hit Italy, that country of rolling hills and ragged mountains, those 300,000 square kilometers on a faultline, on the 6th of April 2009. It killed three-hundred and seven people, injured more than a thousand, and left sixty-five thousand people without a home. *(Tim Small)*

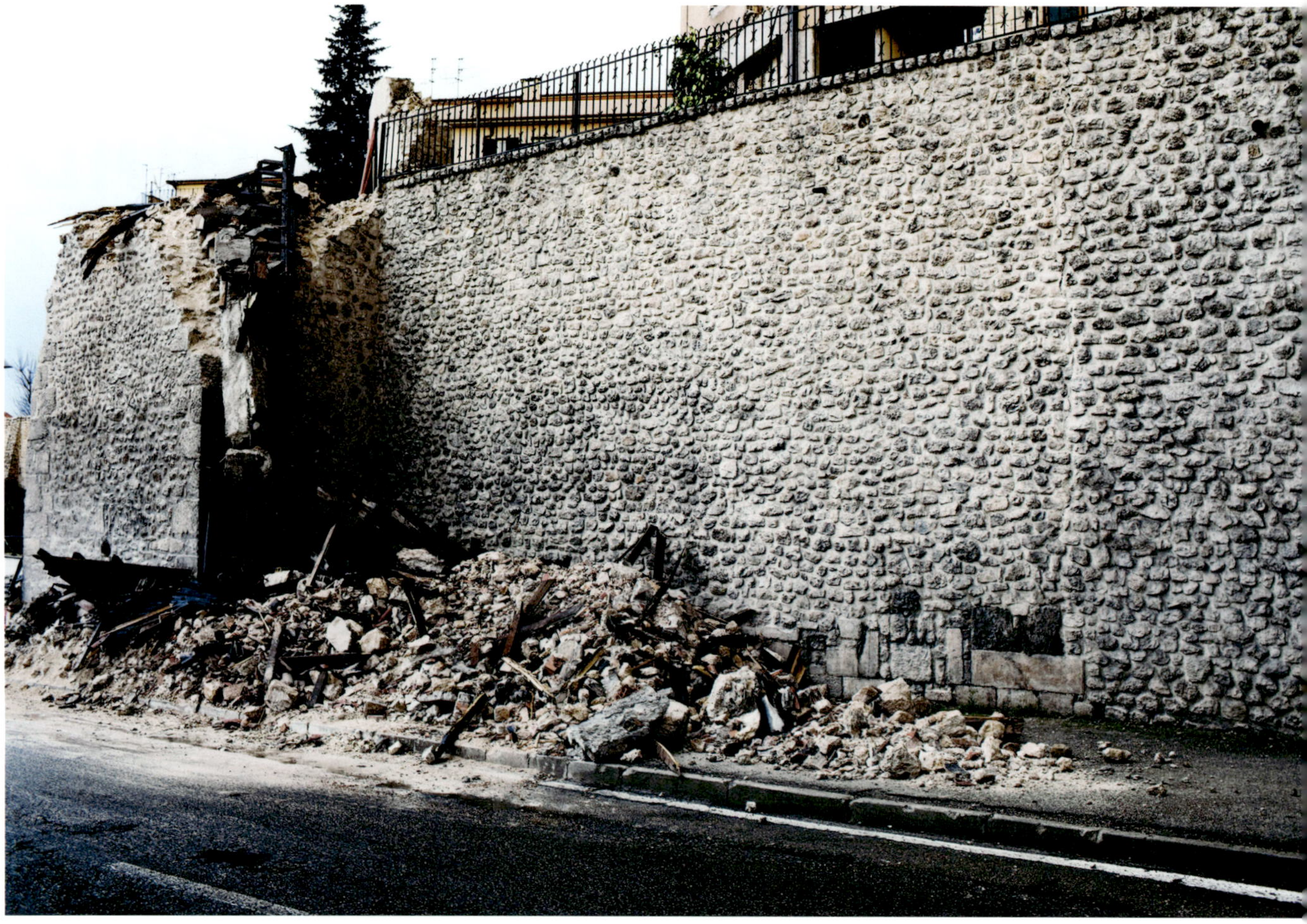

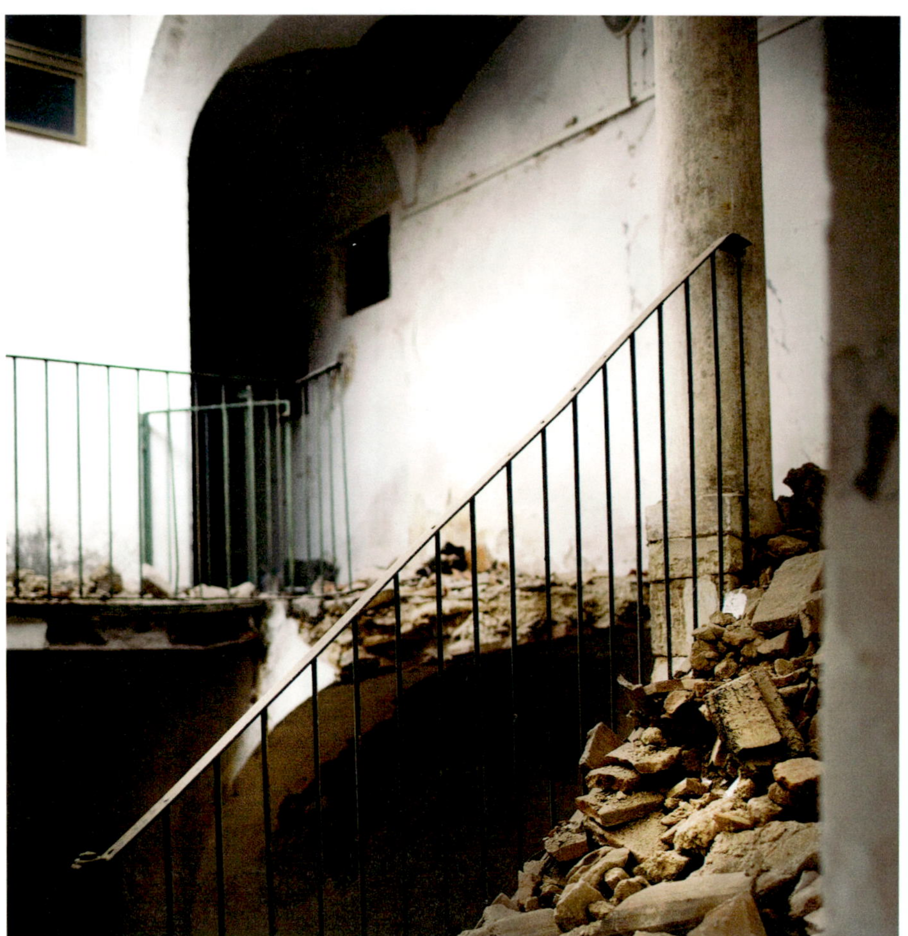

L'Aquila

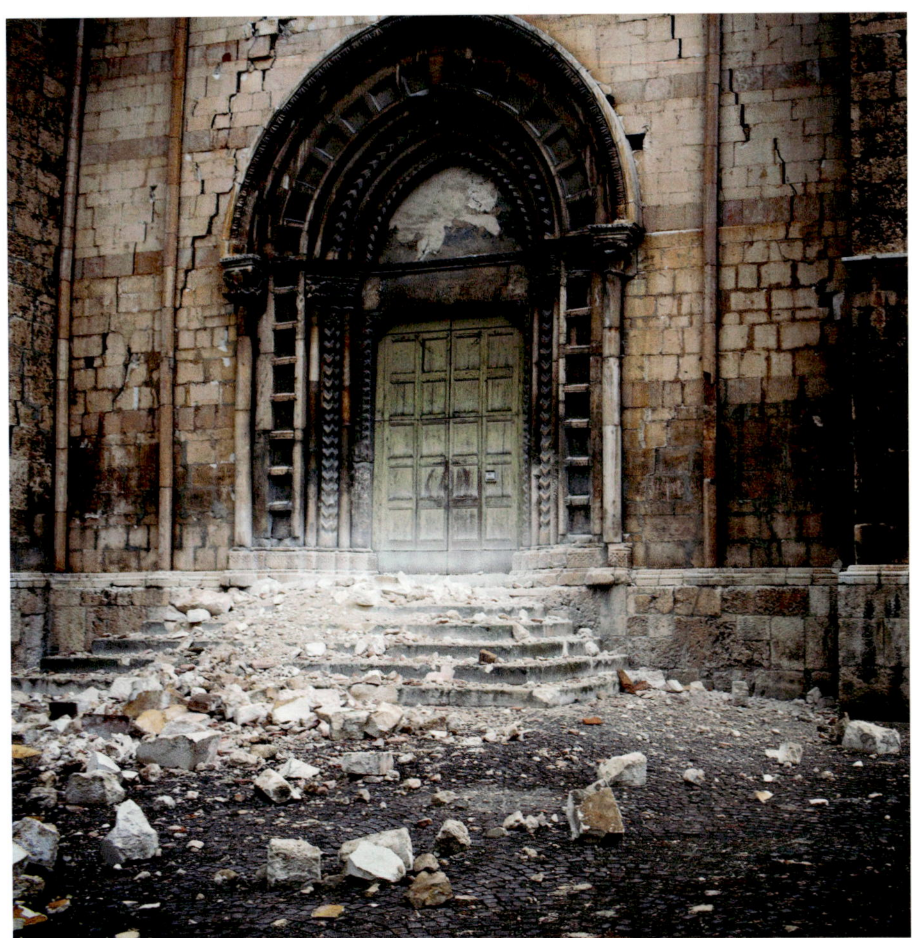

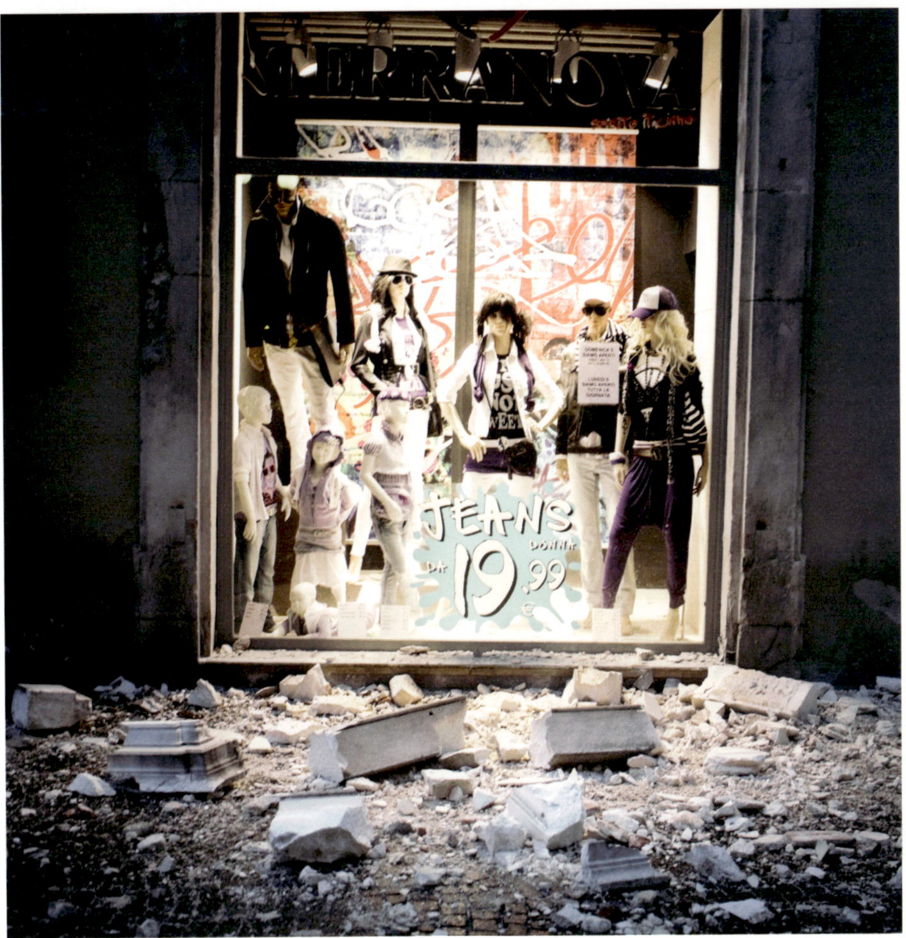
TERRANOVA
JEANS
19,99

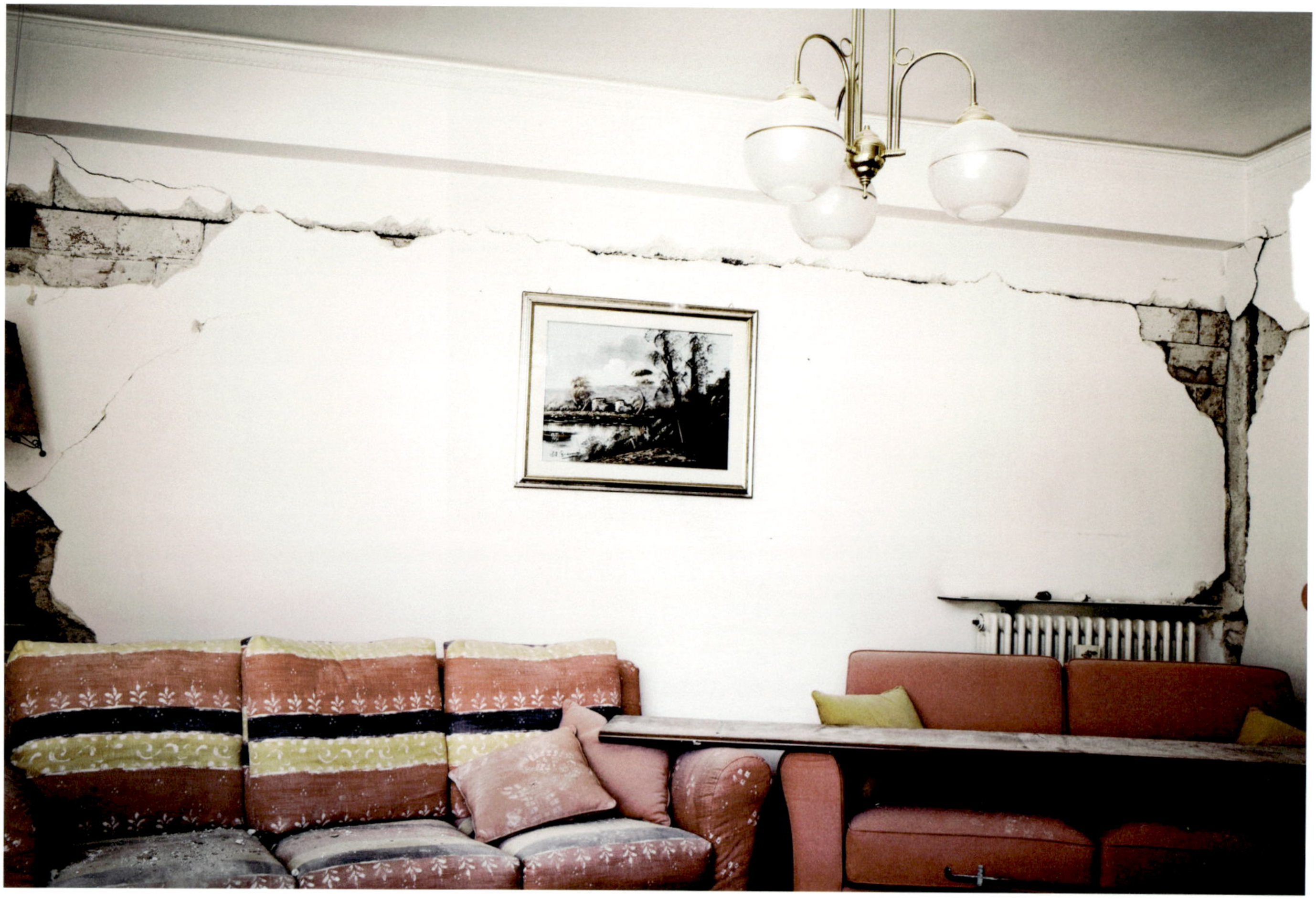

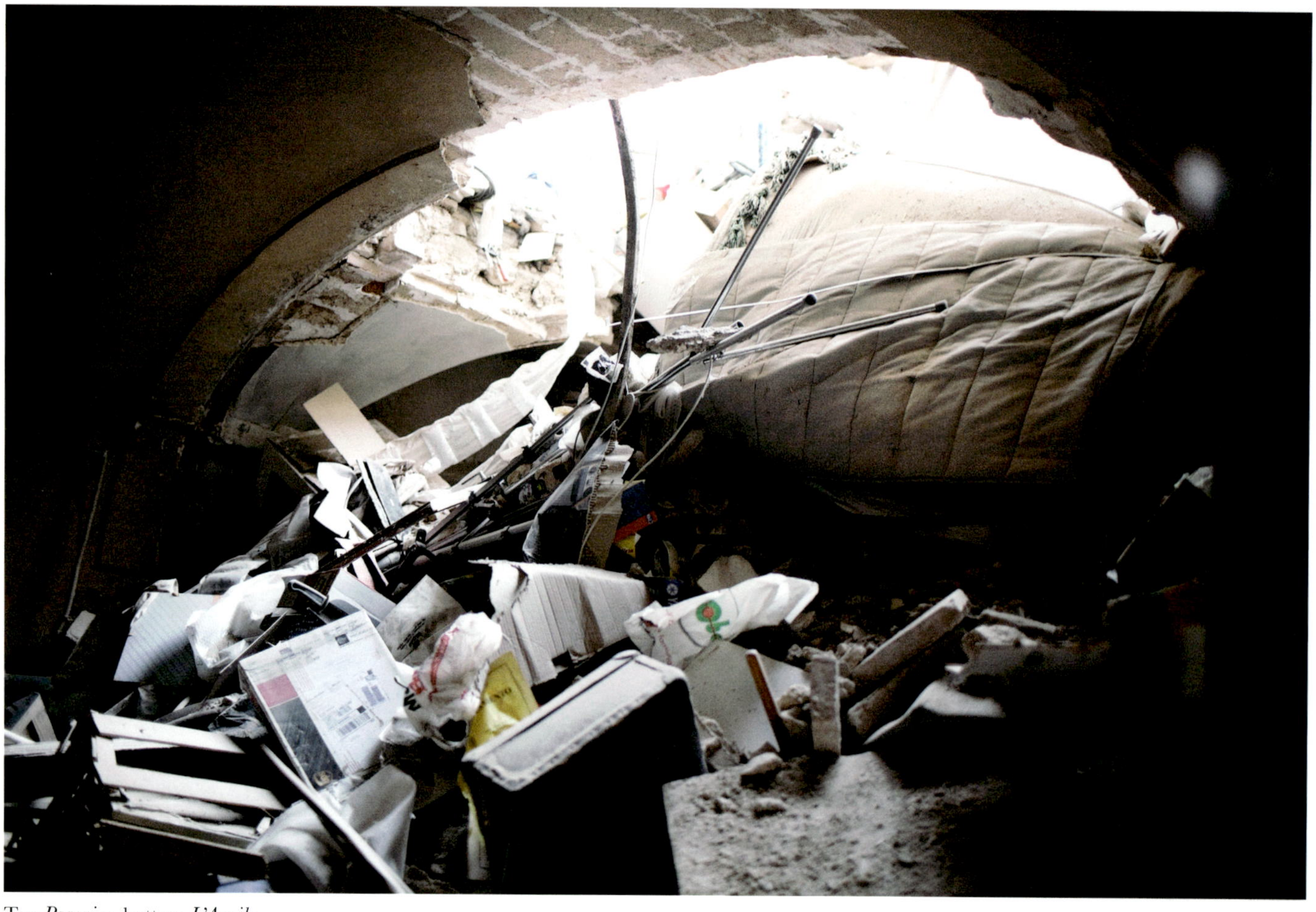

Top *Paganica*, bottom *L'Aquila*

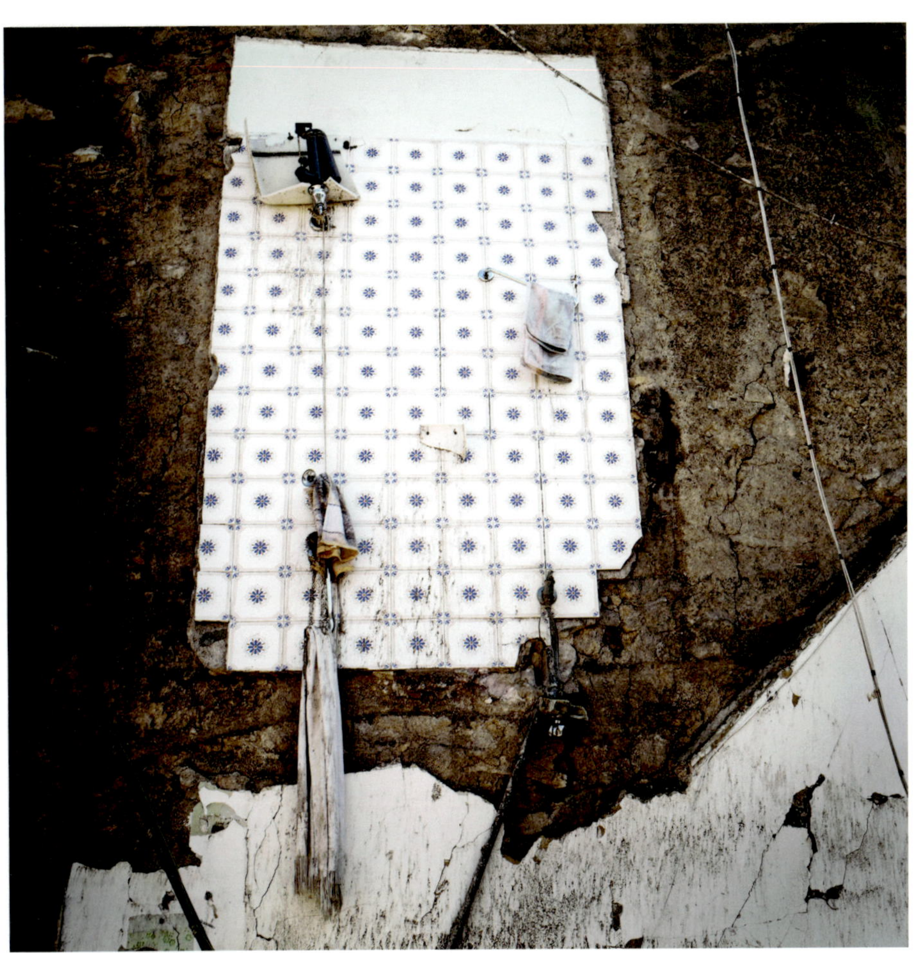

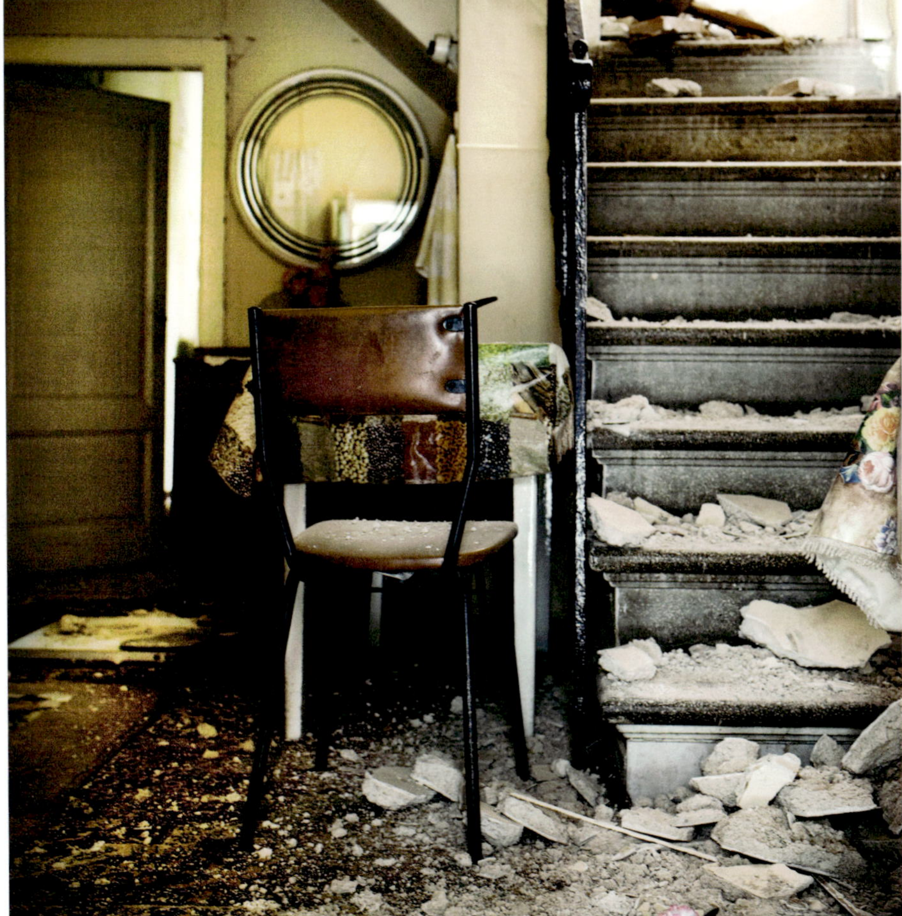

Onna

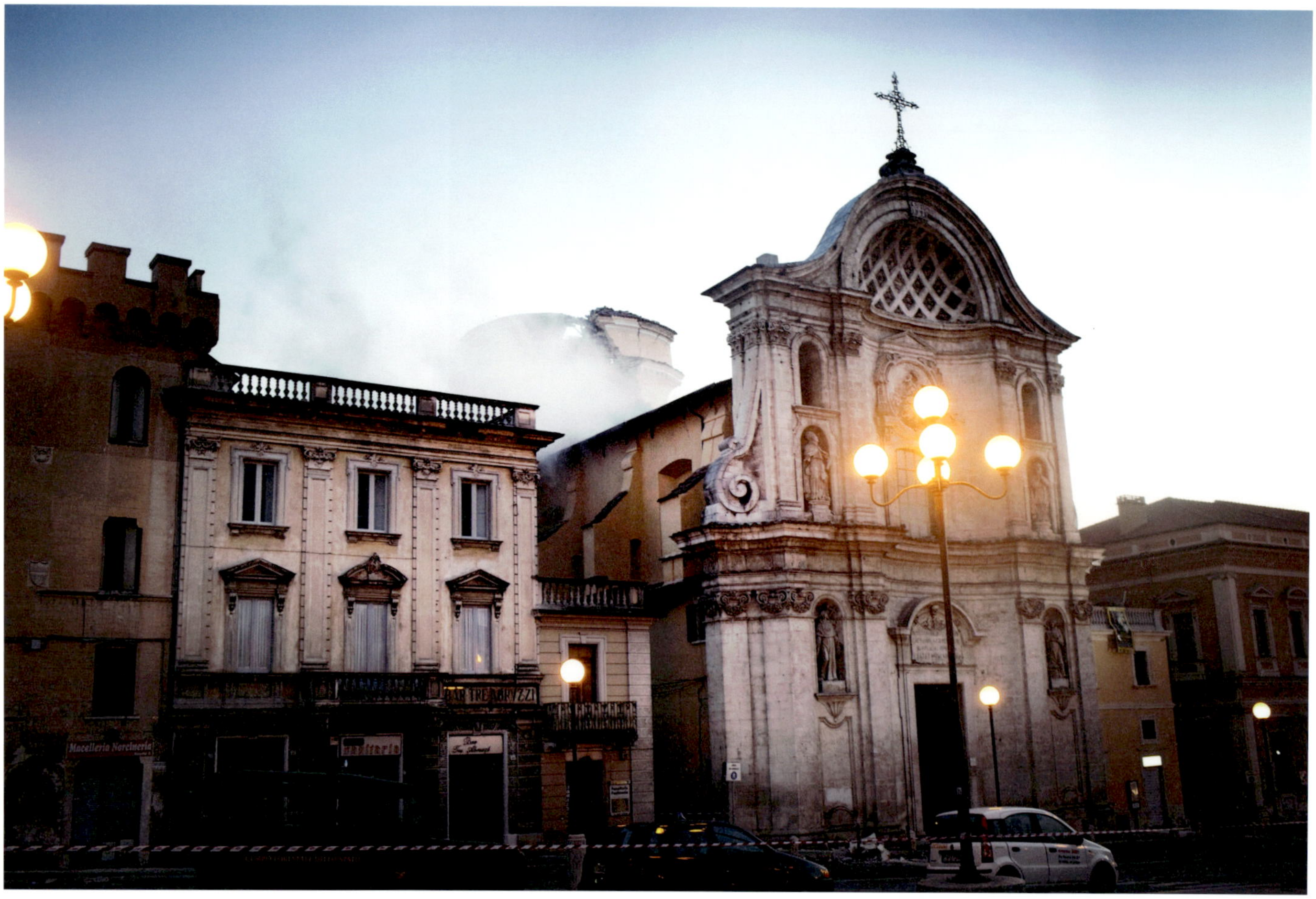

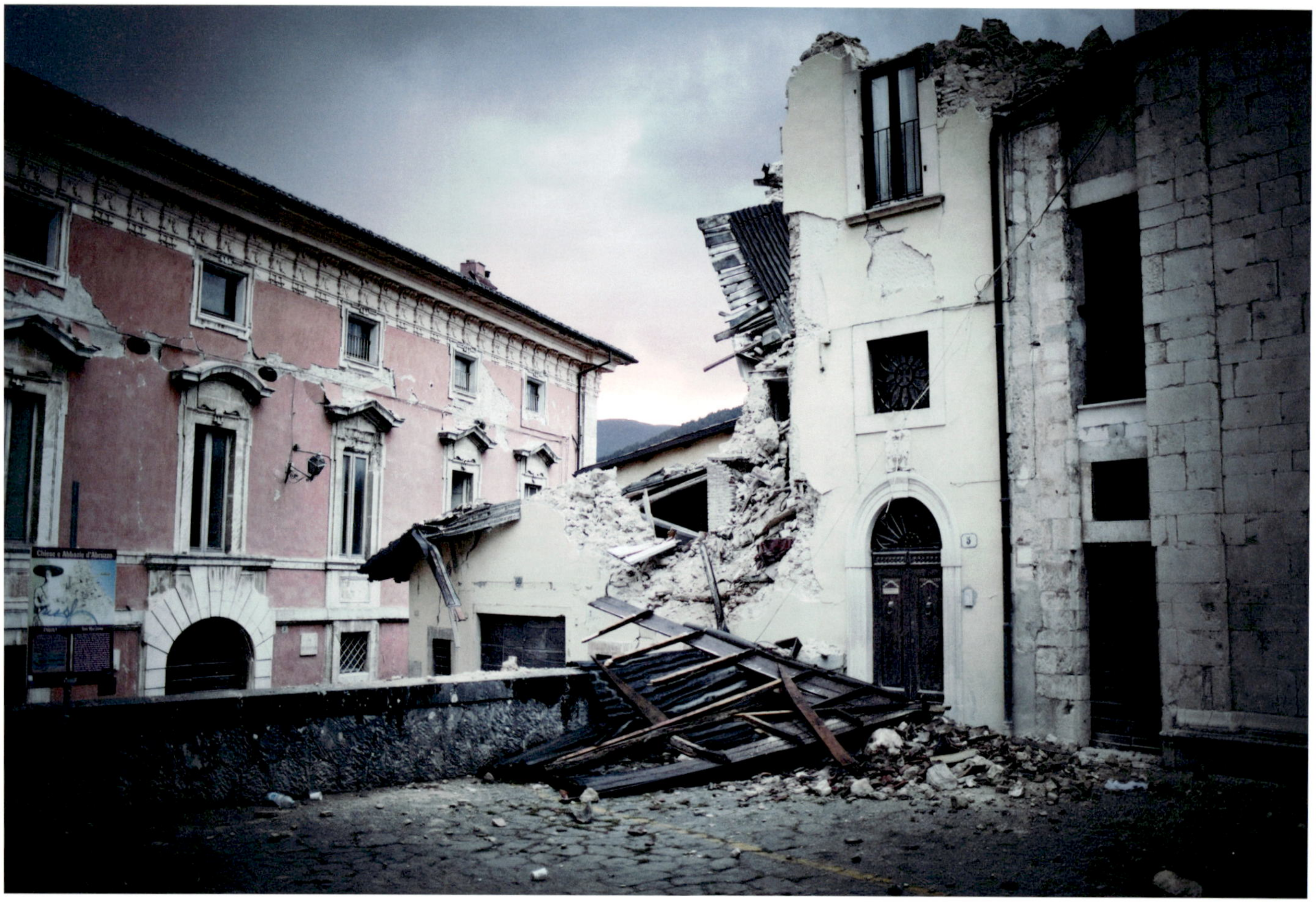

L'Aquila

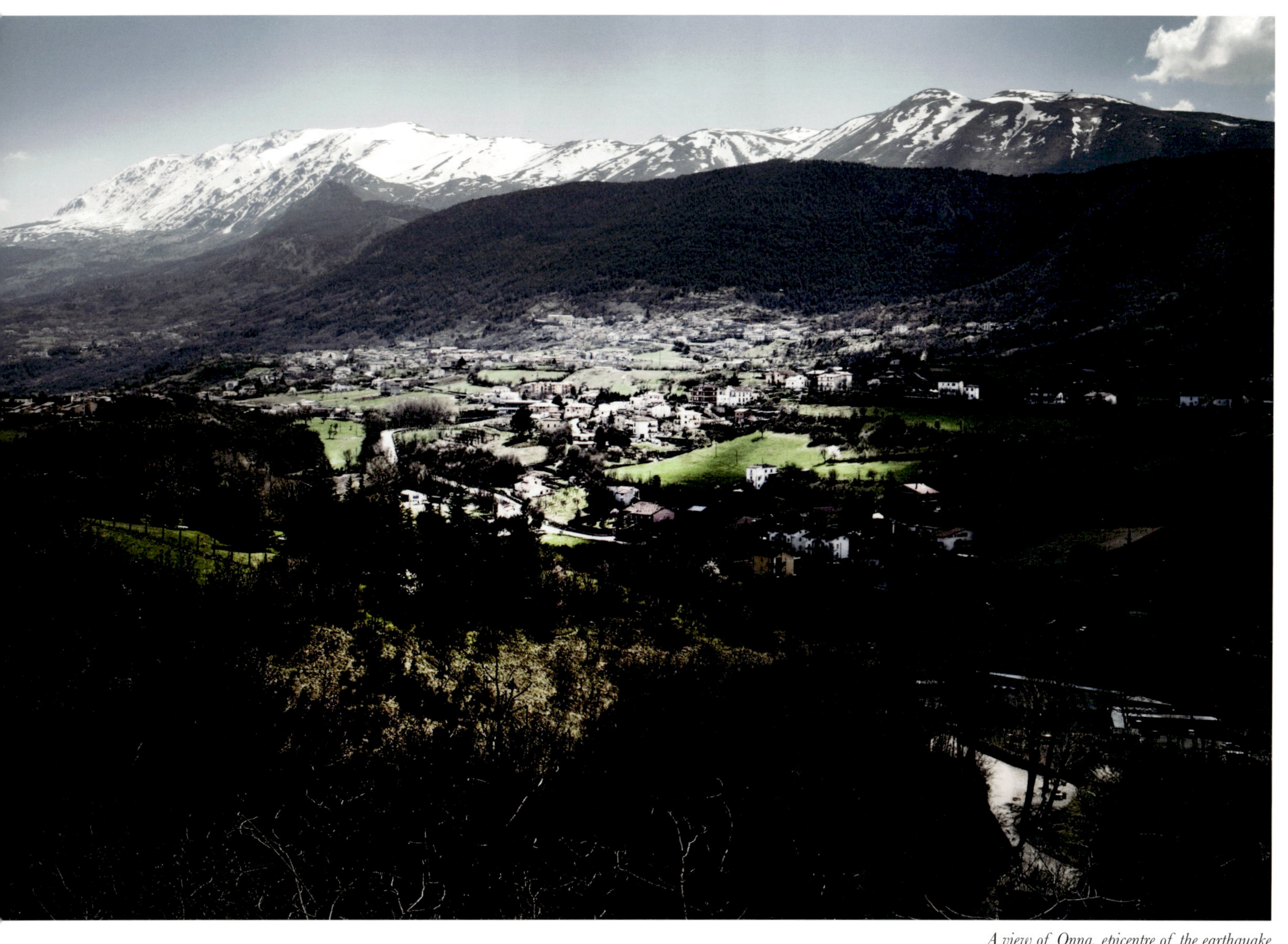

A view of Onna, epicentre of the earthquake

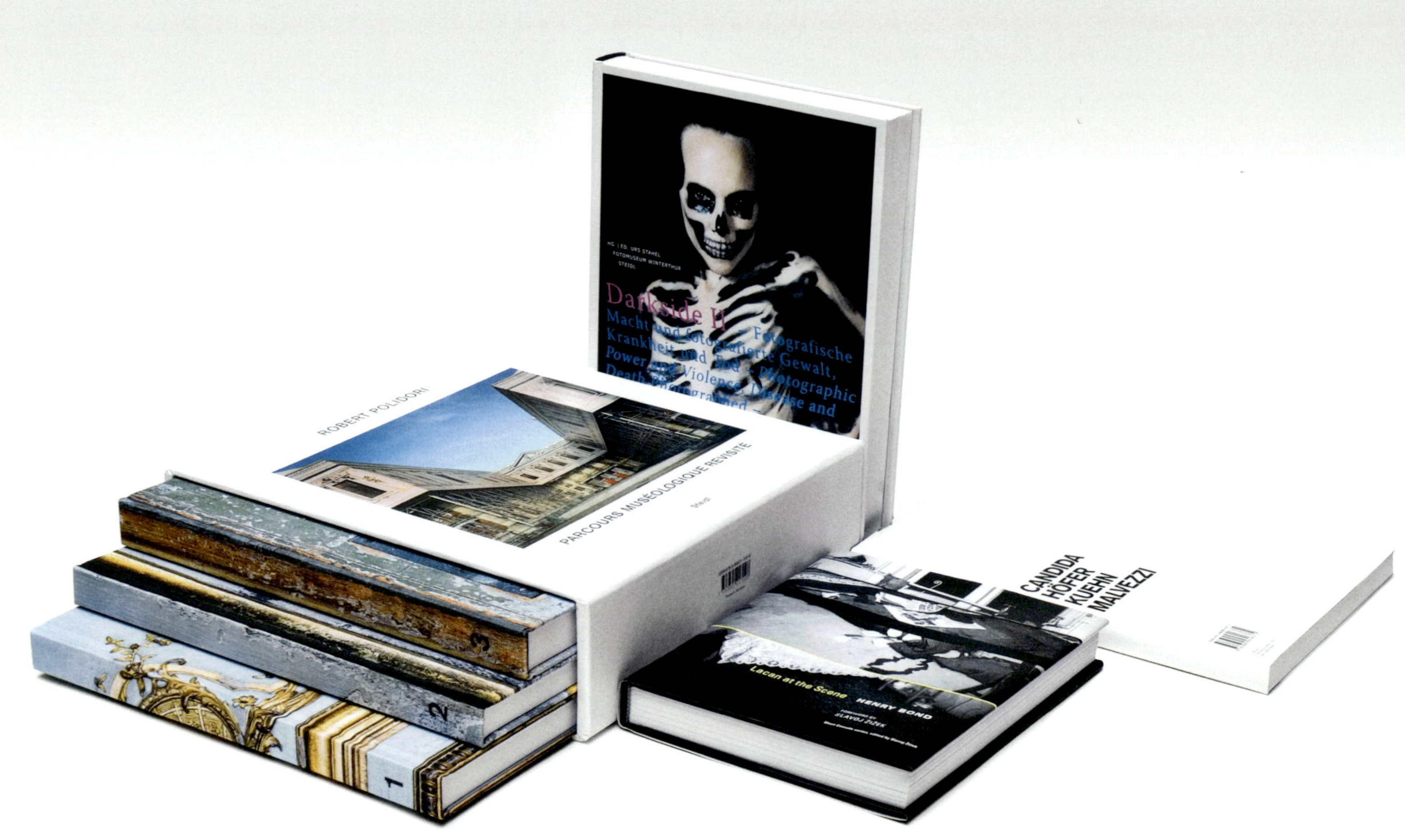

ON OUR SHELVES

From left, clockwise Robert Polidori, *Parcours Muséologique Revisité*, 3 volumes, 744 pages, Steidl (October 2009); *Darkside II - Photographic Power and Violence, Disease and Death Photographed*, edited by Urs Stahel, 368 pages, Steidl (September 2009) *steidleville.com* Candida Höfer, *Kuehn Malvezzi*, text by Chris Dercon, Okwui Enwezor and Axel Sowa, 240 pages, Walther König (May 2009) *buchhandlung-walther-koenig.de* Henry Bond, *Lacan at the Scene*, foreword by Slavoj Žižek, 256 pages, MIT Press (October 2009) *mitpress.mit.edu* (Still life Sean Michael Beolchini)

RICCARDO PREVIDI is the protagonist - with a selection from his 2009 *Test* series - of this issue's *Pop-up* pages. "I found these images typing "print test" in the "search images" of Google, Yahoo and Bing. I am always intrigued by the perfunctory results of this search mode, by the way outcomes are organized, the surprises generated by "intruders". No matter how sofisticated they are, these engines are still at an embryonic stage. I have chosen the images with a certain lightness, the formal aspect being definitively one of the criteria, the other being maintaining a degree of randomness. I have printed them with an A4 printer on sheets that I have crumpled and photographed. The photographs have been then reproduced with an ink jet plotter on deal boards. They question the role of technology (as a medium), its mechanisms, the way they work, the way they get stuck. I am interested in their incompleteness, in the fact that they contain both positive and negative results: print tests are carried out to align printheads, to avoid possible errors, and we crumple up a sheet when we think what is printed on them is wrong. I am interested in the loop generated by the process: connect, research, download, print, modify, photograph, reprint. Marshall McLuan said "the medium is the message"; I began from there, but in my case it is the jammed mechanisms to grab my attention". Riccardo Previdi was born in Milan in 1974. He lives and works in Berlin. *All images courtesy of the artist and Galleria Francesca Minini, Milano - francescaminini.it*

PORZIA BERGAMASCO is an independent journalist, researcher and consultant specializing in design and architecture. An active talent scout and a member of the "Exhibition" committee of ADI-Design Index (Association for Industrial Design), in 2009 she curated for Palermo Design Week the exhibition *Stories of Design: from Idea to Realization*. She lives and works in Milan.

SPARTACUS CHETWYND is an artist living and working in London. Her work mixes avant-garde practices; appropriation and misappropriation of art history and pop culture; anarco-symbolist performances; free associations of sculpture, painting, photography; anything at hand or mind, from Jackson to Giotto. Fashioning a pataphysical, revealing universe that merges rituals and (limping) ceremonies.

ALEX GARTENFELD is an art critic and the Online Editor for *Interview* and *Art in America*. He co-founded an independent gallery space called Three's Company in New York.

GUIDO GAZZILLI was born in 1983 in Rome, where he lives and works. He has extensively traveled throughout Europe to photograph new urban cultures and the independent music scene, and has exhibited and published his work in a number of international galleries and magazines. In 2009 he started a project on drug addiction in Italy. He is currently represented by 7 Minutes Agency. *guidogazzilli.com*

SERGIO GHETTI (Bologna, 1964) is a photographer and architect. Since 1998 he lives between Milano, Venezia and New York. He is the U.S. correspondent of the architecture magazine *The Plan*. His work has appeared in *Amica*, *Style - Corriere della Sera*, *Io Donna*, *Sportweek*, *Marieclaire Italia*, *Elle Decor*, *Riders*, *Gioia*, *Vogue Italia*, *Vogue UK*, *Vogue Brasil*, *Condé Nast Traveller Italia*, *Grazia* and *Grazia Casa*. *sergioghetti.com*

MILTOS MANETAS is an artist who often works with the Internet. In 2009, he launched the first Internet Pavilion at the Venice Biennale *padiglioneinternet.com*, where he invited *thepiratebay.org* to found their Embassy of Piracy *embassyofpiracy.org*. His actions also include the Neen Movement *neen.org*, existential computing, Internet paintings and artworks made with videogames. Manetas lives and works in London. *manetas.com*

BENIAMINO MARINI lives in Milan. After classical and social studies, he became a "creative journalist" mixing writing, creative direction, illustration… in the fields of fashion, art and design. He is now working at *vogue.it* and contributing to *Casamica* and *Zoo*, after having contributed to *Le Monde*, *Corriere della Sera Magazine*, *Io Donna*, *La Gazzetta dello Sport* and *Rodeo*.

FRANCO NOERO opened his eponymous gallery in Turin in 1999. The gallery now operates 3 different exhibition spaces, including La Fetta di Polenta - one of the city's architectural landmarks, built by Alessandro Antonelli around 1840 - a "laboratory for ideas" where the work of Simon Starling that Noero introduces in this issue was conceived and dispayed in April 2008. *franconoero.com*

DENIS PERNET is a curator at the Centre d'Art Contemporain Genève, where he organized monographic exhibitions of Yuri Leiderman, Adrien Missika and Klat. As an indepedant curator, he worked with Maayan Amir & Ruti Sela, Dafne Boggeri and Jean-Luc Manz. In 2008, he curated a solo exhibition of Christodoulos Panayiotou at 1m3 gallery in Lausanne.

JORMA PURANEN is an artist and photographer born and based in Finland. Through the use of different archive materials, he explores the relationships between past and present, histories of representation and the framing of nature by culture. Recent solo exhibitions include *Sixteen Steps to Paradise*, Galerie Anhava, Helsinki and *Icy Prospects*, Purdy Hicks Gallery, London.

ADRIANO SACK German, 42, is a freelance writer living in New York, who works for publications such as *Architectural Digest*, *Monopol* and *Pin-Up*. Sack has a style column in *Welt am Sonntag*, Germany's leading Sunday paper. His latest books include *The Curious World of Drugs and Their Friends* (Plume) and *Gebrauchsanweisung fuer die USA* (Piper), a collection of essays on culture, politics and the social climate in the United States.

TIM SMALL is the editor of the Italian issue of *Vice* magazine and a contributing editor of the international art bi-monthly *Kaleidoscope*. His writings appear regularly in *Rolling Stone*, *The Observer*, *Mousse* and *Satisfaction*, and his documentaries can be seen on *vbs.tv*. He lives in Milan, and despite what most people think, Tim Small is his real name.

COLOPHON

EDITORS
Cay Sophie Rabinowitz, Selva Barni
editorial@fantomeditions.com

CONTRIBUTING EDITOR
Francesco Zanot
francesco@fantomeditions.com

VISUAL EDITOR AT LARGE
Pino Pipoli
pipoli@fantomeditions.com

ART DIRECTOR
Davies Costacurta
sm-work.com

DESIGN ASSISTANT
Francesco Geronazzo

INTERNS
Erin Tao (New York), Stella Paganini (Milano)

ART DIRECTOR *I AM ONE*
Francesco Petroni

TRANSLATIONS
Judith Mundell, Anthony Allen

THANKS TO
Agnese Bossi, Alberto Pellegrinet, Andrea Concina, Angelo Maestroni, Carina Negrone, Christian Rattemeyer, Gialunca Migliarotti, Giorgio Frassi and Sebastiano Pavia, Haidee Findlay-Levin, Luca Cipelletti, Luciano Cirelli, Marta Pozzoli, Mary Skinner, Olivia Gazzarrini, Pasquale Marini, Sergio Ricciardone, Skype, Sofia Sizzi and Iacopo Falai, Stefano Pitigliani, Susanna Cucco and Ivanmaria Vele/Boiler Corporation

FANTOM OFFICE MILANO
Via Nicola Palmieri 34, 20141 Milano, Italy

FANTOM OFFICE NEW YORK
Osmos, 137 Grand Street, 10013 New York, NY, USA

ADVERTISING ENQUIRIES
info@fantomeditions.com

WWW.FANTOMEDITIONS.COM

SUBSCRIPTIONS
International: Bruil & van de Staaij
PO Box 75, 7940 AB Meppel, The Netherlands
T +31 522 261303 - F + 31 522 257827
www.bruil.info

Italia: abbonamenti@fantomeditions.com

DISTRIBUTION
Italia and International: S.I.E.S. Srl
Via Bettola 18, 20092 Cinisello Balsamo (MI), Italy
T +39 02 66030400 - F +39 02 66030269
sies@siesnet.it - www.siesnet.it

North America: D.A.P./Distributed Art Publishers
155 Sixth Avenue, 2nd Floor, 10013 New York, N.Y., USA
T +1 212 627 1999 - F +1 212 627 9484
www.artbook.com

PUBLISHER & EDITOR AT LARGE
Massimo Torrigiani
m.torrigiani@boilercorporation.com

PUBLISHING CONSULTANT
Roberto Rossi Gandolfi

ASSISTANT PUBLISHER
Pier Mario Simula
p.simula@boilercorporation.com

PUBLISHED BY
Boiler Corporation Srl
Fredella & Associati, Piazza Castello 19, 20121 Milano, Italy
www.boilercorporation.com

Printed in Italy by Grafiche Antiga, Via delle Industrie 1
31035 Crocetta del Montello (TV), Italy
www.graficheantiga.it

Prepress: Numerique, Via A. Sciesa 2, 20135 Milano, Italy
www.numerique.it

Periodico registrato presso il Tribunale di Milano
N° 436 del 07/10/2009
Direttore Responsabile: Selva Barni

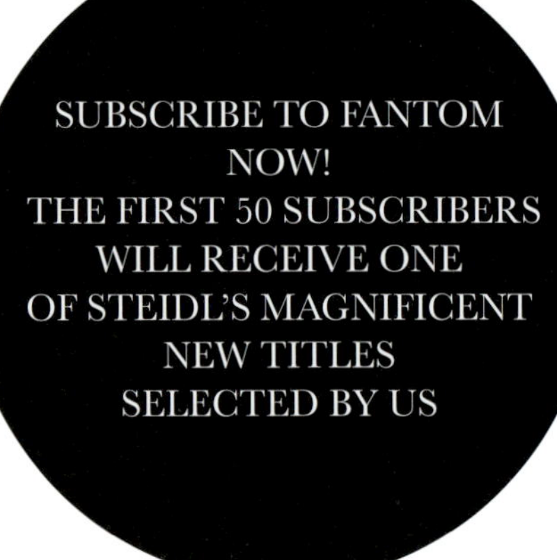

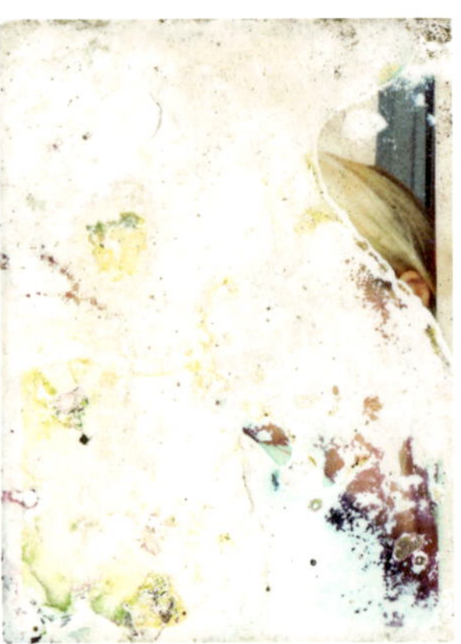

This issue's cover image - 'Dublin, June 2005' - comes from the *Lost Europeans* series, Davis Farrell's collection of found photo booth pictures, which will be featured in our next issue, out in Winter 2010.

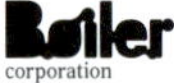

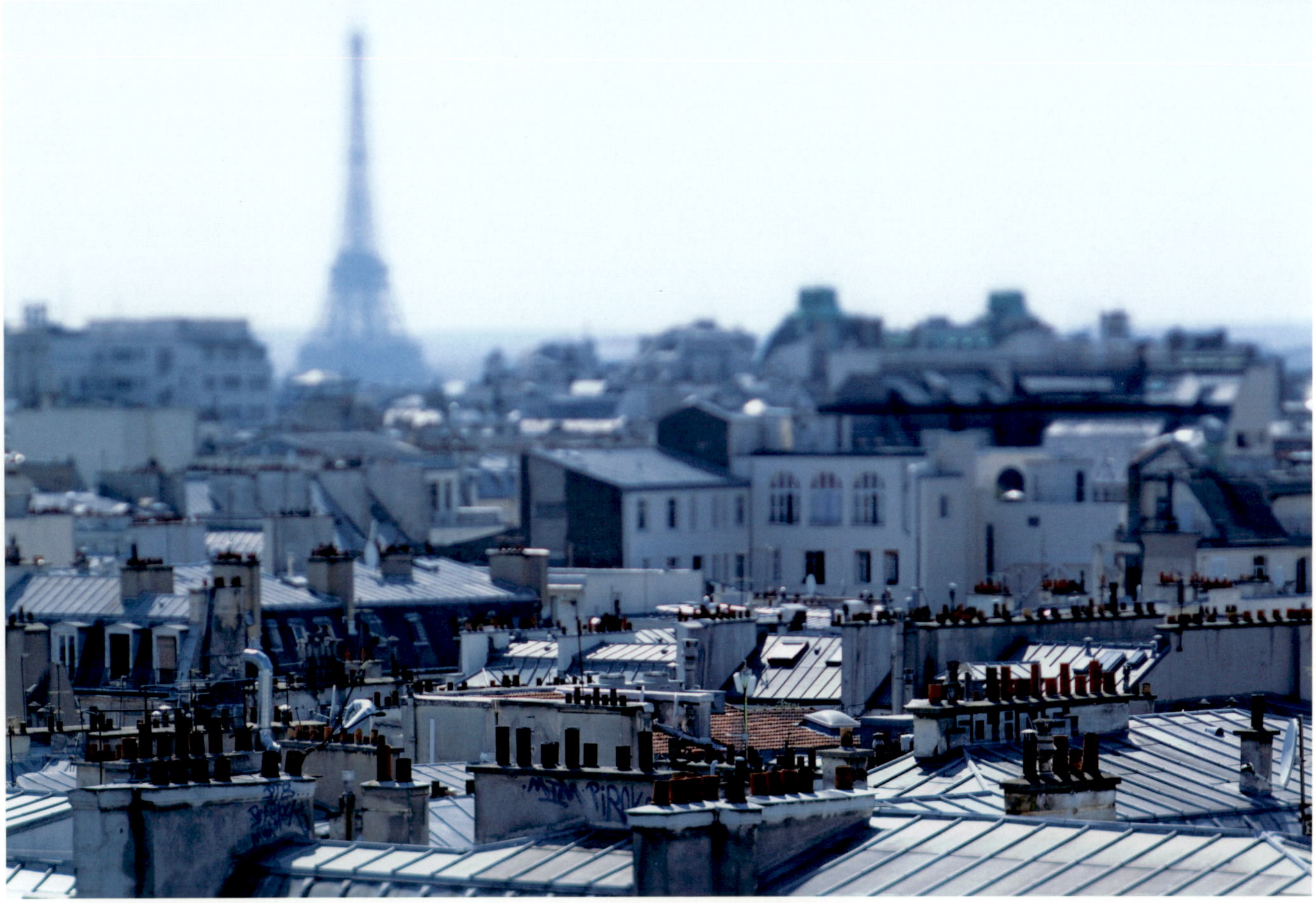

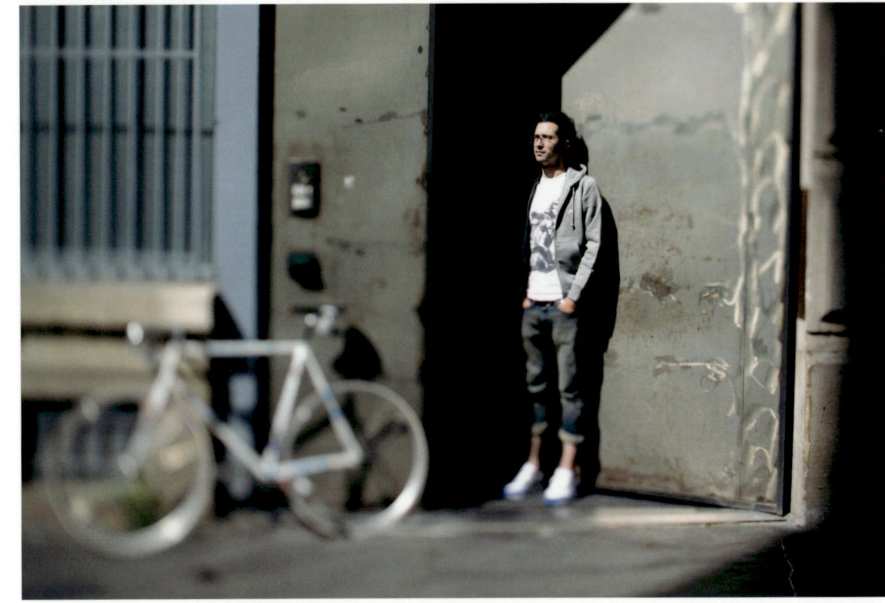

I AM ONE

Photography Paolo Novelli
Courtesy of NIKE
The I AM 1 journey is on
nikesportswear.com

ROMAIN CORVEZ - WEB DESIGNER

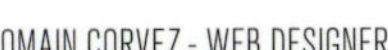

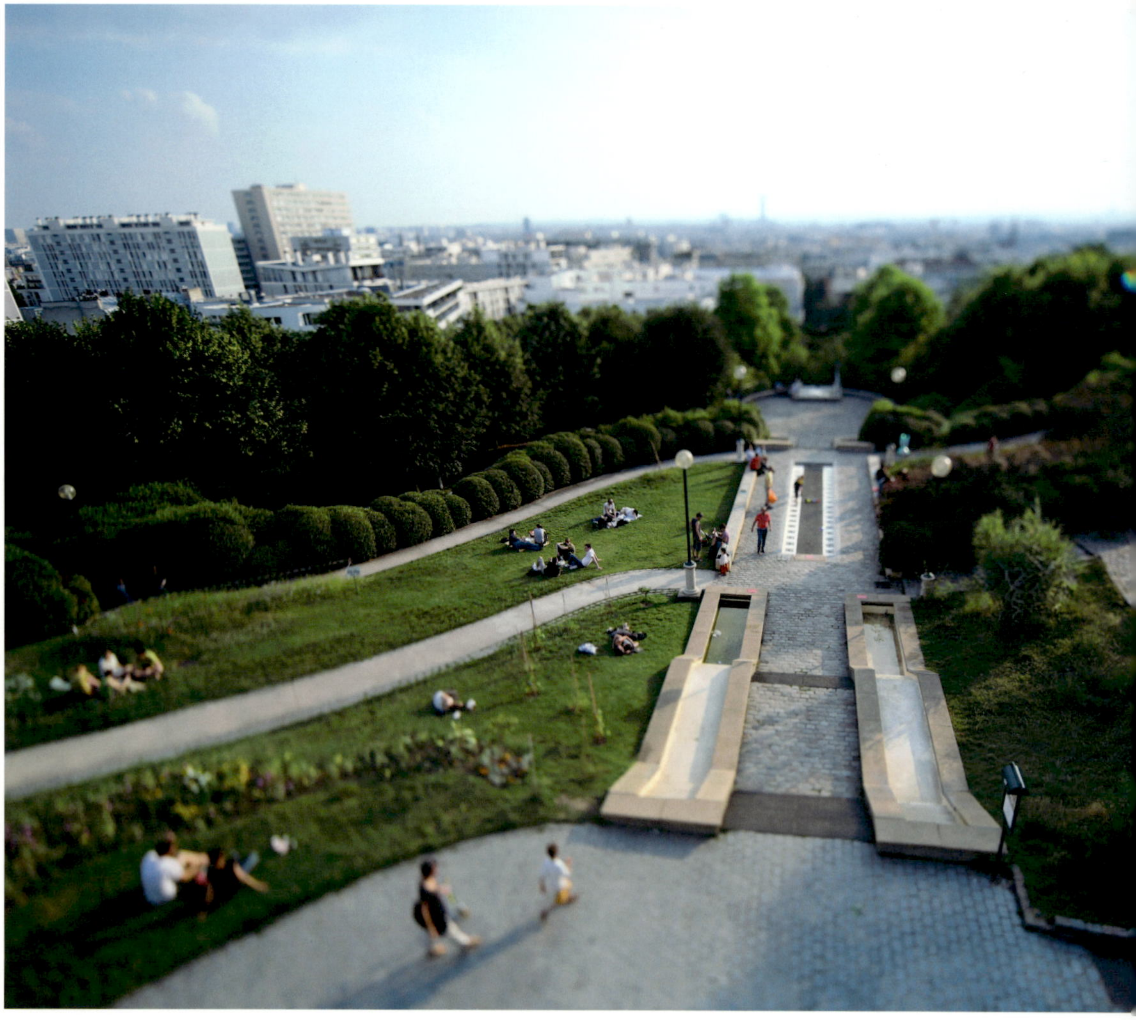

ALBAN TEURLAI - VIDEOMAKER

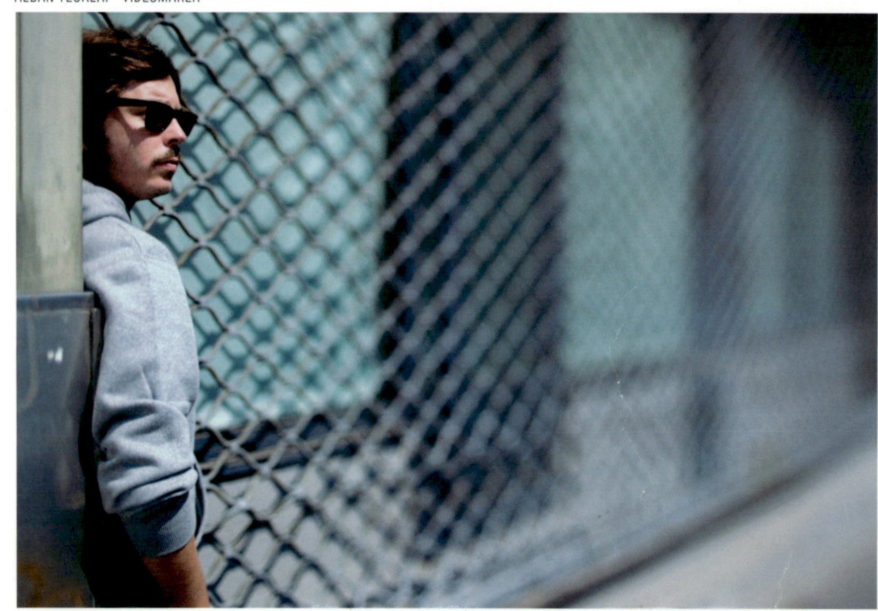

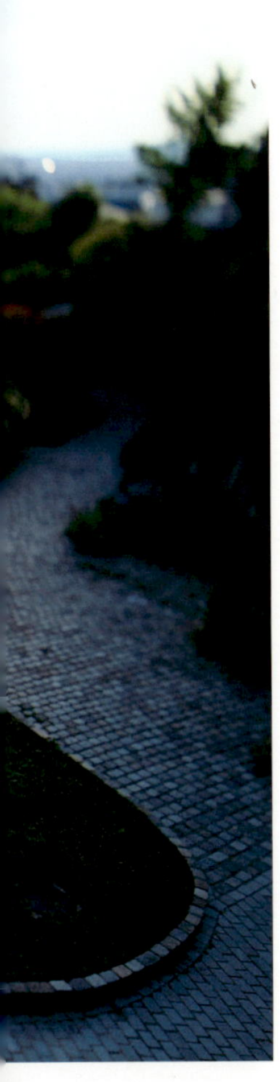
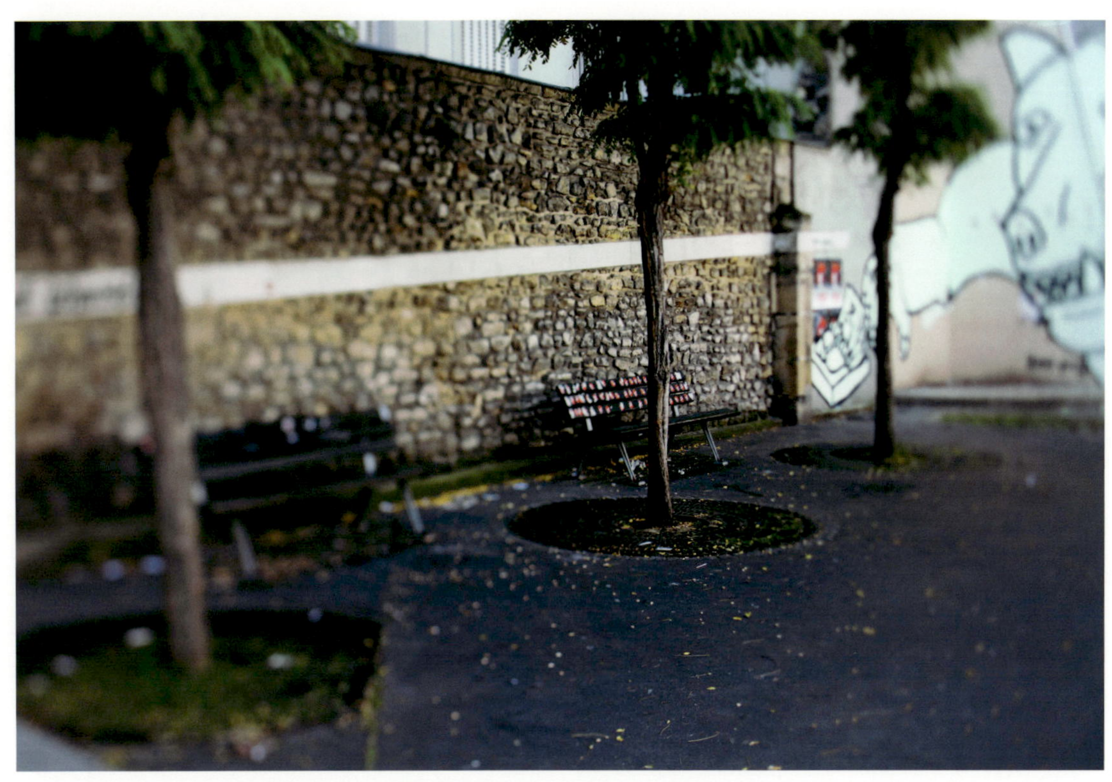

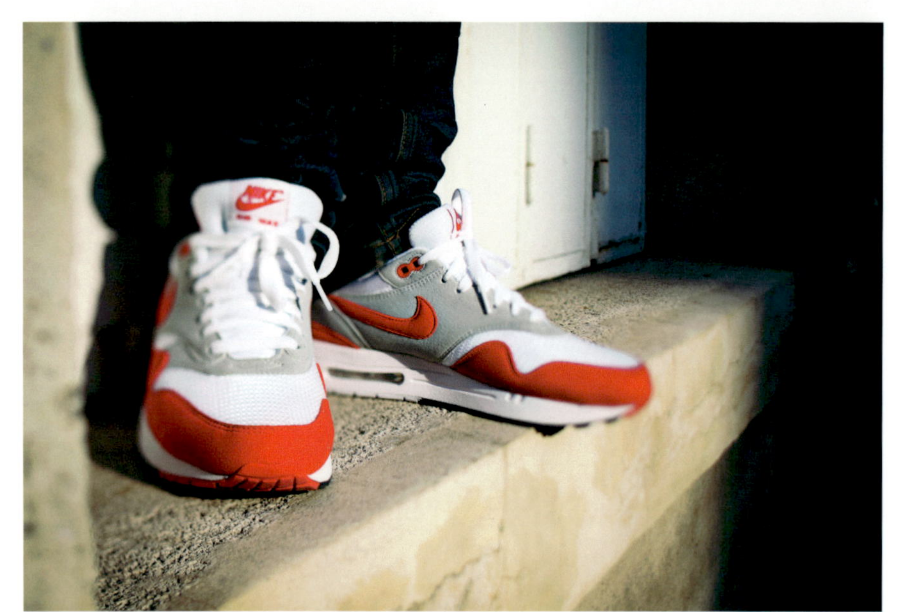

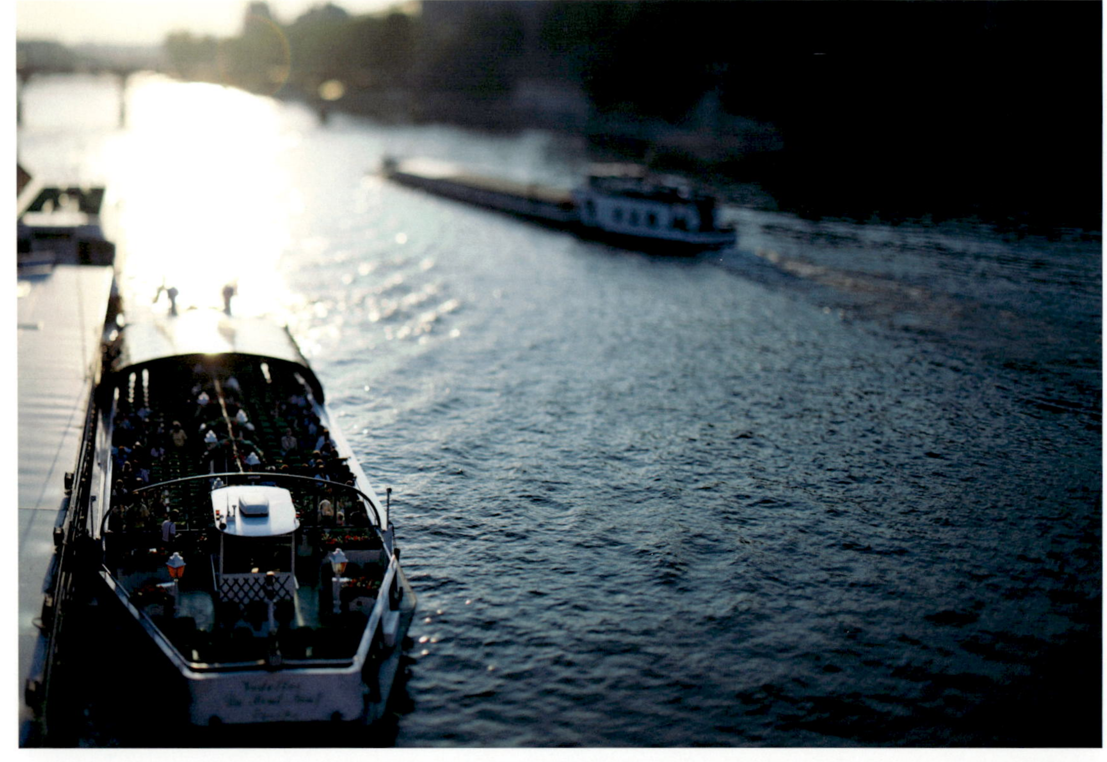

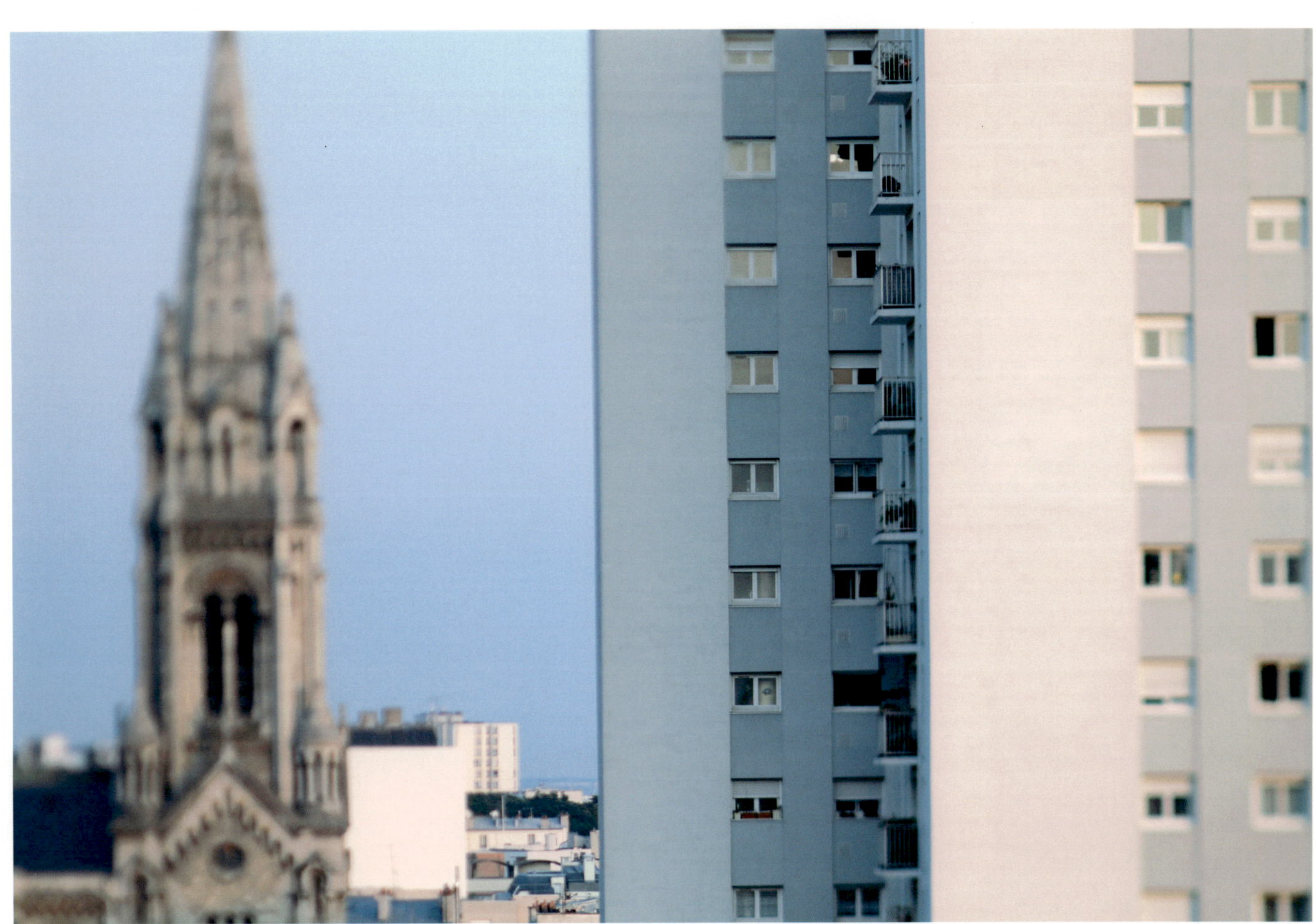

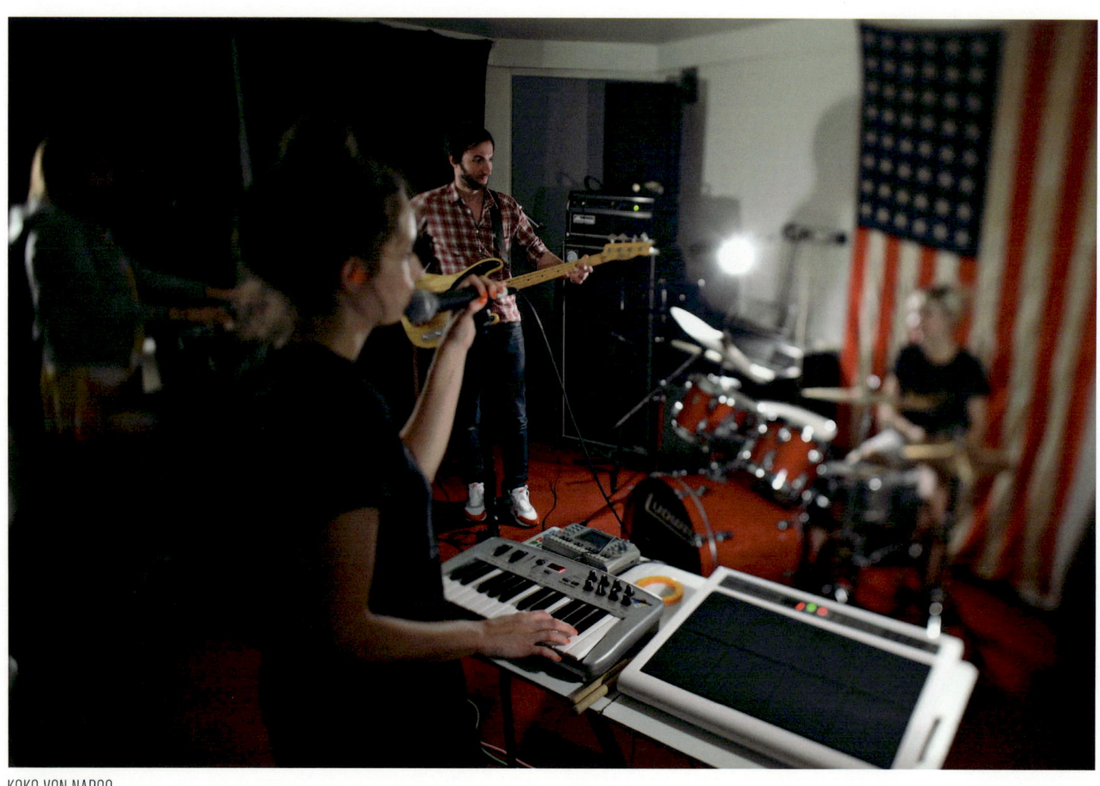

KOKO VON NAPOO

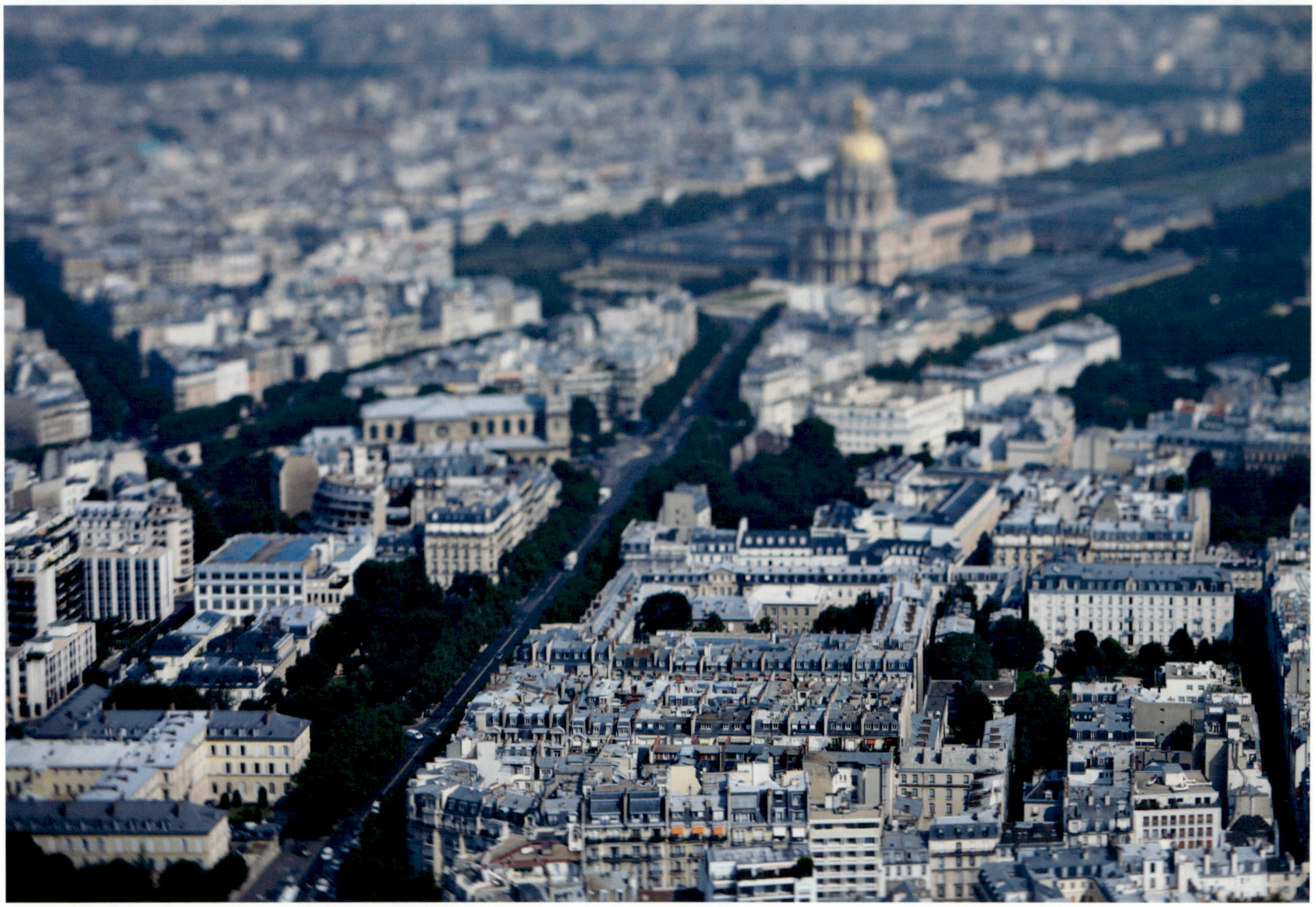

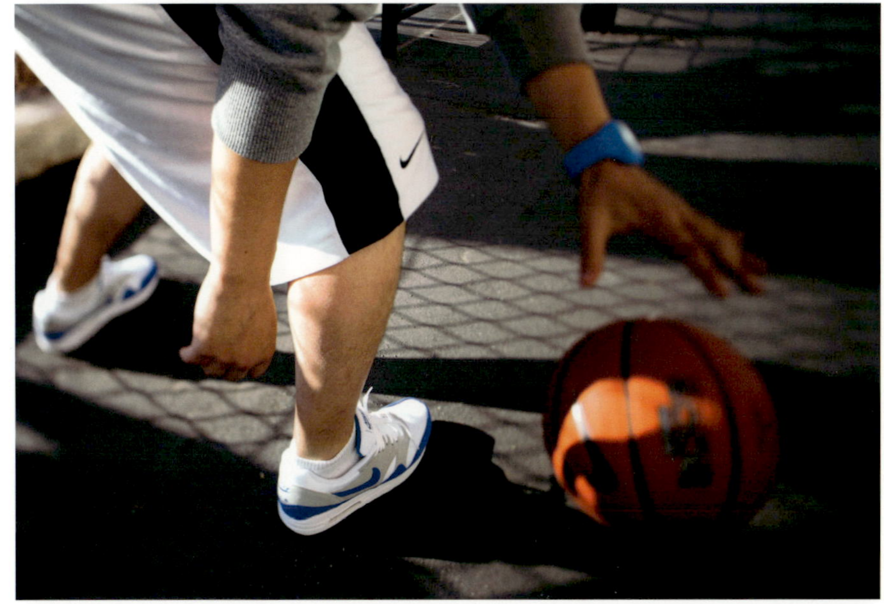

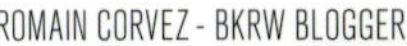

FANTOM *with an F*, is a new international quarterly publication about the uses and abuses of photography. It is about the art of capturing timed effects of light. For practitioners and professionals by professional practitioners, **FANTOM** enframes its content in sectors: **EYE TO EYE** where photographers converse; **SAMPLE SIZE** with ready made discoveries by excellent eyes; **BY APPOINTMENT ONLY** offered by a collector or about a collection; **EYE OF THE BEHOLDER** where gallerists celebrate the time based talents they expose and trade; and **MEANS TO AN END** surveying the unintentional surprises of purposeful image production, i.e. scientic, commercial, surveillance, documentary and the like. Herein the vernacular can take precedence over the artistic and vice versa depending on the value not of a discourse that comes after the image but allowing pictures to lead the discussions. A voyage into photography, **FANTOM** will orient readers and viewers in the scaled horizons drawn by photography and those who critique, exhibit, collect, occupy and emulate it. Found, forgotten and not yet discovered, first and foremost **FANTOM** features the voice of photographers, in interviews, portfolios, and statements alongside the often silent but rarely without a voice medium of *Fotography*.

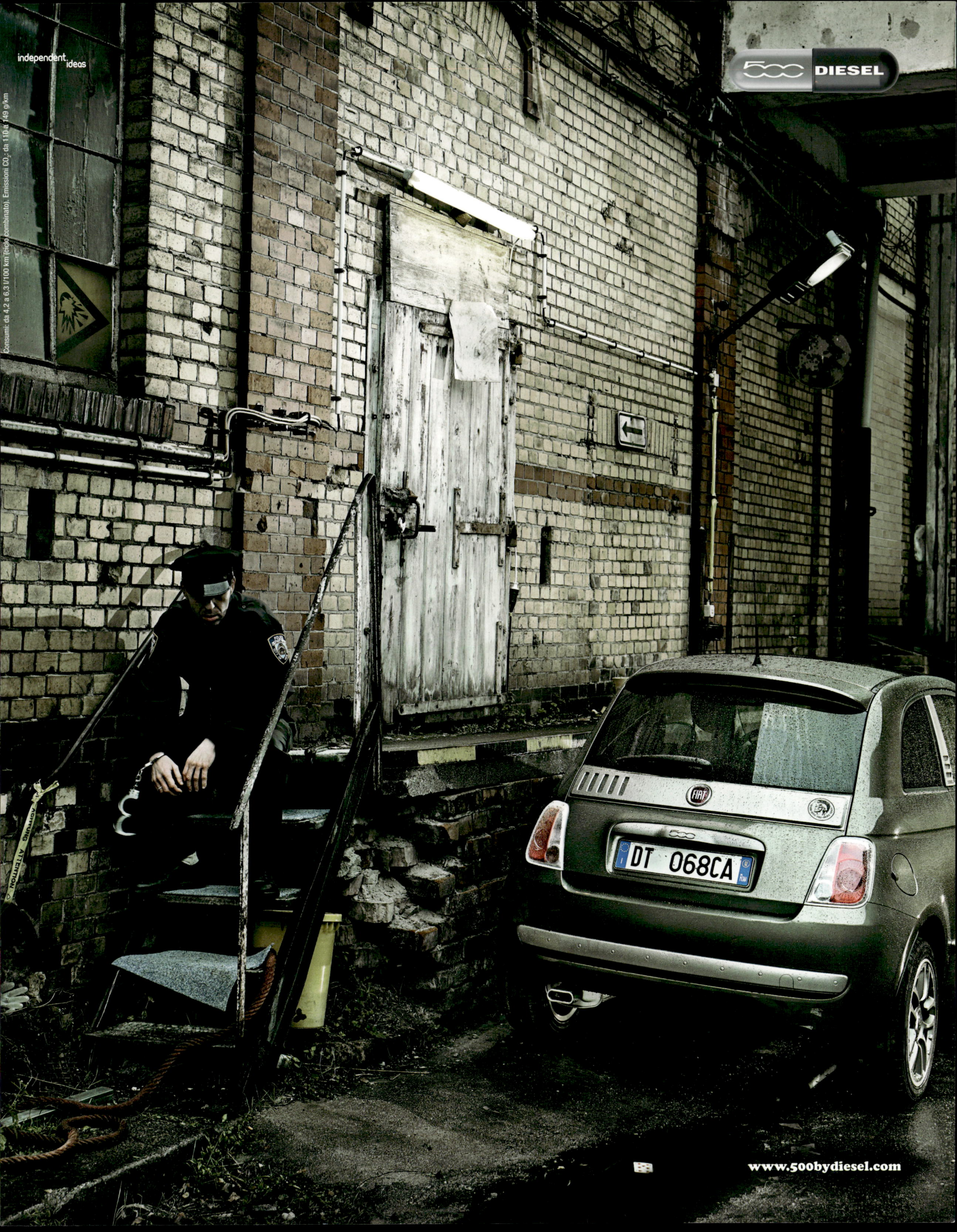
independent ideas
Consumi: da 4,2 a 6,3 l/100 km (ciclo combinato). Emissioni CO₂: da 110 a 149 g/km
500 DIESEL
DT 068CA
FIAT
www.500bydiesel.com

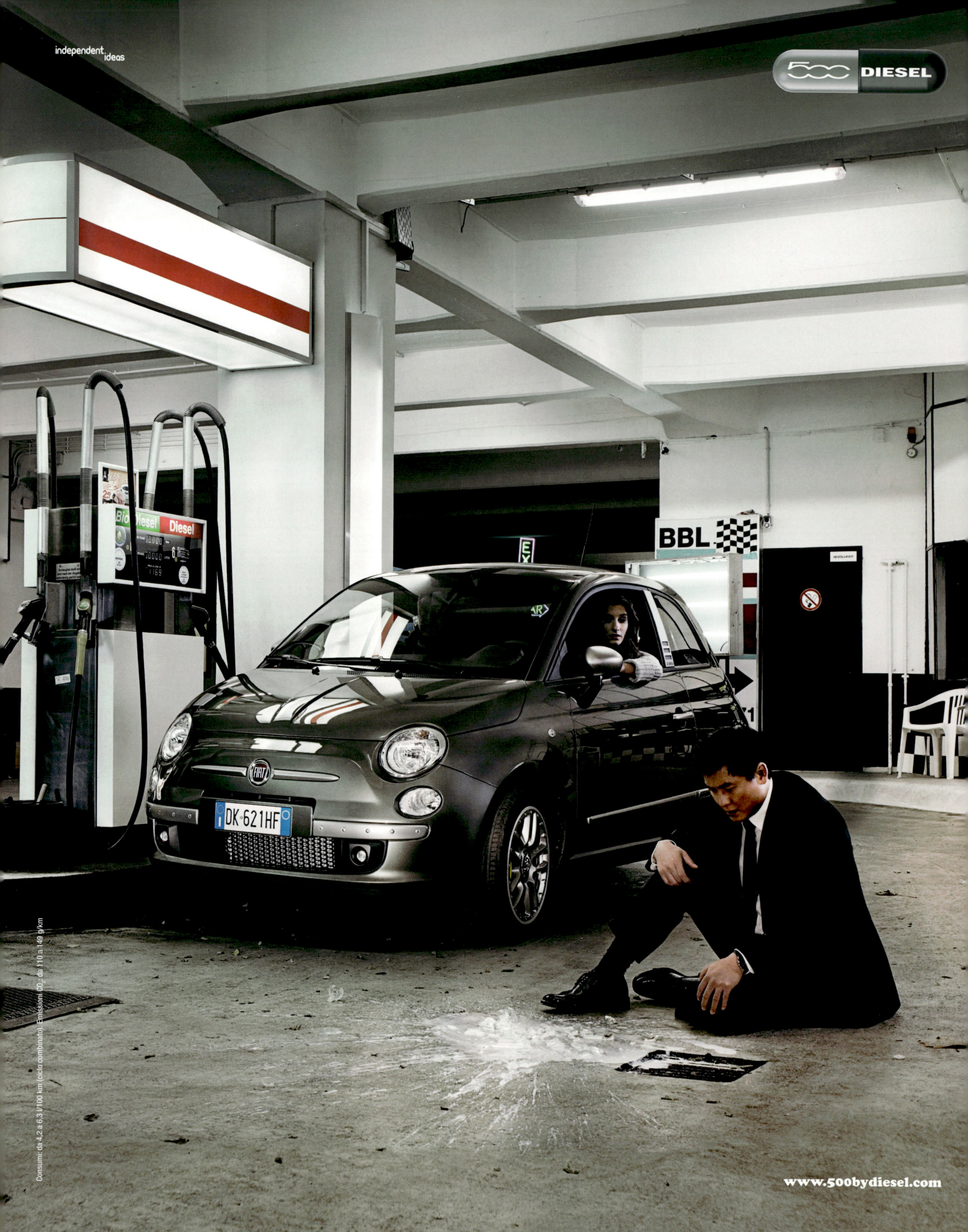

independent ideas
500 DIESEL
Bio Diesel   Diesel
BBL
FIAT
DK 621HF
Consumi: da 4,2 a 6,3 l/100 km (ciclo combinato). Emissioni CO₂: da 110 a 149 g/km
www.500bydiesel.com

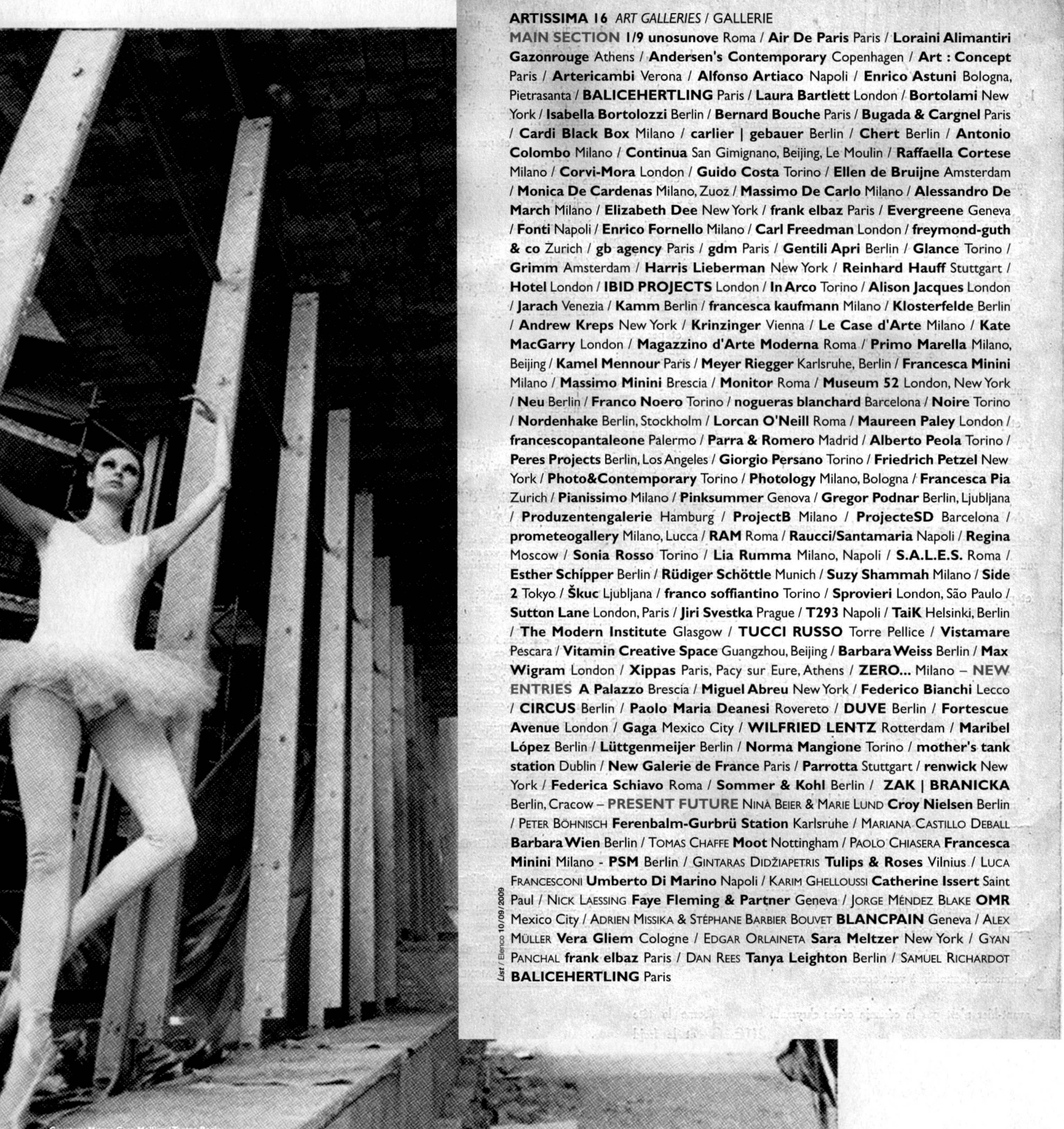

ARTISSIMA 16 *ART GALLERIES / GALLERIE*

MAIN SECTION 1/9 unosunove Roma / **Air De Paris** Paris / **Loraini Alimantiri Gazonrouge** Athens / **Andersen's Contemporary** Copenhagen / **Art : Concept** Paris / **Artericambi** Verona / **Alfonso Artiaco** Napoli / **Enrico Astuni** Bologna, Pietrasanta / **BALICEHERTLING** Paris / **Laura Bartlett** London / **Bortolami** New York / **Isabella Bortolozzi** Berlin / **Bernard Bouche** Paris / **Bugada & Cargnel** Paris / **Cardi Black Box** Milano / **carlier | gebauer** Berlin / **Chert** Berlin / **Antonio Colombo** Milano / **Continua** San Gimignano, Beijing, Le Moulin / **Raffaella Cortese** Milano / **Corvi-Mora** London / **Guido Costa** Torino / **Ellen de Bruijne** Amsterdam / **Monica De Cardenas** Milano, Zuoz / **Massimo De Carlo** Milano / **Alessandro De March** Milano / **Elizabeth Dee** New York / **frank elbaz** Paris / **Evergreene** Geneva / **Fonti** Napoli / **Enrico Fornello** Milano / **Carl Freedman** London / **freymond-guth & co** Zurich / **gb agency** Paris / **gdm** Paris / **Gentili Apri** Berlin / **Glance** Torino / **Grimm** Amsterdam / **Harris Lieberman** New York / **Reinhard Hauff** Stuttgart / **Hotel** London / **IBID PROJECTS** London / **In Arco** Torino / **Alison Jacques** London / **Jarach** Venezia / **Kamm** Berlin / **francesca kaufmann** Milano / **Klosterfelde** Berlin / **Andrew Kreps** New York / **Krinzinger** Vienna / **Le Case d'Arte** Milano / **Kate MacGarry** London / **Magazzino d'Arte Moderna** Roma / **Primo Marella** Milano, Beijing / **Kamel Mennour** Paris / **Meyer Riegger** Karlsruhe, Berlin / **Francesca Minini** Milano / **Massimo Minini** Brescia / **Monitor** Roma / **Museum 52** London, New York / **Neu** Berlin / **Franco Noero** Torino / **nogueras blanchard** Barcelona / **Noire** Torino / **Nordenhake** Berlin, Stockholm / **Lorcan O'Neill** Roma / **Maureen Paley** London / **francescopantaleone** Palermo / **Parra & Romero** Madrid / **Alberto Peola** Torino / **Peres Projects** Berlin, Los Angeles / **Giorgio Persano** Torino / **Friedrich Petzel** New York / **Photo&Contemporary** Torino / **Photology** Milano, Bologna / **Francesca Pia** Zurich / **Pianissimo** Milano / **Pinksummer** Genova / **Gregor Podnar** Berlin, Ljubljana / **Produzentengalerie** Hamburg / **ProjectB** Milano / **ProjecteSD** Barcelona / **prometeogallery** Milano, Lucca / **RAM** Roma / **Raucci/Santamaria** Napoli / **Regina** Moscow / **Sonia Rosso** Torino / **Lia Rumma** Milano, Napoli / **S.A.L.E.S.** Roma / **Esther Schipper** Berlin / **Rüdiger Schöttle** Munich / **Suzy Shammah** Milano / **Side 2** Tokyo / **Škuc** Ljubljana / **franco soffiantino** Torino / **Sprovieri** London, São Paulo / **Sutton Lane** London, Paris / **Jiri Svestka** Prague / **T293** Napoli / **TaiK** Helsinki, Berlin / **The Modern Institute** Glasgow / **TUCCI RUSSO** Torre Pellice / **Vistamare** Pescara / **Vitamin Creative Space** Guangzhou, Beijing / **Barbara Weiss** Berlin / **Max Wigram** London / **Xippas** Paris, Pacy sur Eure, Athens / **ZERO...** Milano – **NEW ENTRIES** A Palazzo Brescia / **Miguel Abreu** New York / **Federico Bianchi** Lecco / **CIRCUS** Berlin / **Paolo Maria Deanesi** Rovereto / **DUVE** Berlin / **Fortescue Avenue** London / **Gaga** Mexico City / **WILFRIED LENTZ** Rotterdam / **Maribel López** Berlin / **Lüttgenmeijer** Berlin / **Norma Mangione** Torino / **mother's tank station** Dublin / **New Galerie de France** Paris / **Parrotta** Stuttgart / **renwick** New York / **Federica Schiavo** Roma / **Sommer & Kohl** Berlin / **ZAK | BRANICKA** Berlin, Cracow – **PRESENT FUTURE** Nina Beier & Marie Lund **Croy Nielsen** Berlin / Peter Böhnisch **Ferenbalm-Gurbrü Station** Karlsruhe / Mariana Castillo Deball **Barbara Wien** Berlin / Tomas Chaffe **Moot** Nottingham / Paolo Chiasera **Francesca Minini** Milano - **PSM** Berlin / Gintaras Didžiapetris **Tulips & Roses** Vilnius / Luca Francesconi **Umberto Di Marino** Napoli / Karim Ghelloussi **Catherine Issert** Saint Paul / Nick Laessing **Faye Fleming & Partner** Geneva / Jorge Méndez Blake **OMR** Mexico City / Adrien Missika & Stéphane Barbier Bouvet **BLANCPAIN** Geneva / Alex Müller **Vera Gliem** Cologne / Edgar Orlaineta **Sara Meltzer** New York / Gyan Panchal **frank elbaz** Paris / Dan Rees **Tanya Leighton** Berlin / Samuel Richardot **BALICEHERTLING** Paris

Fondazione Torino Musei

Regione Piemonte
Provincia di Torino
Città di Torino

Camera di commercio di Torino
Compagnia di San Paolo
Fondazione per l'Arte Moderna e Contemporanea CRT

Main partner
Unicredit Group
Unicredit Private Banking

Partners
Grey Goose
illycaffè
Nationale Suisse
NOVA Investimenti Immobiliari
Depart Foundation

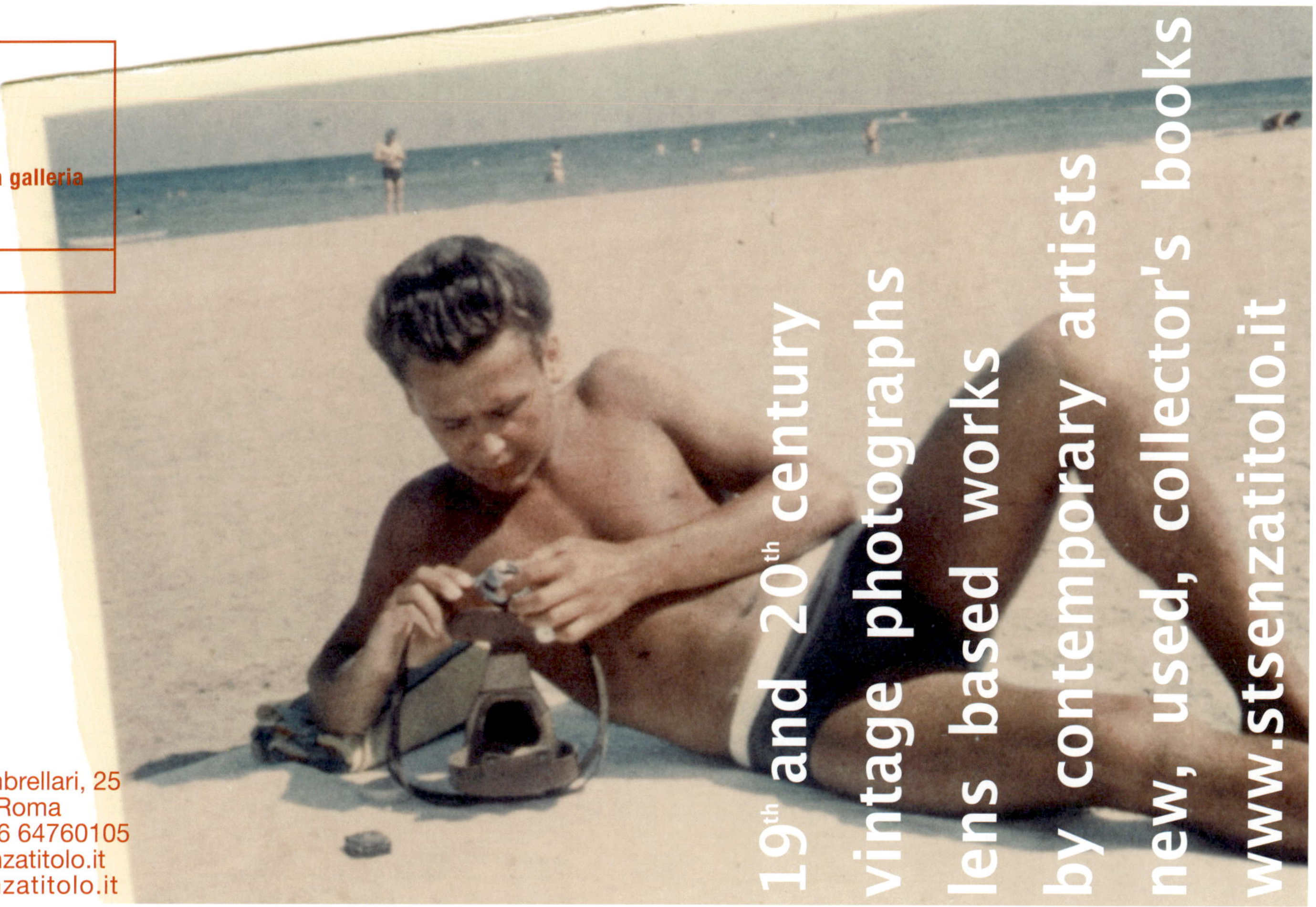

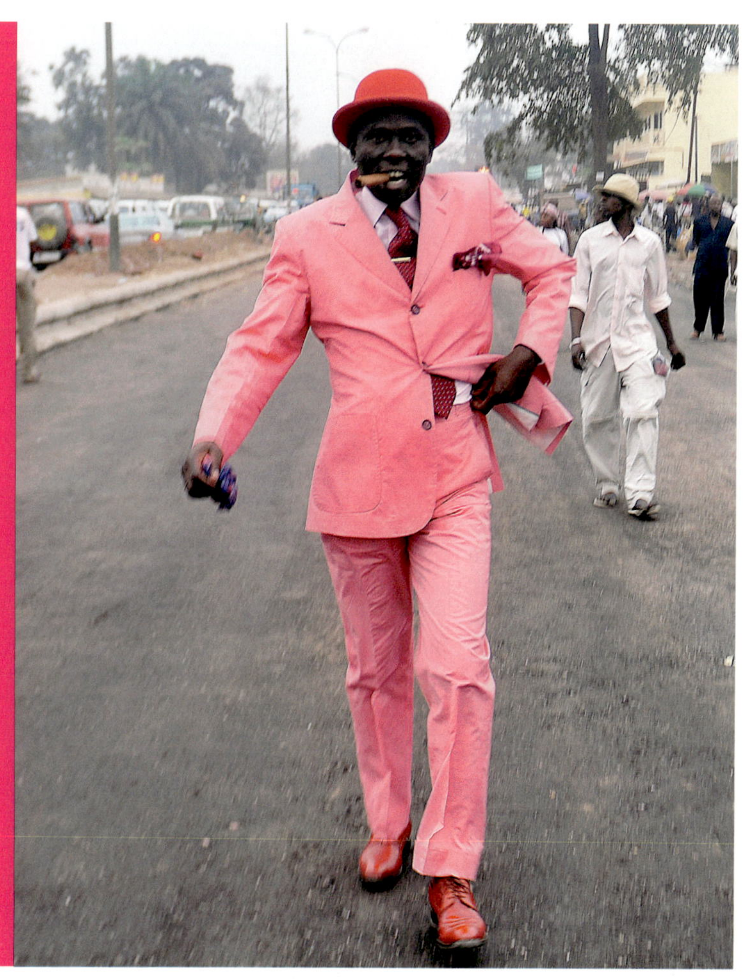